Japanese Hybrid Factories

Also by Tetsuo Abo

HYBRID FACTORY: THE JAPANESE PRODUCTION SYSTEM IN THE UNITED STATES *(editor)*

THE HYBRID FACTORY IN EUROPE: THE JAPANESE MANAGEMENT AND PRODUCTION SYSTEM TRANSFERRED *(editor with H. Kumon)*

Japanese Hybrid Factories

A Comparison of Global Production Strategies

Edited by Tetsuo Abo

In association with The Japanese Multinational Enterprise Study Group (JMNESG)

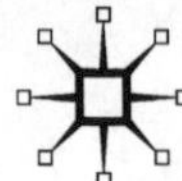

First published 2007 by
PALGRAVE MACMILLAN
Houndmills, Basingstoke, Hampshire RG21 6XS and
175 Fifth Avenue, New York, N. Y. 10010
Companies and representatives throughout the world

PALGRAVE MACMILLAN is the global academic imprint of the Palgrave Macmillan division of St. Martin's Press, LLC and of Palgrave Macmillan Ltd. Macmillan® is a registered trademark in the United States, United Kingdom and other countries. Palgrave is a registered trademark in the European Union and other countries.

ISBN-13: 978–1–4039–9856–9 hardback
ISBN-10: 1–4039–9856–6 hardback

This book is printed on paper suitable for recycling and made from fully managed and sustained forest sources. Logging, pulping and manufacturing processes are expected to conform to the environmental regulations of the country of origin.

A catalogue record for this book is available from the British Library.

A catalog record for this book is available from the Library of Congress.

10 9 8 7 6 5 4 3 2 1
15 14 13 12 11 10 09 08 07 06

Printed and bound in Great Britain by
Antony Rowe Ltd, Chippenham and Eastbourne

Contents

List of Figures

List of Tables

Preface

This book describes the overall research results carried out by the Japanese Multinational Enterprise Study Group* (JMNESG headed by Tetsuo Abo) on the theme entitled 'Japanese Hybrid Factories: Global Transfer of the Japanese Management and Production Systems in Major Regions of the World.' JMNESG organized the Teikyo University System Laboratory Symposium,** on 3 November 2004, to sum up the findings of 20 years of research by the JMNESG members and to seek external evaluations from first-class experts both in Japan and abroad. This book is mainly based on the proceedings and discussions at the symposium.

The research activities were conducted for the last five of those years through the 'Teikyo System Laboratory,'*** as the 'Academic Frontier Promotion Project for Private Universities,' with the support of the Japanese Ministry of Education, Culture, Sports, Science and Technology (directed by Tetsuo Abo) and, for about fifteen years preceding that, conducted with support from the Toyota Foundation (twice), the former Japanese Ministry of Education (several times) and the Japan Industrial Policy Research Institute (once) (directed by Tetsuo Abo and Hiroshi Itagaki) through the Institute of Social Science, University of Tokyo.

JMNESG has been carrying out research on conditions surrounding technology transfer from Japanese automobile and electronics companies to their subsidiaries and affiliated plants (including assembly and parts or components manufacturing) in North and South America, East and South Asia, Western Europe, China, and Central and Eastern Europe.

The focus of this research has been on the problems of the transferability of the Japanese management and production system, especially in terms of its human and organizational aspects. The central part of the system characteristically involves flexible management methods of work organization on the shop floor, and is based upon technologies and skills that have been broadly accumulated at work sites over a long period of time. These are the major factors underlying the achievement of high quality, efficient production in Japan. Since the early 1980s, and with a certain period of stagnation following the breakdown of the bubble economy in the early 1990s, Japanese firms have increasingly undertaken overseas production. The successful transfer of their production systems, which have been almost entirely developed in Japan, constitutes the key to successful local production operations.

Our approach to the transferability issue of the Japanese system to foreign countries utilizes our research and analytical frameworks, the 'Application–Adaptation "Hybrid" Model' and the 'Five-scale Evaluation Method,' in order to measure the degrees of application and adaptation of the Japanese parent systems at the local subsidiary plants. This allows us to deal consistently with research results from various countries and regions and to conduct dynamic comparisons of each result by region and industry (horizontally), as well as chronologically (vertically). We may then be able to consolidate methods to integrate these comparative studies in a way that provides suggestions for the global production strategies of Japanese and other multinational firms.

Perhaps it is now possible to claim that the 'hybrid evaluation method,' which can also be applied to non-Japanese firms introducing Japanese elements into their systems or transferring their own systems to subsidiaries abroad, is an international or global model for the assessment of the transferability of the management and production system of any MNE.

The chapters of this book are written by the editor, Tetsuo Abo (Chapters 1 and 9) and the project leaders of each region: Tetsuji Kawamura (Chapter 2) and Jorge Carrillo (Chapter 3) in North America, Hiroshi Itagaki (Chapter 4) in East and South Asia, Kunio Kamiyama (Chapter 5) in China, Hiroshi Kumon (Chapter 6) in Western Europe and Yuan Zhi Jia (Chapter 7) in Central and Eastern Europe. As shown below in the list of JMNESG's publications**** almost all of them are the editors of the books published or being published on the respective regions. Chapter 8 (edited by Tetsuo Abo) includes the comments and replies between the invited discussants and the presenters and the discussions among them including the main questions from the other participants and the answers at the symposium. And finally in Chapter 9 an overall summary and concluding remarks are given, including the latest data.

Tetsuo Abo
Tokyo

* The Members of JMNESG

(Members permanently resident in Japan, as of 31 October 2005)

Tetsuo Abo, Department of Economics, Teikyo University and Professor Emeritus, University of Tokyo
Hiroshi Itagaki, Department of Economics, Musashi University
Nobuo Kawabe, Department of Commerce, Waseda University
Tetsuji Kawamura, Department of Economics, Hosei University
Hiroshi Kumon, Department of Economics, Hosei University
Etsuo Abe, Department of Management, Meiji University
Hirokuni Tabata, Institute of Social Science, University of Tokyo
Jaw Yann Twu, Department of Economics, Kokugakuin University
Du Sop Cho, Department of Management, Yokohama National University
Yan Shu Hao, Department of Management, Meiji University
Je Wheon Oh, Center for Design and Manufacturing, Department of Economics, University of Tokyo
Yuan Zhi Jia, Department of Economics, Rissho University
Wooseok Juhn, Department of Management, Chukyo University
Rolf Schlunze, Department of Management, Otemon Gakuin University
Shinya Orihashi, Department of Economics, Tohoku Gakuin University
Toshihiko Miyaji, Department of Information Business, Teikyo University Junior College
Koji Serita, Kushiro Public University of Economics
Nobuyuki Yamada, Department of Sociology, Komazawa University
Tadahiro Takeno, Department of Humanities & Social Sciences, Nagoya Institute of Technology
Katsuo Yamazaki, Department of Management, Shizuoka Sangyo University
Mitsuru Takahashi, Department of Economics, Teikyo University
Masatake Wada, Department of Economics, Teikyo University
Sizhi Guo, Energy Strategy Department, The Institute of Energy Economics, Japan

** Profiles of the main presenters (authors), discussants and chairs at the Teikyo System Lab Symposium

Etsuo Abe, Professor, Meiji University, *Keieishi (History of Management)* (2002).

Tetsuo Abo, Professor, Teikyo University (ed.), *Hybrid Factory: The Japanese Production System in the United States* (1994).

Robert Boyer, CEPREMAP, Director, CNRS (co-eds), *Between Imitation and Innovation: the Transfer and Hybridization of Productive Models in the International Automobile Industry* (1998).

Jorge Carrillo, Dr, Chief Research Fellow, El Colegio de la Frontera Norte, Mexico (eds), *Cars. Carriers: The Future of Motor Vehicle Production* (2004).

Takahiro Fujimoto, Professor, University of Tokyo, *The Evolution of a Manufacturing System at Toyota* (1999).

Hiroshi Itagaki, Professor, Musashi University (ed.), *The Japanese Production System: Hybrid Factories in East Asia* (1997).

Kunio Kamiyama, Professor, Josai University, The Society for Industrial Studies, Japan (ed.), *Sengo Nihon Sangyo-shi (Industrial History in Postwar Japan)*, edit committee (1995).

Tetsuji Kawamura, Professor, Hosei University, *Gurobaru Keizai ka no Amerika Nikkei Koujo (Japanese Factories in the USA under Global Economy)* (2004).

Martin Kenney, Professor, University of California, Davis (ed.), *Locating Global Advantage* (2004).

Hiroshi Kumon, Professor, Hosei University, 'Nissan: From a Precocious Export Policy to a Strategic Alliance with Renault,' in Freyssenet, M., *et al.* (eds), *Globalization or Regionalization of the American and Asian Car Industry?* (2003).

Toshihiko Miyaji, Professor, Teikyo University, 'Joho-ka to Bijinesu Jitsumu no Henka' ('Changes in the development of information technology and business practices'), Teikyo Daigaku Tanki Daigaku Kiyo, vol. 21 (2001).

Yasuo Okamoto, Professor, Bunkyo Gakuin University & Professor Emeritus, University of Tokyo (eds), *Hokubei Nikkei Kigyo no Keiei: Managemnt at the Japanese Firms in North America* (2000).

Koji Okubayashi, Professor, Kobe University, 'The Japanese style of management of Japanese affiliates in Germany and UK,' in Thorpe, R. and Little, S. (eds), *Global Change: The Impact of Asian in the 21st Century* (2001).

Stanislaw Strzelczak, Ass.Dean for Int'l Education, Professor, Warsow University of Technology (ed.), *Economic and Managerial Developments in Asia and Europe: Comparative Studies* (2004).

Takahashi, Mitsuru, Professor, Teikyo University, *Chuka Shin Keizai System no Keisei (China's New Economic System)* (2004).

Hideo Tamura, Senior Staff Writer, Nihon Keizai Shinbun, Inc., *Jinmin gen, Doru, Yen (People's Yuan, US Dollar and Yen)* (2004).

Jaw-Yann Twu, Professor, Kokugakuin University (ed.), *East Asian Economic Regionalism and Japan (Higashi Ajia Keizai Chiiki-shugi to Nihon)* (1999).

Masatake Wada, Professor, Teikyo University (co-authored), *Shijou Keizai Ikou Shokoku no Risou to Genjitsu (The Idea and Reality for the Countries in the Transitional Market Economies)* (2003).

Katsuo Yamazaki, Associate Professor, *'Nikkei Jidosha Buhin Maker no Keiei Senryaku (Management Strategy of Japanese Auto Parts Makers)'*, The Japan Society of International Economics, *Kokusai Keizai*, vol. 55 (2004).

Zhi Jia Yuan, Professor, Rissho University, *Chugoku ni Ikiru Nichi-Bei Seisan Sisutemu: Handoutai Seisan Sisutemu no Kokusai Iten no Hikaku Bunseki (Japanese and American Production System in China: A Comparative Study of the International Transfer of Production System of Semi-conductors)* (2001).

Shuying Zhang, Director, Chinese Academy of Social Sciences (ed.), *Japanese Economy After the Cold War.*

*** The Teikyo University Sytem Laboratory

The Teikyo University System Laboratory ('Teikyo System Lab') was selected as one of the Academic Frontier Promotion Projects aided by the Ministry of Education, Culture, Sports, Science and Technology. It is the main institution to promote research studies on 'Global transfer of the Japanese management and production systems,' by the Japanese Multinational Enterprise Study Group (JMNESG). It has study meeting rooms with a network system, which makes most of the information accumulated, and analysed by the study group.

Development of the database and its managing system on the information have been carried out. The information for the system includes confidential matter from companies. The leaking of such information to the outside would be detrimental to the enterprise concerned and would create great difficulties in the future research activities Therefore, a firewall has been installed between the network and the Campus LAN and the server of the database is accessible only to the researchers concerned.

The data gathered ranges from primary data such as company interview records, factory questionnaire records, to generalization lists and diagrams that are evaluated and formed according to 'five-point evaluation models for application and adaptation hybrids.' The database system offers an easy and effective entering function of data, and searching and analysing function of information from the database, meeting the demands of the researchers.

The database system uses the database software ACCESS on Windows for the researchers' convenience. One of the constituent units of the overall database is made from the investigation of one company during a single visit and consists of the standardized data indicating industry, company, area/country; numerical data such as capital amount, investment share, etc. with which comparison on the basis of numerical value and analysis are possible; character (string) data that concretely describe the evaluation subject items, which should be expressed in sentences and secondary data of evaluation scores of the researchers.

The database offers the following various search and reference functions. For example, the company search function offers company searches by economic area, operating country, field of business, and searches by the company conditions, the key word input, item key word, and detail condition input. The relevant information search of more than one company from the database and its display on the same screen make possible comparative examination, so researchers are able to give more time and effort to analysis of the information, instead of searching for it.

The web site is http://appsv.main.teikyo-u.ac.jp/~jmnesg/index.html

Toshihiko Miyaji
Professor, Teikyo University Junior College

**** The main publications of JMNESG

Abo, T. (ed.), *Nihon Kigyo no Amerika Genchi Seisan: Jidosha to Denki; Nihon-teki Keiei no 'Tekiyo to Tekio'* (1988).

Abo, T. (ed.), *Local Production by Japanese Automobile and Electronics Firms in the United States; The 'Application and Adaptation' of Japanese Style Management*, The Institute of Social Science, University of Tokyo, Research Report No 23 (1990).

Abo, T., Itagaki, H., Kamiyama, K., Kawamura, T. and Kumon, H., *Amerika ni Ikiru Nihon-teki Keiei-Seisan Shisutemu*, Toyo Keizai Shinpo Sha (1991). *(Japanese Management and Production System Thrives in the United States).*

Abo, T. (ed.), *Hybrid Factory: The Japanese Production System in the United States* (1994).

Abo, T. (ed.), *Nihon-teki Keiei-Seisan Shisutemu to Amerika* (*The Japanese Management and Production System and America)* (1994).

Itagaki, H. (ed.), *Nihon-teki Keiei-Seisan Shisutemu to Higashi Ajia* (1997a) (*The Japanese Management and Production System in East Asia).*

Itagaki, H. (ed.), *The Japanese Production System: Hybrid Factories in East Asia* (1997b).

Kamiyama, K. and JMNESG (eds), *Kyodai-ka Suru Chugoku Keizai to Nikkei Haiburiddo Kojo* (*Toward Gigantic Chinese Economy and Japanese Hybrid Factories*) (2005).

Kawamura, T. (ed.), *Gurohbaru Keizai-ka no Amerika Nikkei Kigyo* (Toyo Keizai Shinpo Sha (2005) (*Japanese Firms in the United States under the Globalizing World Economy*).

Kumon, H. & Abo, T. (eds), *The Hybrid Factory in Europe: The Japanese Management and Production System Transferred* (2004).

Kumon, H. & Abo, T. (eds), *Nihon-gata Keiei-Seisan Shisutemu to EU: Haiburiddo Kojo no Hikaku Bunseki* (2005) *(The Japanese Style Management and Production System in EU).*

Wada, M. and Abo, T. (eds), *Chu-Tohoh no Nihon-gata Keiei-Seisan Shisutemu: Po-rando/Surobakia deno Juyo* (2005) (*The Japanese Style Management and Production System in Central and Eastern Europe: The Reception in Poland and Slovakia).*

Yuan, Z. J. and JMNESG (eds), *Chu-Tohoh no Haiburiddo Kojo: Kakudai EU ni Mukau Iko-Keizai ni okeru Nikkei Kojo* (forthcoming) *(Hybrid Factories in Central and Eastern Europe: The Japanese Plants in the Transitional Economies toward Enlargement to the East of EU).*

Acknowledgements

Since the begining of our research in the early 1980s there have been a great many individuals and organizations to whom we owed an enormous debt of gratitude for assistance and support in bringing a large numbers of our projects and the publications of their results to fruition.

First, now we have reached a point where we can sum up the overall research results carried out for almost twenty years, it would be relevant to list the main research foundations and organizations who have continually supported us. The Academic Frontier Promotion Project for Private Universities with the support of the Japanese Ministry of Education, Culture, Sports, Science and Technology and Teikyo university has been the most important foundation that has aided our project financially at the 'Teikyo System Lab' for the last five years (2000–2004). For about fifteen years preceding that our research was conducted with the support of the Toyota Foundation (1986, 1988–89), the former Japanese Ministry of Education (1992–93, 1998, 2000–2001) and the Japan Industrial Policy Research Institute (1997) at the Institute of Social Science, the University of Tokyo, and Teikyo University (also see the Preface).

Here, we would like to express our appreciation only to the individuals and organizations who have directly supported the present project and publication. At Teikyo university, 'Teikyo System Lab' (described above) was built as a research center for our project activities and the Teikyo System Laboratory symposium on 3 November 2004, and the publication processes such as the tape transcribing works of simultaneous translation have also been aided financially by the above Academic Frontier Promotion Project. At the symposium Mr Yoshihito Okinaga, the President of the university, and Professor Yutaka Tanabe, Dean, Department of Economics, participated and gave speeches, and many professors, graduate students and office staff contributed greatly in its preparations and administration.

In addition to the commentators and chairs who played admirable roles in the symposium (see the Preface), we would like to express our thanks to the sincere efforts of Professor Mira Wilkins, Florida International University, who is a foreign member of our group and tried to attend the symposium as a commentator but regrettably had to cancel. At Palgrave Macmillan, we wish to say particular thanks to Jacky Kippenberger, Editor, Pash Rebecca, former Assistant Editor and Ann Marangos, Copy-editor, who have been so kind and flexible in their scrupulous checking of the progress of our book. We are also grateful to the various translators: from Japanese manuscripts to English, to Ms Junko Yamaga and the translators at Lingua Gild Ltd, Miss Mitsuko Najima, and, at the symposium, to the simultaneous interpretors led by Ms Choko Harada at Diplomat, Inc.

Last but not least, we would like to take this opportunity to express our sincere thanks to the surveyed companies we visited. The following are the names of the Japanese and foreign firms that have been the most important supporters of our worldwide research activities for the last twenty years. Most of them welcomed us many times both at their parent and at their subsidiary companies. As mentioned later the total number of the plants we visited both in Japan and foreign countries is more than 600.

Japanese firms

Aikawa Press Co. Ltd
Aisan Industry Co. Ltd
Aisin Seiki Co. Ltd
Akebono Brake Industry Co. Ltd
Alps Electric Co. Ltd
Araco Corporation
Asahi Breweries, Ltd
Brother Industries, Ltd
Calsonic Kansei Corporation
Canon Inc.
Clarion Co. Ltd
Delta Kogyo Co. Ltd.
Denso Corporation
Eagle Industry Co. Ltd
Exedy Corporation
Hitachi, Ltd
Hitachi Cable, Ltd
Honda Motor Co. Ltd
Isuzu Motors Ltd
JETRO
Kenwood Corporation
Komatsu Ltd
Kyocera Corporation
Mabuchi Motor Co. Ltd
Matsushita Electric Industrial Co. Ltd
Mazda Motor Corporation
Minebea Co. Ltd
Mitsuba Corporation
Mitsubishi Electric Corporation
Mitsubishi Heavy Industries, Ltd
Mitsubishi Motors Corporation
NEC Corporation
NHK Spring Co. Ltd
Nissan Motor Co. Ltd
Ogihara Corporation
Olympus Corporation
Pioneer Corporation
Rohm Co. Ltd
Sanshin Electric Co. Ltd
Sanyo Electric Co. Ltd
Sharp Corporation
Shinwa Corporation
Showa Denko K.K.

Suzuki Motor Corporation
Takata Corporation
TDK Corporation
Toko Inc.
Toray Industries, Inc.
Toshiba Corporation
Toyota Gosei Co. Ltd
Toyota Motor Corporation
Victor Company of Japan, Ltd (JVC)
Yazaki Corporation
YKK Corporation
Yokogawa Electric Corporation

Major foreign firms

[China] Zongshen Group
[France] Renault Co. Ltd, PSA Peugeot Citroen SA
[Germany] Daimler-Benz AG, Volkswagen AG, BMW AG, Adam Opel AG
[Italy] Fiat Auto SpA
[Korea] Daewoo Public Motors Co. Ltd, Hyundai Motor Co. Ltd, Kia Motors Corp., L. G. Electronics Inc., Samsung Electronics Co., POSCO Ltd
[UK] MG Rover Group, Ltd, Ford Motor Co. Ltd (UK)
[USA] General Motors Corp., Ford Motor Co., Chrysler Corp., Motorola, Inc., IBM Corp., Texas Instruments, Inc., Delphi Auto System
[Sweden] Volvo Car Corp.
[Poland] Thomson Multimedia Polska Sp.zo.o., FWP 'VIS' S.A.

List of Abbreviations

AFTA	ASEAN Free Trade Association
ASEAN	Association of South-East Asian Nations
CD	Compact Disc
CKD	Completely Knocked Down
CQD	Cost, Quality and Delivery
CRT	Cathode Ray Tube
CTV	Color Television
EC	European Community
EU	European Union
FA	Factory Automation
FDI	Foreign Direct Investment
FPD	Flat Pack Display
FTA	Free Trade Agreement
GERPISA	Group d'Etude et de Recherche Permanent sur l'Industrie et les Salaries de l'Automobile (Permanent Group for the Study of the Automobile Industry and Its Employees)
IC	Integrated Circuit
IE	Industrial Engineer
ISO	International Standards Organization
JC	Job Classifications
JETRO	Japan External Trade Organization
JIT	Just In Time
JMNESG	Japanese Multinational Enterprise Study Group
JMPS	Japanese Management and Production System
JPS	Japanese Production System
JR	Job Rotation
JV	Joint Venture
M&A	Merger and Acquisition
MNE	Multinational Enterprise
OEM	Original Equipment Manufacturer
OJT	ON-the-Job Training
QA	Quality Assurance
QC	Quality Control
QCC	Quality Control Circle
R&D	Research & Development
SCM	Supply Chain Management

SKD	Semi-Knocked Down
TNC	Transnational Corporation
TPM	Total Productive Maintenance (or Total Preventive Maintenance)
TQC	Total Quality Control
VAT	Value Added Tax
VCR	Video Cassette Recorder
ZD	Zero Defect

1

Comparison of Japanese Hybrid Factories in the World: Generalities and Peculiarities of Patterns in the International Transfer of the Japanese Management and Production Systems

Tetsuo Abo

Introduction

The objectives of the Teikyo University System Laboratory Symposium (Teikyo System Labo) were to sum up the findings of research studies hitherto conducted by the Japanese Multinational Enterprise Study Group (JMNESG) on the theme entitled 'Global transfer of the Japanese management and production systems in major regions of the world: Japanese hybrid management (factories),' and to seek external evaluations from first-class experts both in Japan and abroad. The findings are the result of 20-years of effort by the JMNESG members, and particularly of research activities conducted during the past five years at the Teikyo System Laboratory as an 'Academic Frontier Promotion' project aided by the Ministry of Education, Culture, Sports, Science and Technology.

Japanese manufacturers' overseas operations, which entered into a fully fledged expansion phase in the later half of the 1980s, against the backdrop of intensifying trade friction and the rising value of the yen, are continuing to grow today though there was a temporary setback following the burst of the economic bubble in the early 1990s. The overseas production ratio of Japanese manufacturers – those which were called 'reluctant multinationals' in the early 1980s – has since risen remarkably, with electric machinery and car industries reaching a level above 50 per cent in recent years. In tandem with this, the Japanese management and production systems have been steadily spreading in various parts of the world. Figure 1.1 shows changes in

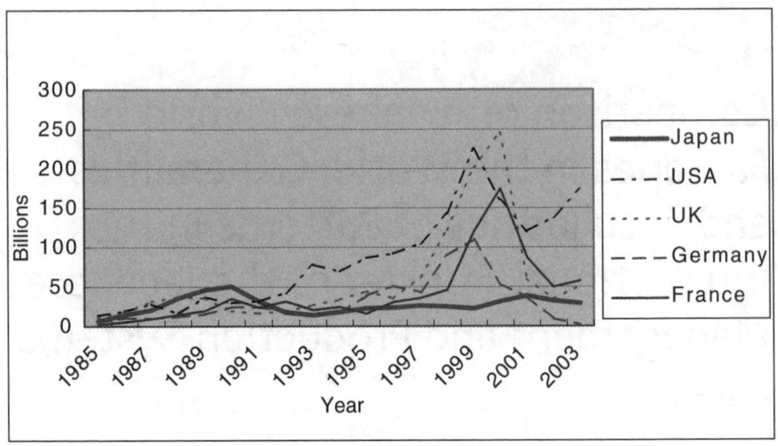

Source: IMF, *International Financial Statistics, Yearbook*, 1998 and September 2004.

Figure 1.1 FDIs by major countries

Japan's foreign direct investment (FDI), and gives macroeconomic statistical data that provides an insight in to Japanese companies' overseas operations.

This remarkable expansion is basically attributable to the international competitive advantage of Japanese companies and their highly flexible adaptability to different operational conditions. However, on the other side of the coin, Japanese companies have been faced with a range of tough challenges in adapting to local environments because of the organizational cultural traits of the Japanese system, which also is the very factor underlying their competitive advantage. Thus, the same question has been persistently asked. Just to what extent is the Japanese system internationally applicable? In other words, it is the question of generalities and peculiarities of the Japanese business and management systems that translate into different degrees of applicability when they are internationally transferred. Indeed, a number of scholarly arguments have been made on this subject. If we could clearly identify and extract factors representing the general or universal aspects of the Japanese system, it would help us – at least to some extent – to quantify the degree of international transferability of the Japanese system. And then, we would be able to address the practical needs of Japanese companies seeking to further expand operations overseas. However, the more we proceeded with our research, the more we were assured that the competitive advantage of the Japanese system is greatly attributable to the very peculiarities of the system. Based on this observation, we decided that both our points of interest and our tasks in this project should be to examine various factors constituting the Japanese system, to classify them into two groups – general factors that have relatively high applicability and specific factors that do not – through comparative analysis of the results of our extensive on-site surveys at factories across the world, and then, more importantly, to find out, both empirically and theoretically, how these specific elements have been transferred to various parts of the world and how they demonstrate strength in the respective countries and regions.

As such, since the mid-1980s, at the JMNESG we have been conducting systematic and extensive on-site surveys on Japanese factories overseas with special focus on those in major regions and countries. The focal points of our research studies are as follows. Our primary focus is on how the Japanese management and production systems – which have been developed on the social and business environments of Japan – can be transferred to various countries and regions in the world, each of which has different social and business environments, and what modifications had and have to be made to the Japanese systems even when they are transferable. More specifically, we shed light on Japanese companies' workplace-based approaches in the management and operations of factories, i.e. flexible work organizations, the fostering of worker technologies and skills in a build-up manner, quality control and facility management systems based on the principle of participation by all the workers, forging of long-term counterpart relationships with suppliers, and so forth. These are the factors underlying the strength of Japanese companies, and they have been developed and operated on the basis of participation-oriented personal relationships where cooperation and competition coexist. We have examined how these approaches have been transferred to and taken root in various regions and countries. Furthermore, we have tried to find out to what extent foreign companies would be able to adopt the strength factors of the Japanese system and under what conditions.

Since its launch in the mid-1980s, the JMNESG has come to embrace several tens of member researchers and collaborative researchers both in Japan and abroad. Research activities had taken place primarily at the University of Tokyo's Institute of Social Science up until 1998 and from then onward the Teikyo University System Lab had been serving as a base station for research activities. We have so far conducted 10 rounds of full-scale on-site surveys with the participation of all the research members, visiting some 400 overseas factories – mostly automobile and electric machinery assembling factories – in eight regions and 30 countries (including those visited more than once). The total number of factories subjected to our survey exceeds 600 if domestic factories as well as overseas factories visited by individual members or groups of members are included (see the Teikyo University website at http://appsv.main.teikyo-u.ac.jp/~jmnesg/index.html).

When we proceed further with these research activities, we would probably be able to clarify the state of transfer and spread of the Japanese management and productions systems under various social and management environments around the world and thus to obtain a comparative picture of system attributes and industry-by-industry differences. And through this, we do hope that we will be able to make a sizable contribution to research developments in various academic fields, for instance, to the development of international comparative study on management systems, technology transfer theory, Japanese system theory, and the theory of economic/management geography (Abo, 2004a). Not only that, we believe that our efforts would provide Japanese companies and entrepreneurs with significant guidelines in developing management strategies for both domestic and overseas operations in the era of globalization in which the ratio of overseas operations exceeds 50 per cent at many companies. As an analytical framework for examining the above-described research subjects, the JMNESG developed a 'five-point evaluation model for application and adaptation hybrids' (to be described later). This framework enables us to sort out and evaluate – in a consistent and integrated manner – information and data collected first-hand through our surveys on various companies and factories across the world. With this, we can perform a comparative dynamic analysis both quantitatively and qualitatively by plotting area values – such as inter-regional, inter-industry and inter-company – on the horizontal axis and time-series values on the vertical axis. It is no exaggeration to say that this model – which is now being used also for analysing foreign companies' adoption of the Japanese system – has now become a kind of international standard for evaluating the transfer of management and production systems by multinationals.

Overall research trend and our research concerning the international transfer of the Japanese management and production systems

A considerable volume of research and studies have been made over years to investigate the competitive advantage of the Japanese management and production systems and the possibility of their international transfer. Here, however, I would like to touch on the overall development of such research and studies but limit my discussion to considering the recent arguments related to the theme of this Symposium. Research activities in this field have been carried out in the form of arguments on the so-called Japanese management theory. A series of pioneering research works, which were carried out as discovery attempts when the competitive advantage of the Japanese system was not so visible, include Abegglen (1958) in the late 1950s, Dore (1978), Ozawa (1979), Koike (1977) in the 1970s. These were followed by Takamiya (1981), Trevor (1982), Cole (1981), Aoki (1989), Kagono *et al.* (1983), Itami (1987), Abo and JMNESG (1990,1988), Oliver and Wilkinson (1988), and the MIT Industrial Productivity Studies Committee (1989) in the 1980s, which together expanded the scope of research and studies in this field. This trend was carried further into the 1990s. Against the backdrop of the remarkable performance of the Japanese economy and Japanese companies' expansion both at home and abroad in the 1980s, the publication of research works that positively evaluate the Japanese system culminated in work by Womack *et al.* (1990), Porter (1990), Clark and Fujimoto (1991), Abo and JMNESG (1991), Hashimoto (1991), Adler (1993), Kenney and Florida (1994), Okubayashi *et al.* (1994), Elger and Smith (1994), and so forth. Almost at the same time, however, the reversal of economic conditions in Japan and the US, with Japan plunging into economic doldrums over a decade and more, following the burst of the economic bubble in the early 1990s on one hand and the US enjoying the booming economy led by IT revolution on the other, gave rise to another trend of studies. Specifically, market fundamentalism based on the American standards and entailing skepticism over the entire Japanese system – as seen in a range of 'Japan-is-no-good' arguments and those calling for 'structural reforms' – have permeated from the mass media into academia at an astounding pace. (*Manifest for a Market-Oriented Economy* published in 1997 by the Japan Association of Corporate Executives is one typical example of this trend.) Yet, even against this backlash, steady and persistent research efforts have been made not to overlook the comparative advantage of the Japanese system as seen in the works by MacDuffie (1996), Fujimoto (1997), Abo, Itagaki, Kamiyama, Kumon, Kawamura (JMNESG) (1994, 1997, 1998, 2005), Boyer *et al.* (1998), Liker *et al.* (1999), Beechler and Bird (1999), Okamoto (2000), Keeley (2001), Saka (2003), Hood (2003), Elger and Smith (2005), and so forth. And now into the 21st century, the IT bubble has run its course and

entered a new stage, and the strength of the Japanese management system and industrial technologies – as demonstrated by automotive-related sectors and in the field of digital electronic appliances – are now being re-evaluated, though in a more relative light.

Now, let me define the meaning and positioning of our studies against the backdrop of this overall research trend. The fundamental viewpoint, upon which our studies are based, can be described as an 'organizational culture approach.' It is based on the 'organizational principles,' an idea upon which Dore (1973) and others have constructed their arguments. At the same time, however, we emphasize 'culture' as a factor that determines the qualitative nature of an organization in characterizing the business management system of Japanese companies. The organizational principles, with their unique logic, give influence to the universality of the market principle (as seen in the internalization theory formulated by Coase [1937] and Williamson [1975]). When cultural factors – those determined by the historical and social backgrounds of each region – are added to them, certain differences come to light on the way organizations and institutions are shaped and what functions they play. We believe that the comparative advantage of the Japanese management and production systems is related to certain elements of the Japanese culture (Abo, 2004a), which has been formed by the 'homogeneous and inward-looking' people in an East Asian, insular environment. Therefore, we assume that any attempt to transfer these Japanese systems, and have them take root in a regional society with different cultural and business environments, would cause gaps and friction, and certain modifications would inevitably have to be made.

To check the validity of the 'organizational culture approach' discussed above, let me introduce and examine two major arguments in the field of management theory.

Somewhat surprisingly, Porter's theory on competitive advantage, based on how I understand it, shows a strong characteristic of a theory of 'social and cultural dependency.' To begin with, the very title of his book, *The Competitive Advantage of Nations* (Porter, 1990), indicates that a nation (region) is the basic unit in defining competitive advantage. It is a comparative advantage theory in which countries are compared in terms of their advantage with respect to a specific industrial sector. And in this sense, it is very faithful to the Ricardian theory. The book is famous for the 'diamond,' a model showing factors that determine the competitiveness of a country. This, however, should be taken as secondary in view of the original intention of the book. Porter's 'diamond' lists four types of conditions – factor conditions, demand conditions, related and supporting industries, and strategy, structure and competition – as key components of environment under which companies of a country compete. These are relatively common sense propositions, though they are useful as a reference.

Porter sets out that the competitive advantage of a country tends to concentrate in a specific industry (or a cluster). His theory of competitive advantage of nations starts from the Ricardian model that has established the basic theory of international trade from this idea of industry-based comparative advantage. Porter argues that the Heckscher–Ohlin model or the factor-endowment model – which is an attempt to reinforce the simple Ricardian model – is insufficient. And then, while emphasizing the dynamic roles played by companies such as seen in technology development and competition strategies, he insists on the importance of roles played by their home country that provide a regulatory influence on corporate behaviors. In other words, while corporate strategies and behavioral norms differ from one sector to another, all of these factors are subject to the influence of features unique to each country (national attributes) such as the type of skills in which employees are trained, the nature of domestic demand, and the goal of investors. Porter says it is these unique features of a country that enable companies to avow a certain strategy, give them an impetus, and help them continuously upgrade the sources of their competitiveness. The question is what factors determinate such national attributes. And according to Porter, 'national economic structures, values, cultures, institutions and histories' are the major determinants (op.cit., pp.19, 129). In particular, Porter argues that cultural factors – which form the overall social and business environment and, by way of determinants, come into play – are important because they are slow to change and difficult for outsiders to emulate, and therefore, any differences in these factors last forever.

It seems to me that this argument of Porter's shows that he was deeply conscious of Japan in writing this particular book. This is apparent from his remarks in the preface of the book, in which he says that he, for the first time in his research history, became consciously aware of the significance of the existence of nations in his framework, when he was appointed to serve on President Ronald Reagan's Commission on Industrial Competitiveness, an experience that has subsequently led Porter to include the concept of national competitive advantage into his research framework. The commission was formed in 1985 when the Japanese management model was receiving a great deal of world attention. Its primary mandates were to study the Japanese model and to rethink the importance of 'industrial policy' as a means to counter competition from Japan.

Certainly, however, it is not the case that Porter consistently maintains his theory on culture as key determinant throughout the chapter in which he discusses Japan. While Porter repeatedly points to the 'cultural and ethnic homogeneity' (ibid., p. 401) of Japan as a determinant of the competitive advantage of Japanese companies, some portions of his account in the same chapter negate such cultural theory. For instance, he maintains that cooperative labor–management relationships are not a phenomenon that is naturally born out of certain cultural circumstances (ibid., 409) and that 'cultural' factors are often attributable to the 'diamond' (p. 420). Furthermore, in his more recent studies on Japan (in his Japanese book [2000], with Takeuchi), it seems that the cultural approach has receded with the downturn of the Japanese economy and emphasis is now placed more on 'showing that the same principles for success in competition, which are universally seen across the world, apply to Japan' (ibid., p. 30).

Okamoto's dichotomic analysis of management structure

A study on Japanese companies' management of their subsidiaries' in North America conducted by the 'Okamoto group' of researchers (Okamoto, 2000) presents a classification system for sorting out features of various management structures and their argument therein relates to the generalities and peculiarities of the Japanese management system in terms of their international transferability. Chapter 2 of the book (written by Mikio Anzai) divides the overall features of management structures into two groups – 'non-Japanese' factors and 'Japanese' factors (as classified by T. Burns, etc.) – with the former categorized as 'mechanistic system' and the latter as 'organic system.' In Chapter 9 (here, 'American' versus 'Japanese'), Okamoto further divides the features classified as the Japanese-style organic systems into two types of dimensions, i.e. functional rational dimensions and groupism, affective dimensions. Okamoto then defines the group-ism, affective dimensions – such as small group activities and the so-called '5-S' quality control activities – as the peculiar aspects of Japanese-style organizations on one hand, and the functional rational dimensions – diversification of skills performed by a single worker, built-in quality control, and multifunctional supervisors as elements constituting an overall workplace mechanism – as representing the general aspects of these organizations on the on the other (op.cit., pp. 223, 237–43, 247–8, in Japanese).

More specifically, he says:

> The organic structural features of Japanese companies, though in some aspects they were originally formed by social and cultural factors unique to Japan ... have been able to deliver reasonable achievements by proactively seeking functional rational factors, i.e. greater adaptability to changing environment based on greater discretion and flexibility in organizational factors. In cases of Japanese affiliates in North America, the affective dimensions of the Japanese system have been suppressed through a sort of cross-pollination ... and now flowers showing more preference for functional rationality are beginning to bloom ... (ibid., p. 223).

It is deemed that because the group-ism, affective dimensions are irrational at least outside Japan and thus do not have general applicability, Japanese companies – in transferring their management system overseas – should select strategically the functional rational dimensions and combined them with local resources to create a 'Japan plus alpha' composite system.

The most critical question that arises in relation to our argument is whether we can conclude readily that general and rational factors applicable to the rest of the world can be derived by simply removing all the group-ism, affective dimensions from the Japanese organizational features. Can those 'functional rational' factors, as defined in the above context, attain 'rationality' so easily when they are detached from the Japanese social and cultural environment? Indeed, Okamoto himself points to various 'conflicts' between the Japanese personnel management system and American-style practices for personnel and labor management. For instance, he cites the strong influence of the American-style job task-based wage payment system (pp. 226–7), the difficulty of diversifying skills performed by a single worker (p. 228), and the institutionalized differences (clear task demarcation) between general factory workers and mechanics (pp. 239, 254–5). Meanwhile, regarding the 'built-in quality control system' and 'multifunctional supervisors,' the survey conducted by the Okamoto group (in which respondents were asked to do all the evaluations) has found that North American affiliates have achieved a level that is close to the average of major Japanese companies. Our survey to be described later, however, has found that there still exist substantial gaps between North American subsidiaries and their parents in Japan.

This kind of difficulty faced in duplicating the Japanese system is not a matter that simply concerns segmental issues such as whether small group activities can be implemented or whether a union exists. Instead, we should assume that the difficulty stems from the fundamental differences in the underlying 'principles of organization' (here, represented by task segmentation and other demarcation problems) that provide foundation in building institutions. Yet, in considering this difficulty involving the international transfer of management and production systems, which stems from differences in social and cultural environments, it is not appropriate to take a fatalistic approach. I would like to examine this point in the summary section at the end of this chapter.

As such, theoretical assumptions underlying our study on the possibility of international transfer of Japanese management and production systems are neither optimistic nor pessimistic focusing solely on difficulties. The basic framework of our research can be described as follows: First, we formulate some basic models of the Japanese system based on thorough observations and analysis of Japanese companies and their factories. Next, through systematic and extensive surveys on overseas factories, we closely examine how the organizational cultural characteristics of Japanese companies differ from those of local companies that are under the influence of the local communities and management environment of the respective regions to which the Japanese system is transferred. Then, using the aforementioned 'application– adaptation (hybrid) evaluation model,' we attempt to evaluate and analyze, in a concrete and theoretical manner, what types of management and operation systems – in terms of the extent to which the Japanese systems are mixed with local systems – have been realized in each region.

International comparison of hybrid factories

'Application–adaptation (hybrid) evaluation model' and 'five-point grading system': analytical framework for research

This survey seeks to investigate the management and production systems of major Japanese manufacturers with comparative advantage such as automakers and electric and electronics machinery makers, compare the situation of mother factories in Japan with those of subsidiaries' factories abroad, and then, measure and evaluate the degree of overseas transfer of Japanese systems by utilizing the 'application–adaptation (hybrid) evaluation model' and the 'five-point grading system.' For this purpose, an ideal model for the composition of Japanese management and production systems (see Table 1.2 'Six-group, 23-item hybrid evaluation') has been developed based on the results of our surveys on Japanese parent factories. The introduction and transplanting of each factor item constituting the Japanese system into an overseas factory is referred to as 'application,' whereas any modification made to an original factor in accordance with the local management environment is called 'adaptation.' The 'five-point grading system' is designed to show quantitatively the results of the application–adaptation evaluation. For instance, if an overseas factory is found to have implemented a certain factor of the Japanese system 100 per cent, an application ratio score of '5' (meaning zero modification, and consequently, the adaptation ratio score of '1') will be given to that factory, while an application score of '1' (meaning 100 per cent modification into the local system, and consequently, an adaptation score of '5') will be given if no transfer of Japanese factors has been made (see Figure 1.2 and Appendix). Any scores referred to hereinafter represent application scores unless otherwise specified.

For this, let us turn to the 'four-perspective evaluation system,' another useful method developed by us to evaluate and judge the substantive content of international transfers of management systems and technologies. To begin with, of the six-group, 23-item hybrid analysis framework, 21 evaluation items are taken and classified in accordance with two dimensional factors, namely, 'Methods', which refers to the transfer of intangible elements such as technique and know-how

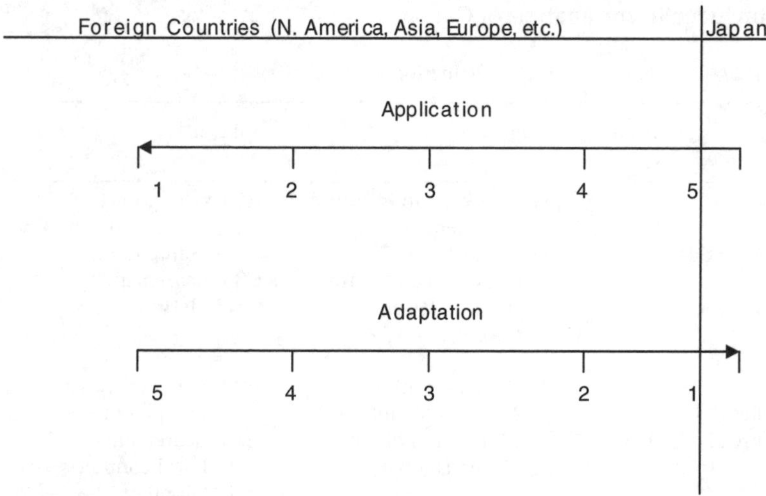

Figure 1.2 Concept of application–adaptation evaluation method

required in building an organization and implementing personnel administration and 'Results', which concerns the transfer of machinery, parts and any other visible elements of 'ready-made' hardware including the dispatch of Japanese expatriates. Then, each of these two types of perspectives is further divided into two groups, i.e. 'Human' and 'Material,' thereby forming a four-way matrix to evaluate the degree to which a certain system has taken root in a local community (see Table 1.1). (For more details see Abo, 1994, chs 1 and 2, Itagaki, 1997, ch 1).

Table 1.2 summarizes the major portion of the evaluation results. By analyzing data listed in this table, it is possible to examine the degree to which various factors composing the Japanese system have been transplanted in to Japanese factories overseas and to compare the situations by region or country and by industry, or between different points of time. This 'six-group, 23-item evaluation' is an orthodox, performance-oriented approach focusing on efficiency and quality which examines – from the viewpoint of Japanese parent companies and their factories in Japan – to what extent their competitive advantage has been transplanted into subsidiaries' factories overseas. On the other hand, the 'four-perspective evaluation system' is used as a means to analyze situations from the viewpoint of each host community, shedding light on the substance and nature of technology transfer.

In this symposium, we take five specific countries and regions, each of which will be discussed later. Of these, however, China and Central and East Europe are not included in Table 1.2 (but these two are included in the analysis of Chapter 9).

Table 1.1 Four perspective evaluation method

Element / *Method*	*Human*	*Material*
Methods	G1 Work organ.& admin. • All items: 1 ~ 6 G4 Team sense • All items: 14 ~ 16 G5 Labor relations • All items: 17 ~ 20	G2 Production control 8 Quality control 9 Maintenance G3 Procurement 13 Methods
Results ('ready-made')	G6 Parent–subsidiaries 21 Ratio of Japanese 23 Position of local managers	G2 Production control 7 Equipment G3 Procurement 11 Local content 12 Suppliers

Source: Table 1.2.

Table 1.2 Application ratios of the Japanese production systems at overseas Japanese plants

	N. America (01)	*N. America (89)*	*UK (97)*	*Continental Europe (98)*	*Korea/ Taiwan (92)*	*Southeast Asia (93)*
I Work organization and administration	3.2	2.9	3.4	3.0	3.7	3.3
1. Job classification	4.1	3.7	4.4	3.2	4.9	4.5
2. Multi-functional skills	3.0	2.6	3.3	2.8	2.9	2.6
3. Education and training	3.7	2.9	3.5	3.1	3.4	3.3
4. Wage system	2.3	2.4	2.8	2.8	3.9	3.1
5. Promotion	2.9	3.1	3.4	3.1	3.7	3.1
6. Supervisor	3.2	2.9	3.4	3.1	3.4	2.9
II Production Control	3.4	3.3	3.5	3.1	3.5	3.4
7. Equipment	3.9	4.3	3.9	3.4	3.5	4.0
8. Maintenance	3.1	2.6	3.0	2.8	3.3	3.0
9. Quality control	3.4	3.4	3.6	3.1	3.6	3.2
10. Process management	3.5	3.0	3.6	3.2	3.5	3.2
III Procurement	2.6	3.0	2.5	2.8	3.2	3.2
11. Local Content	1.8	2.7	1.9	2.8	2.9	3.1
12. Suppliers	2.9	3.9	2.7	2.9	3.5	3.8
13. Methods	3.1	2.5	2.9	2.8	3.2	2.8
IV Team Sense	3.3	3.2	3.3	2.7	3.4	3.2
14. Small group	2.6	2.5	2.7	2.5	3.2	2.9
15. Information sharing	3.6	3.6	3.6	2.8	3.5	3.3
16. Sense of unity	3.7	3.5	3.7	2.8	3.6	3.3
V Labor Relations	3.7	3.6	3.6	3.2	3.4	3.1
17. Hiring policy	3.6	3.4	3.3	3.1	3.0	3.1
18. Long-term employment	3.5	3.4	3.4	3.2	3.3	3.0
19. Harmonious labor Relations	4.2	4.4	4.2	3.5	4.0	3.3
20. Grievance	3.7	3.3	3.0	3.1	3.2	3.1
VI Parent–subsidiary relations	2.8	3.6	2.8	3.0	2.3	2.9
21. Ratio of Japanese	2.1	3.7	2.4	2.6	1.5	1.6
22. Delegation of power	3.1	3.6	3.0	3.2	2.7	3.2
23. Position of local managers	3.1	3.6	3.0	3.1	2.7	3.8
Total average of 23 items	3.2	3.3	3.3	3.0	3.3	3.2

Note: Scores are only those of application
Source: From the data base of JMNESG (research year).

Characteristics of the Japanese management and production systems: in the light of international transfer models

Let me briefly explain the basic way the Japanese model described above should be understood. What needs to be pointed out here is the relationship between the reversal in economic fortunes in the 1990s and the change in the status of the Japanese management system. More specifically, while the whole Japanese economy slumped following the burst of economic bubble in the early 1990s, the IT revolution progressed throughout the 1990s particularly in the United States. And against this backdrop, there emerged a tendency to degrade the conventional Japanese models and we began to hear a chorus of calls for 'structural reforms.' In this context, I do acknowledge that the Japanese models had their heydays in the mid-1980s and that our prototype of Japanese management and production systems has been developed from those systems developed in such a prime period. However, I do not believe that the international competitiveness of these Japanese systems has totally collapsed since. That is not the case with regard to such sectors as automobile and auto parts, electric and electronics machinery parts, and precision machinery. Therefore, although it is necessary to pay due attention to the recent moves made by some leading Japanese companies (primarily by major electric and electronics machinery assembly companies whose business performance temporarily deteriorated) to overhaul the lifetime employment system and/or the age-based remuneration system and to carry out a large-scale restructuring, I do believe that these Japanese systems still remain sufficiently valid as a prototype of the Japanese model so far as the sectors of industry and the nature of technology are adequately defined. This is to say that while building such an ideal type that represents each stage of the times, we also need to measure the distance from the ideal type as a methodological means to evaluate the current state of affairs.

The characteristics of the Japanese management and production systems (Abo, 1994; Itagaki, 1997) lie, first and foremost, in the way of defining authority and responsibility broadly and loosely. This would allow substantial versatility for each worker of a factory to divide and/or combine job tasks with other workers, consequently, enabling the factory to turn out a wide range of products in small lots and respond to the changing needs of market quickly and flexibly. To make this happen, however, each member needs to be fully familiar with the rules of the company to which he or she belongs as well as with the condition of the workplace. And then, in order for workers to demonstrate a certain degree of competency for making judgment so that they can cope with any changes in the condition of their workplace (*genba shugi*, or shop floor-oriented system), each one of them must be equipped with adequate and broad knowledge and skills in accordance with his or her assigned position at the workplace (Koike, 1977 in Japanese, 1988 in English). But having employees trained for multiple kinds of company-specific job skills cannot be achieved through ready-made professional education and training programs. This necessitated companies to nurture employees through in-house on-the-job training (OJT) based on the premise of 'lifetime employment,' which led to the establishment of a 'person-centered' job performance evaluation system (as compared to American-style 'job task centered' wage system). The introduction of such person-centered system – a kind of ability-based grade system that combines a merit-rating system and a seniority system – has enabled the formation and utilization of human resources in a 'made-to-order' or 'homemade' manner, hence, the formation of an internal labor market system. The system is suitable for the type of sectors and businesses in which relatively homogeneous and inward-looking people get together to carry out certain tasks while balancing competition and cooperation. This is an area where product differentiation and meticulous quality control – even in an environment of mass production – hold the key to success and therefore many of those in the workplace are required to have a substantial ability to make judgments and a willingness to improve themselves.

To borrow terms used in a taxonomy of technologies (Fujimoto *et al.*, 2001; also Table 8.1 in ch. 8), this particular Japanese system is also suitable for industries with 'integral-type' production system, for instance, the automobile industry where the designing and manufacturing of a product requires the fine-tuned 'suriawase (tight coordination)' of technologies by each member being involved in the process ranging from the designing of molds to the final stage of assembling and inspection. This system is distinguished from the 'modular-type' production system – such as 'Dell production system' for computers that has been receiving much attention in conjunction with the IT revolution – which is to assemble ready-made parts and materials procured from outside market on an as-needed basis and in a cost-oriented manner.

Six-group, 23-item evaluation

With regard to Table 1.1, I would like to go directly to the evaluation results, omitting the explanation for each item or group (Abo, 1994; Itagaki, 1997).

Meaning of the average scores of 23 items

In Table 1.1, each region's average score of the 23 items falls in the range 3.0–3.3. This means that some sort of 'hybrid management' system – in which a little more than half the elements are of Japanese with the remaining elements reflective of local characteristics – is being implemented in Japanese factories operating in each of these regions. Or, by focusing on the fact that the average scores for all the regions – including North America where Japanese factories have been operating for more than a decade along with relatively new destinations such as China and the Central and East Europe (Table 9.1 in Chapter 9) – remain within this range, we can assume that, as far as average scores are concerned, there is little likelihood of overseas Japanese factories getting substantially closer to the level of their parent factories in Japan. In a sense, these evaluation results may provide a concrete clue in determining the limit of the generalization with regard to the internationalization of Japanese production systems. However, average scores themselves are no more meaningful, for instance, higher scores for Equipment, Local content (rate of locally procured materials and parts), and JPN ratio (ratio of Japanese expatriates to total employees) indicate a greater likelihood of achieving production efficiency that is comparable to that of parent factories in Japan. At the same time, however, this can be interpreted negatively because, as to be discussed later, such a situation – characterized by high scores for both 'Material–Results' and 'Human–Results,' i.e. heavy reliance on the transfer of ready-made materials and personnel from Japan – is undesirable from the viewpoint of adaptation to local environment. What is more important from the standpoint of 'cultural approach,' which is the prime theme of this chapter, is to examine the semantic content of various differences, which I will discuss in the following.

Regional comparison across the world in six groups

Figure 1.3 provides the most succinct picture of regional differences in the situations of hybrid factories focusing on the six aspects of their characteristics. Major points of arguments derived from this are as follows:

Different patterns. Conspicuous regional differences in scores for the six groups of characteristics and the shapes of hexagons are observed between the following groups of countries and regions:

(a) North America (89) and Continental Europe versus South Korea, Taiwan and Britain.

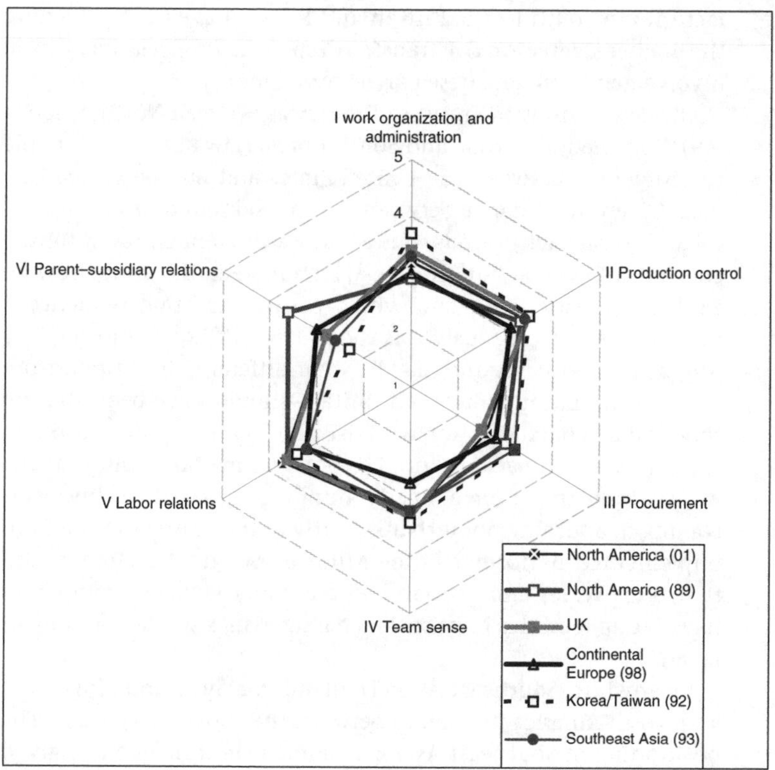

Source: Table 1.2.

Figure 1.3 Comparison of Japanese hybrid plants in the world

What is noteworthy here is a sharp contrast between these two groups of regions and countries with factory patterns for North America (89) and Continental Europe being almost mirror opposites of those for South Korea/Taiwan and Britain. Specifically, North America (89) and Continental Europe have relatively low scores for G-I Work organization/administration, which forms the 'core personnel-related portion' of the Japanese system, and high scores for G-VI Parent/subsidiary, whereas South Korea/Taiwan and Britain post high scores for G-I and low scores for G-VI. That is, the degree of transfer of G-I remains rather modest in North America (89) and Continental Europe despite the considerable involvement of Japanese parent companies as indicated by the high ratios of Japanese expatriates to total employees. On the other hand, hybrid factories in South Korea/Taiwan and Britain have been achieving the higher degree of G-I transfer despite having relatively little involvement from Japanese parent companies.

Of these contrasting results, differences between North America (89)/Continental Europe and South Korea/Taiwan are attributable to differences between the United States and Europe versus East Asia. Given the distance between the two sides in terms of historical and social backgrounds, this is quite a convenient result for the cultural approach. But the big question remains as to how to explain the case of Britain which shows the same tendency – though less conspicuously – as those of South Korea/Taiwan. The Anglo-Saxon background may be what differentiates Britain from Continental Europe. But then, Britain should have been sharing the similar characteristics with North America which also has the Anglo-Saxon background. For now, let me point out that the British industry, after a nearly hundred years of decline, was coming to a turning point thanks partly to the drastic social reform implemented by former Prime Minister Margaret Thatcher, and that both Wales and Scotland where many Japanese companies have set up factories have social characteristics similar to those of Japan.

Meanwhile, Southeast Asia (Thailand, Malaysia and Singapore) and North America (01) fall in between the above two groups. The positioning of Southeast Asia is to some extent imaginable given the background of this region which, while historically influenced by Europe, has a sizable population of overseas Chinese. But the case of North America (01) came as a bit of surprise because the result of the 2000–2001 survey shows that the situation of this region has changed substantially since 1989 when we conducted the previous survey there, and that the hexagon for North America (01) has become similar in shape to that of Britain. (As we are still trying to determine the meaning of this, I will not discuss this further: see Chapter 2)

(b) South Korea/Taiwan, Southeast Asia, and North America (89) versus Britain and North America (01).

Differences can be found with regard to G-III Parts procurement for which South Korea/Taiwan, Southeast Asia and North America (89) scale conspicuously high application scores while Britain and North America (01) have low scores and Continental Europe comes in between. The situation is somewhat complex for G-III because the meaning of scores can be different depending on to which of the items within the group the scores are attributable. Generally speaking, however, the high scores for Southeast Asia reflect the fact that the region does not have a sufficiently developed domestic parts industry and therefore Japanese factories need to rely on parts imported from Japan and/or those procured from Japanese affiliated suppliers operating in the region. In contrast, the presence of a well-established domestic parts industry and the implementation of strict local content requirement (particularly in the 1990s when the survey was conducted) are deemed to have contributed to the high scores for Europe. Here again, the 2000–2001 survey on North America revealed a sharp drop in the application score (sharp increase in the adaptation score) as compared to the results in the previous survey (Chapter 2). This is attributable to the expansion and deepening of local production, particularly in the automobile sector, and the subsequent reinforcement of supply bases for procuring the relevant parts and material.

Common patterns

(a) *A group for which all the regions have scores close to each other.* Regardless of region and time, scores for G-II Production control are, almost without exception, close to each other. This is because production control represents the 'core portion of Material' of the Japanese production system, a key condition that is required and has a direct impact in bringing in the strength of the system. Indeed, this group is composed of the kind of items upon which companies would place great emphasis. As shown in Table 1.1, many of the production equipments are either made-in-Japan products or those made by local affiliates of Japanese equipment makers with some adjustments made so that they fit the needs of each user company, thus, resulting in almost equally high scores across the board. Also, Japanese expatriates are substantially involved, either directly or indirectly, in both quality control and operation management to realize conditions that are as close as possible to – though not perfectly same as – the Japanese system and to ensure that no problems arise. With respect to maintenance, a considerable gap is observed between North America (89) and Continental Europe, which is attributable to the difference in the education and training systems of the two regions. However, the score for this item in North America (01) has reached a level comparable to that of Britain. It is noteworthy that such a significant change is observed after more than 10 years since Japanese factories began to operate in the region because this indicates the possibility that a certain degree of change can be made to the existing regional patterns.

(b) *Continental Europe versus the others.*
For G-IV Team sense, Continental Europe has a conspicuously low score (2.7) while scores for all the other regions are at or around 3.3. Certainly, a closer look at the detailed breakdown results based on the 23-item classification in Table 1.3.1 and 1.3.2 shows that scores for small group activities are concentrated at the lowest level ranging between 2.5 and 2.7 except for South Korea/Taiwan and Southeast Asia. But all the regions but Continental Europe posted high scores for the other two items – Information sharing and the Sense of unity – and this resulted in the above-mentioned outcome for G-IV. In Continental Europe, there still exists the traditional idea of dichotomy in the division of social classes, which translates into the division between labor and management. And under such labor–management relations, there would be a limit to the introduction of personnel policies or the formation of human relationships based on the principle of unanimous participation and cooperation. On the other hand, it seems quite natural that many aspects of the Japanese system – such as a company cafeteria, parking lots, and company parties for all employees – are welcomed in many regions, that is, as long as these aspects do not require the 'self-sacrifice' of time and labor on the part of employees under a sort of 'peer pressure' as is the case with small group activities.

Inter-industry comparison in six groups

As discussed earlier in relation to Porter's arguments, the competitive advantage of industry differs by country and/or by region. Therefore, a certain industry whose comparative advantage lies in the Japanese system have different 'compatibility' with different regions to which the system is transferred, which is more or less reflected in the patterns of hybrid factories.

Although I do not want to discuss this at length, Table 1.3.1, Table 1.3.2, Figure 1.4.1, and Figure 1.4.2 show that North America and Southeast Asia are somewhat symmetrical to each other in the relational patterns between two major industries, i.e. automobile assembly, and electric and electronics machinery assembly. In the case of North America, overall application scores and thus the size of hexagon for automobile assembly factories far exceed those for electric

Table 1.3.1 International comparison of auto assembly hybrid plants – 6 group

	N. America (01)	*UK*	*Continental Europe*	*N. America (89)*	*Korea/ Taiwan*	*Southeast Asia*
I Work organ./ admin.	3.4	3.8	3.2	3.3	3.9	3.4
II Production control	4	3.3	3	3.4	3.6	2.9
III Procurement	2.7	1.9	2.4	3	3	3.1
IV Team sense	3.6	3.3	2.5	3.9	3.9	2.9
V Labor relations	4.3	3.8	3.1	4.2	3.6	3.2
VI Parent–subsidiary relations	2.8	2.6	2.9	3.5	2.2	2.4
Total average	3.5	3.4	2.9	3.5	3.5	3

Source: From JMNESG's database.

Table 1.3.2 International comparison of electric/electro assembly hybrid plants – 6 group

	N. America (01)	*UK*	*Continental Europe*	*N. America (89)*	*Korea/ Taiwan*	*Southeast Asia*
I Work organ./ admin.	2.5	3.4	3	2.3	3.8	3.2
II Production control	2.7	3.8	3.3	3	3.7	3.4
III Procurement	3.3	2.8	2.7	2.6	3.1	3.1
IV Team sense	3	3.3	3	2.3	3.4	3.3
V Labor relations	3.1	3.5	3.5	2.7	3.8	3.1
VI Parent–subsidiary relations	2.5	2.8	2.7	3.1	2.1	3
Total average	2.8	3.3	3.1	2.6	3.4	3.2

Source: From JMNESG's database.

and electronics machinery assembly factories both in the 1989 and 2000–2001 surveys, though there are some notable differences in the shape of hexagon between the two surveys. In contrast, in Southeast Asia (Thailand, Malaysia and Singapore), application scores for electric and electronics machinery assembly factories are higher than those for automobile assembly factories although the difference is not so large. Meanwhile, no significant gaps between the two industries are observed in Britain, Continental Europe, South Korea and Taiwan. For here, I will cover only the key points of the background and factors

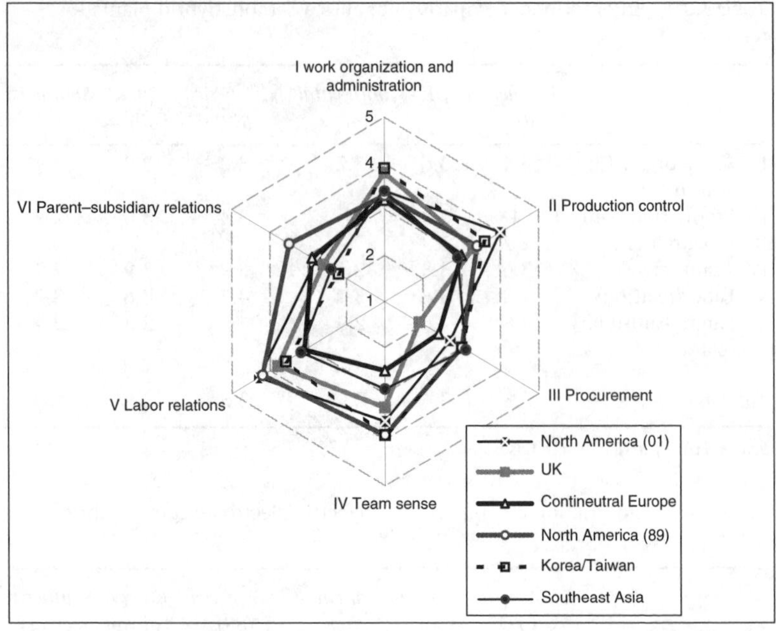

Source: Table 1.3.1.

Figure 1.4.1 International comparison of auto assembly plants – 6 group

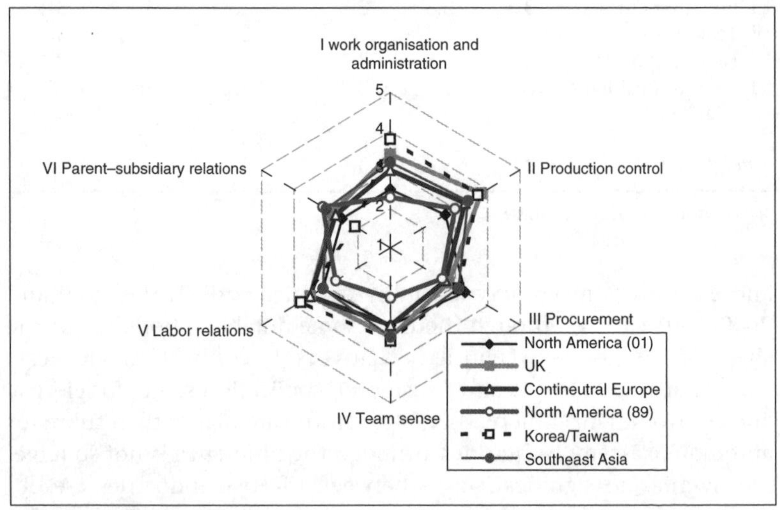

Source: Table 1.3.2.

Figure 1.4.2 International comparison of electric and electronics assembly hybrid plants – 6 group

behind these differences, leaving it to each of the researchers in charge of the respective regions to provide more detailed explanation concerning the differences.

To be successful in automobile assembly, factors concerning market and strategy, which are to be discussed later, are surely important. As a comprehensive machinery industry, however, it also requires a certain level of engineering technology standards as well as good compatibility between technology and technical skills on the part of production system. In North America and Europe, all these conditions – except for some shortcomings in the compatibility of production system – have been basically met. In contrast, Asia, as of the time of our survey, had yet to fulfill prerequisites both in the market-related aspect and the level of engineering technology standards. Certainly, there was no Japanese automobile assembly factory with significant presence in Continental Europe in the late 1990s when we conducted the survey there (Toyota Motor Corporation's factory in France began to operate in 2002), and none existed in South Korea (scores for automobile assembly for the region are solely those of Taiwan). Therefore, the regional comparison of patterns of hybrid factories may not be very precise. Still, we believe that the clear differences observed between North America and South Asia would provide sufficient foundation for the above-mentioned explanation.

Meanwhile, in the case of electric and electronics machinery assembly, East Asia had all the conditions necessary to become a major battlefield for Japanese electric and electronics machinery makers. That is, all the following conditions fit for or existed in the region: (1) because of the very nature of electric and electronics machinery products, which are an 'aggregation' of pieces of segmental technology and technical skills (i.e. a 'modular type' product in Fujimoto's definition as discussed earlier), all that is necessary is to bring in high function, high quality parts and materials along with machinery equipments of a certain level, thus, there was no need for local industries to attain high-level engineering technologies; (2) the region had human resources available at extremely low cost and readily adaptable to the Japanese production system that has comparative advantage in assembly industry; and (3) an extensive market, especially for home electric and electronics appliances, was being formed. All these factors were the case primarily for Southeast Asia at the time of survey and they best fit for China today. But basically, they also hold true for South Korea/Taiwan. That is, the gaps between electric and electronics machinery assembly and automobile assembly in these regions are not as conspicuous as those of North America.

One reason why electric and electronics machinery assembly factories in Britain and Continental Europe, unlike their counterparts in North America, achieved the level of application comparable to that of East Asia is that the Japanese systems – both in the application of Human and Material–Methods as indicated in the aforementioned 'four-perspective evaluation' – are more familiar in Britain and Continental Europe than in North America. In addition, it can be pointed out that while Central America and Asia were serving as low-cost production bases for North America, both Britain and Continental Europe had no such bases in the nearby area as of the time of survey. Also, while forming an economic community that is protected by the common trade barriers, each country and region in Europe retains its own telecommunication system and regulations, thus creating a unique market environment where Japanese companies can take full advantage of their technologies and know-how to produce a wide variety of product in small lots.

Comparison of strategic typologies

It is a common-sense management theory that apart from the regional and inter-industry differences discussed above, individual companies' independent decisions – i.e. different management strategies – result in differences in the patterns of hybrid factories. However, instead of focusing on some individual cases, here, I would like to point out that even such strategic decisions made by individual companies are governed by macroeconomic market conditions and can be captured as a general trend that is common to specific region and/or industry.

This is particularly true with the automobile industry in the US. As of 1989, when we conducted the first round of *large scale* survey on North America, the Japanese production system was not necessarily in the transferable form of hybrid but Japanese automakers stirred themselves to move into the US market in the face of intensifying US–Japan trade friction. Subsequently, however, seeing a clear benefit of having a foothold in the US, a country that embraces an enormous domestic market, a total of seven Japanese assembling makers – including Toyota, Honda and Nissan, but not counting those in the supporting industry – have launched operations there. Today, automobiles locally produced by Japanese automakers account for some 25 per cent of the US market. And the consistent accumulation of efforts to adapt to the local environment has resulted in the aforementioned modification of hybrid patterns toward those of Britain, South Korea and Taiwan, as shown in the result of 2000–2001 survey.

Meanwhile, in Europe, Japanese companies' operations have not been necessarily profitable. However, they have been able to cope with such difficulties by trying to overcome problems right in front of them – trade barriers, segmented markets, and so forth – in the prospect of rapid market integration in the European Union, supported by the unique capacity of Japanese companies to pursue a long-term strategy. With regard to automobile manufacturing, there are only few Japanese factories operating in Continental Europe (Spain, Belgium, France, etc.) and the hybrid patterns of these factories are not necessary of an easy-to-manage type (Kumon and Abo, 2004). Yet, it is expected that the overall situation – including that of Central and Eastern Europe – will begin to improve in due time. After all, Japanese electric machinery and precision machinery makers – except for those in semiconductor-related fields – have been able to survive against various odds encountered in the course of their operations.

In East Asia, automakers are now seeing not only the potential for market growth but also the formation of an engineering technology base. Thus, following the lead of electric machinery makers that have been blessed with all the conditions from the very beginning, Japanese automakers have begun to focus on the establishment of fully fledged local production bases. Their targeted destinations have been shifted from South Korea, Taiwan and the ASEAN countries to China, and now India is emerging as yet another target.

Summary and prospects

Up to this point, I have summarized the results of our research and surveys, which have been conducted across the world in the past 20 years, presenting them in the form of international comparison along the lines of our research theme concerning the international transferability of the Japanese management and production systems. Specifically, I have clarified the geographic distribution of Japanese hybrid management and factories across the world and categorized their respective features either as generalities or peculiarities observed in various patterns of international transfer of these systems. What has become apparent is that each business management system has a certain degree of organizational cultural traits that are unique to the country or region in which the system has been developed, and that it is inevitable for the Japanese system, in which such traits are particularly strong, to be substantially transformed or modified in accordance with the management environment in the country or region to which it is transferred.

From the standpoint of practical application in corporate management, a company cannot sufficiently secure its competitive advantage simply by transferring only the easily applicable 'general' aspects of the management and production systems. Rather, the success or failure of its local management hinges largely on how various factors constituting the specific aspects of the Japanese management and production systems can be modified and transplanted into local operations in a way to effectively retain the merits of the systems. Therefore, no progress can be made by highlighting differences, peculiarities, or the difficulty of transplanting the systems. What is of utmost importance is how to overcome the difficulty in practice. I do hope that the findings of our research on hybrid factories will provide some suggestions and guidance to help companies overcome such a difficulty.

Theoretically, there is no ruling out the possibility that we find, through our analysis and evaluation of various hybrid factories, cases that exhibit an interesting blend of different management systems or those in which hybridization has been proactively pursued. So, in what follows, I would like to discuss, based on the above-described results of our study, the possibility of a 'desirable hybrid model' or a 'practical hybrid model' in the international transfer of the Japanese system, looking into the situation of hybrid factories in several different patterns of hybridization.

Extraction of common patterns – 'minimum program'

The quickest way to transfer internationally the Japanese management and production systems is to extract – out of the six groups and 23 items explained above – the factors in which relatively small regional differences are observed and high scores are posted, create a transfer model by incorporating such factors, and then, put the model into practice in each region as the 'minimum program.' Of all the items, 'equipment' within G-II Production control is the most important. This item is meant to be a transfer of 'Material–Results' factors within the above-described four-perspective evaluation framework, i.e. a ready-made hardware that has been produced by a Japanese equipment maker and used by a parent factory whereby usability features and know-how regarding the use of the equipment have been fully developed and incorporated. And for this, it is required, to some extent, to bring in 'Human–Results' in the form of the involvement of Japanese expatriates and/or staff sent by the equipment maker. In other words, it is possible to make an immediate and significant impact to improve efficiency in a substantial portion of a local factory by directly transferring some 'ready-made' assets on the both Material and Human aspects. But this is not enough to firmly implant 'Human–Methods' factors concerning the Japanese-style maintenance and quality control systems based on universal employee participation, which is necessary to enable local workers to fully utilize equipment and keep the occurrence of defective products to the minimum.

Extraction of models by region and industry – management environment adaptive models

This approach also utilizes the results of our research and surveys. However, contrary to the first approach described above, this approach seeks to build a 'general model' with limited applications for hybrid factories under certain conditions by typifying the differences in the hybrid patterns of each region and industry. This requires very detailed typological classification and would not produce any universally applicable standard manual. Instead, however, this could be used to help realize a low-risk factory management system that is adaptive to local management environment. For instance, when both the timing and changes in market conditions are taken into account, the following typological patterns are possible: (a) automobile and electric and electronics machinery industries in North America, for both of which the situations changed substantially between 1989 and 2001; (b) automobile and electric and electronics machinery industries in East Asia, which may be further subdivided into South Korea/Taiwan, Southeast Asia, China, India and so forth; (c) automobile and electric and electronics machinery industries in Britain; and (d) automobile and electric and electronics industries in Continental Europe, which may be further subdivided into Germany, Central South Europe, and Central Eastern Europe.

'Flexible generalized model' – from East Asian and British patterns to global convergence

In comparison to the above-described two approaches, this method seeks to build a more 'flexible general model.' Rather than simply detecting and extracting common traits, this approach attempts to take out the patterns of hybrid factories that show a more 'desirable' or 'practical' combination of application and adaptation as a model, using a specific type of patterns actually detected as a platform. And then, patterns observed in various regions would be analyzed and evaluated against such 'desirable' or 'practical' patterns, which thus serve as a yardstick in searching for a direction that should be pursued. This is a model that companies would risk choosing, even if it takes time and costs money, banking on the prospect of future expansion of market and going beyond common-sense responses to the given management environment with certain social and cultural backgrounds. In this sense, this model is deemed to have fairly strong strategic adaptability.

Specifically, the East Asian patterns (particularly those of South Korea/Taiwan) and the British patterns fit the definitions of such a model. Simply put in terms of our four-perspective evaluation, this model is designed to promote the application of the Japanese system by increasing the 'Methods application' of Human and Material factors while restraining the 'Results application' of them. In South Korea, Taiwan and Britain, situations closer to such a desirable state have been achieved without much effort. As opposed to this, in the case of the US, the initial situation was at the other end of the spectrum and it took 10 years to get closer to the desirable state.

As apparent from the fact that the aggregate averages of application scores for South Korea, Taiwan and Britain – which fall within the range between 3.2 and 3.3 – are not much different from scores for the other regions, a desirable pattern of hybrid factories cannot be achieved simply by raising the ratio of various Japanese factors. Instead, it is more like a result attributable to the differences in the composition of management and production systems. That is, a desirable pattern is a result obtained by reducing the direct transfer of 'ready made' assets (Results) such as Japanese expatriates, parts and material, and equipments from Japan (promotion of localization, i.e. adaptation to local personnel, material and institutions) as well as by implementing flexible cooperation- and team-oriented systems for operations and management, and making efforts to formulate labor–management relationship based on cooperative participation to achieve that end (promotion of the application of Japanese-style 'Methods').

From the viewpoint of our 'cultural approach,' trying to realize such desirable hybrid patterns is for a company to 'overreach' and 'take a risk' in managerial decision making, and thus, it would require a certain degree of preparedness and strategic responsiveness on the part of the management. In reality, however, such hybrid patterns have taken root not only in East Asian countries which have substantial cultural affinities with Japan but also in Britain that has undergone considerable social changes in the later half of the 20th century. Not only that, even the US has begun to head for that direction in recent years. Furthermore, it seems that these patterns developed overseas are now being re-imported into Japan in the form of 'internal internationalization' amid the mounting calls for 'structural reform' and the wave of social changes. Should it be the case, it may be no exaggeration to say that all these phenomena are pointing to the direction of global convergence of Japanese-style hybrid systems.

Here, let me call this emerging pattern of hybrid systems an 'internationalization model of Japanese management and production systems.' A major challenge in applying this internationalization model is how to keep the cost at or below the expected level of benefits, particularly, in transplanting the system in a country or a region that is culturally separated by a great distance from Japan. Strenuous strategic efforts and various schemes must be required to achieve that end. In this respect, we have encountered a few cases that are both interesting and valuable in the course of our on-site survey visits to a number of factories. In what follows, I will introduce some of such cases.

Program-type education and training system

To the best of my knowledge, this system ('apprenticeship program') was first developed at Company T's automobile plant in Kentucky in the late 1980s and it is one typical example of Japanese companies' ingenious schemes designed to provide Japanese-style education and training in substance while taking the form of an American-style education and training system. The basis of the Japanese-style employee training is an on-the-job training (OJT) system in which employees are to acquire skills and knowhow while they carry out actual tasks at workplace. This forms the core of '*genba shugi* (shop floor-oriented system)' of personnel training in a sense that company-specific job skills are internally procured through OJT. What is indispensably important here is multi-skill training through systematic job rotation, a system under which employees are transferred from one post to another within the relevant work process in a way to enable them to expand the scope of knowledge and skills required in the workplace. The opposite, American perception is it that knowledge and skills are something that should be basically attained through external programs provided by special educational institutions. Thus, companies are to define job tasks for a certain post and externally recruit ready-made employees who are already equipped with necessary knowledge and technical skills to carry out the tasks.

Thus, the 'program-type education and training system,' which can be described as 'manualization' of shop floor-oriented system, has been developed by analyzing the Japanese OJT process designed to train maintenance workers, decomposing the process into functional fragments, and then reorganizing these fragments into an in-house special education and training program which would take three years or so to complete. Employees who have applied for a maintenance post are assigned to take the program. The program is composed equally of classroom lectures and practical training with those on practical training being treated somewhat differently from ordinary workers. When we visited the same plant three years later, we were told that less than 20 per cent of the applicants had been able to achieve their intended goal to get fully assigned to the maintenance post. This outcome indicates that the attempt has been a case of a long trial and error experience. However, we have also learned that Company T has since adopted the same kind of system in its factories in Canada and Britain, and even in some of its factories in Japan. Given this, it is fair to say that this particular system is now being accepted as an internationalization model.

'Segmentation of an assembly line'

This is once again a case of Company T. The system, called 'self-fulfillment line,' received considerable publicity in 1992 when it was implemented on a full scale in the company's plant in southern island of Kyushu and then in the Motomachi Plant in Aichi Prefecture. Before that, however, a series of attempts had been made to virtually introduce the system in factories both in Japan and abroad. Under this system, an assembly line for the final phase of automobile production is divided into 10 or so smaller sets of work procedures, with buffers to hold several units of cars in between. It was a remarkable change from the conventional serial production lines based on a single-line formation, and particularly far removed from the basic principles underlying the so-called T Production System (TPS), a very lean system featuring a formation designed to realize efficient operations throughout the production process by eliminating waste thoroughly in the production line, for instance, by ensuring maintenance of a good balance between different stages of the work process and minimizing waste motions of line workers. Against all these odds, however, the company introduced the new system as the company recognized the need to improve overall working conditions. Initially prompted by the growing difficulty of recruiting young workers who are unwilling to take up any type of the so-called 'three-K' job (that translates into the 'three D' in English, meaning physically demanding, dirty and dangerous), the company allocated buffers so as to alleviate the strain of working on the line and tried to give employees the sense of accomplishment

(Volvoism?) by having each group of employees perform a coherent set of tasks ('self-fulfillment line'). The introduction of the system is also aimed at creating a 'human-friendly' labor environment in due consideration of the needs of elderly and female workers.

As it turned out, this system seems to have produced a greater effect in overseas factories than in those in Japan. The system was launched in around 1988 when the assembly lines in certain section of the company's Tahara Plant in Japan as well as in Kentucky Plant in the US were divided into seven segments (segmentation of the assembly line). Of these two cases, I believe that the one in Kentucky was more important as an experiment because, at that time, production activities at the Tahara Plant were led by the cutting-edge automated production lines that had been installed by Company T at immense cost. (By the way, this massive investment came under critical review within the company after the burst of the economic bubble, which has resulted in the acceleration of shift to 'self-fulfillment lines' in which 'people are the main player'.) Indeed, the system has spread at a far greater pace in overseas plants than in Japan. In so far as I know, the system was introduced in Australia in 1994, Britain by 1997, Indonesia in 1999 and India in 2001. The system has been gradually spreading in Japan, adopted at the Kyushu Plant, and then in the production line for the RAV4 models in the Motomachi Plant, but the overall pace of spread remains modest. One major reason behind this lies in the clarity and definiteness on the scope of responsibility for each work group under this system. This represents a significant modification to the Japanese system that has been made by incorporating Euro-American-style demarcation barriers, which has effectively reduced stress and strain for workers by relieving them from the continuous pressure of 'unlimited responsibility' under the single-line production system. It is deemed that the adoption of the segmented production system, coupled with the introduction of buffers, has smoothed the way for transplanting the Japanese system into overseas factories. Also, it is quite suggestive that in Japan, the system has been introduced in Kyushu, a region which is unfamiliar with auto production and located far from Toyota City where the company has headquarts, and as a new production line for the RAV4 cars, a model with peculiar features, in the flagship Motomachi Plant in Toyota, Aichi Prefecture. The implication is that the introduction of the segmented production system has an aspect of 'internal internationalization.'

Of course, being a modified version of the Japanese system does not necessarily mean that the segmented production system is inferior to the original Japanese system in terms of operating efficiency and product quality. The sense of accomplishment derived from completing a certain segment of tasks in a small group can serve as a motivation to work harder. It has been also pointed out that the presence of buffers provides an opportunity to check the quality of products in process, thus, offering an advantage that may more than offset the loss caused by allowing some 'waste motions' of line workers.

Simplified small group activities

With regard to the implementation of the quality control circle (QCC) system, a typical case observed in Japan is the one in which all the employees are expected to 'voluntarily' participate in QCC activities after regular work hours without any payment. This, however, can be accepted nowhere in the world but in Japan. And even in Japan, in recent years, there have been an increasing number of cases in which QCC activities are conducted during regular work hours with pay. Thus, as far as QCC activities at overseas factories are concerned, Japanese companies would generally consider that 20 to 30 per cent participation rate is satisfactory in case emphasis is on voluntary participation. And if companies want to assure 100 per cent participation, they would arrange QCC activities to be carried out during regular work hours and instruct employees to participate as part of their job duties. Either way, the original intention of the QCC system would be substantially diminished. Yet, at least to some extent, an effect can be expected. Our surveys found that more than 90 per cent of Japanese factories operating overseas are adopting either one of the above two methods.

Modified and upgraded versions of Euro-American-style Japanese systems

In addition to various models developed by ingenuity of Japanese companies in various overseas locations, there are quite a few successful standard models that have been developed by American and other foreign companies as a modified and/or upgraded version of the Japanese system. Although I am not going to explain the details of each model, such foreign-made popular models include ISO9000 (integrated international standards for quality control procedures), Six Sigma (systemized manual for on-site management of participation-oriented activities such as small group activities), supply chain management or SCM (integrated logistics management system derived from 'kanban' or just-in-time [JIT] systems), and so forth. These systems are being employed by many Japanese companies, particularly, in their overseas operations.

As described above, this 'flexible general model' has the possibility of evolving into the third hybrid management model by proactively incorporating foreign systems while retaining factors of the Japanese system to some extent. For the moment, this cannot be presented in the form of a single integrated system and all we can do is to explore the possibility based on the accumulation of specific cases, taking the patterns of East Asia and Britain as a cue. But it can be said that all these specific cases are pointing to the direction of 'flexible generalization.'

Finally, I would like to summarize our findings, while keeping the above-three patterns in mind, and present as a tentative theory on the selection of a 'desirable' or 'practical' model for hybrid factories in the international transfer of the Japanese management and production systems.

First, the initial model which is created simply by extracting common patterns is just a systematic generalization and does not have much substance. This may have a certain degree of usability as a ready-made method under situations in which some sort of management decision must be made with limited resources and in a limited time frame, for instance, when Japanese companies need to quickly make a series of decisions concerning their overseas operations. However, based on what is perceived to be appropriate evaluation and judgment from the viewpoint of our hybrid management model theory, a combination of the second model – which incorporates factors peculiar to each region and type of industry – and the third one – 'flexible general model' that is dependent on the trend of global convergence – would be the way seems to be the direction to head for. And based on this premise, final decision by each company would be made as a strategic choice with an eye on market conditions (scale, diversity, etc.) and cost factors (local factors and conditions).

References

Abegglen, J.C. (1957) *The Japanese Factory,* MIT Press.

Abo, T. 'The Emergence of Japanese Multinational Enterprise and the Theory of Foreign Direct Investment', in K. Shibagaki, M. Trevor and T. Abo (eds) (1989) Japanese and European Management, Tokyo University Press.

Abo, T. (ed.) (1994) *Hybrid Factory: The Japanese Production System in the United States.* NY: Oxford University Press.

Abo, T. (2000) 'Spontaneous Integration in Japan and East Asia', G.L. Clark, *et al.*, (eds), *The Oxford Handbook of Economic Geography,* Oxford University Press.

Abo, T. (2003) 'Japanese Hybrid Factories in Germany: Survival in a Different Environment', S-J. Park, and S. Horn, *Asia and Europe in the New Global System,* Palgrave Macmillan.

Abo, T. (2004a) 'An Integrated Theory of Mangement Geography: Japanese Hybrid Factories in the Three Mager Regions', V. Gupta, (ed.), *Transformative Organizations*, Response Books.

Abo, T. (2004b) 'A Shortened Path to Transplant the Japanese Management System', in S. Strzelczak, (ed.), *Economic and Managerial Developments in Asia and Europe: Comparative Studies*, Kramist.

Adler, P.S. (1993) 'The Learning Bureaucracy: New United Motors Manufacturing,Inc.,' in B.M. Staw and L.L. Cummings (eds), *Research in Organizational Behavior*, JAI Press.

Aoki, M. (1989) *Information, incentives, and bargaining in the Japanese economy*, Cambrige University Press.

Aoki, M. (2000) *Information, corporate governance, and institutional diversity: competitiveness in Japan, the USA, and the transitional economies*, Oxford University Press.

Beechler, S.L. and Bird, A. (1999) *Japanese Multinationals Abroad*, Oxford University Press.

Boyer, R., E. Charron, U. Jürgens and S. Tolliday (eds) (1998) *Between Imitation and Innovation: The Transfer and Hybridization of Productive Models in the International Automobile Industry*, Oxford University Press.

Clark, Kim B. and Takahiro Fujimoto (1991) *Product Development Performance*, Harvard Business School.

Coase, R.H. (1937) 'The Nature of Firm,' *Economica*, N.S.1937, 4.

Cole, R.E. (ed.) (1981) The Japanese Automobile Industry, Michigan Papers in Japanese Studies, No. 3.

Dore R.P. (1973) *British Factory – Japanese Factory*, University of California Press.

Elger, Tony and Chris Smith (ed.) (1994) *Global Japanization: The Transnational Transformation of the Labour Process*. NY: Routledge.

Elger, T. and Smith, C. (2005) *Assemling Work*, Oxford University Press.

Fujimoto, T. (1999) The evolution of a manufacturing system at Toyota, Oxford University Press.

Fujimoto, T., Takeishi, A. and Aoshima Y. (2001) *Bijinesu Ahkitekucha (Business Architecture)*, Yuhikaku.

Hall, E.T. (1976) *Beyond Culture*, Anchor Books.

Hood, N. (2003) *The Multinational Subsidiary*, Palgrave Macmillan.

Institute of Social Science (Abo, T., ed.) (1990) *Local Production of Japanese Automobile and Electronics Firms in the United States*, Research Reports no. 23, University of Tokyo.

Itagaki, H. (ed.) (1997) *The Japanese Production System: Hybrid Factories in East Asia*, Macmillan Press.

Itanii, H. (1987) *Jinpou-shugi (Peoplism)* (Chikuma-shibo).

Kagono, T. *et al.* (eds) (1983) *Nichibei Kigyo no Keiei Hikaku* (*Composition of Management Between Japanese and American Firms* (Nihou Keizai Shinbun-sha)).

Keeley, T.D. (2001) *International Human Resource Management in Japanese Firms*, Palgrave Macmillan.

Kenney, M. and R. Florida (1994) *Beyond Mass Production*, Oxford UP.

Koike, K. (1988) *Understanding industrial relations in modern Japan*, Macmillan.

Kumon, H. and Abo, T. (2004) *The Hybrid Factory in Europe: The Japanese Management and Production System Transferred*, Palgrave Macmillan.

Liker, J.K., Fruin, W.M. and Adler P. (1999) (eds) *Remade in America: Transplanting and Transforming Japanese Management Systems*, NY: Oxford University Press.

MacDuffie, J.P. (1996) 'International Trends in Work Organization in the Auto Industry: National-Level vs. Company-Level Perspectives', in K.S. Wever and L. Turner (eds), *The Comparative Political Economy of Industrial Relations, IRRA Series.*

The MIT Commission on Industrial Productivity (1989) *Made in America; Regaining the Productive Edge,* The MIT Press.

Okamoto, Y. (ed.) (2000) *Hokubei Nikkeikigyo no Keiei (Management of Japanese Affiliated Firms in North America),* Dobunkan.

Oliver, N. and Wilkinson, B. (1988) *The Japanization of British Industry.* Oxford: Blackwell.

Ozawa, T. (1979) *Multinationalism, Japanese Style,* Princeton Univ. Press.

Porter, M. (1990) *The Competitive Advantage of Nations,* New York: The Free Press.

Porter, M. and Takeuchi, H. (2000) *Can Japan Compete?,* London: Palgrave Macmillan (*Nihon no Kyoso Senryaku,* Tokyo: Daiamondo-sha.).

Saka, A., (2003) *Cross-National Appropriation of Work Systems,* Edward Elgar.

Trevor, M. (1983) *Japan's Reluctant Multinationals,* Frances Pinter.

Williamson, O.E. (1975) *Market and Hierarchies,* New York: The Free Press.

Womack, J.P., Jones, D.T. and Roos, D. (1990) *The Machine that Changed the World,* Rowson Associates, Macmillan.

2

Hybrid Factories in North America: Changes of the Japanese Management and Production System in the United States Between 1986 and 1989 and 2000 and 2001

Tetsuji Kawamura

Introduction

In 2000–2001, the Japanese Multinational Enterprise Study Group (JMNESG) conducted extensive field research on the management and production systems of the Japanese transplants, mainly in automobile and electronics industries in North American, 10 years after the previous one in 1986–89.[1] Based on the outcomes of the latest survey, this chapter aims at elucidating the present situations of 'hybridization' of their management and production systems. It focuses on the transferability of Japanese-style management and production systems in North America, the main battlefield of global mega-competition.

This chapter discusses mainly the following two points: first, the current positions of the 'application–adaptation' relationship and the 'hybrid pattern' in the United States and the characteristics of their major changes that have taken place during these 10 years after the 1989 survey; secondly, the factors that have influenced the transfer of Japanese management and production systems to Japanese transplants in North America, especially the specific ones to the United States. It includes the main changes in the economic and managerial environment in North America during this period as well. Through these arguments, we try to single out the major problems and tasks that the Japanese transplants have faced in North America, thereby shedding light on the transferability of Japanese-style management and production systems in North America.

Characteristics of the economic and managerial environment surrounding Japanese transplants in North America in the 1990s

Of the circumstances that affected the business and local production strategy of Japanese companies in North America since the early 1990s, three stand out. First, the competitive advantages of Japanese companies have been progressively shaken and faced major challenges at home and abroad. Secondly, the pressures of global 'mega-competition' have intensified. Thirdly, the US economic expansion lasted for an extraordinary period of time during 1990s.

The initial cause stemmed primarily from the deterioration of corporate earnings amid the dire straits of the Japanese economy, rather than from problems of the micro-structure of the Japanese management and production system. The most important factors were: (1) the deflationary trend of the economy and (2) intensified competition at home and abroad, which had become glaringly evident since the early 1990s. The Japanese economy lapsed into a deflationary spiral due to the protracted *Heisei* recession that followed the collapse of the 'bubble economy' in the late 1980s. The rise of the break-even point for major manufacturers amid the 'bubble economy' also played a part. Consequently, high costs at home put significant pressures on Japanese companies.

Then, global 'mega-competition' impacted the Japanese economy. While competition with Western companies grew intense, especially Korean, Taiwanese and other Asian companies were catching up rapidly, not only in the fields of commodities and medium technology products such as television sets, audio equipment, other general consumer electronics, automobile, steel and ordinary machinery, but also in the high-tech sectors including semiconductors, personal computers and liquid crystal panels. In the latter half of the 1990s, competition intensified with low-cost products made in China (mainly produced locally by Japanese and other foreign companies). In the semiconductor sector, Japanese companies lost global market shares of memory chips, which used to be the mainstay of Japanese semiconductor plants in North America, to Samsung and other Korean companies and Taiwanese firms. In the automobile industry, including auto parts, competition among Japanese automakers as well as competition with

General Motors, Ford, DaimlerChrysler, and Volkswagen and other European automakers increased in intensity not only in North America and other industrial country markets but also in emerging markets of Latin America and Asia. In North America, the hollowing out of the manufacturing base in the US electronics industries and increased competition with Asian companies significantly affected local production operations by Japanese companies in the United States. Since the previous survey, there have been many transfers of production to Mexico, and further to East Asia and China for TV assembly and many of other electronics products. At the same time another conspicuous trend has appeared, i.e. the revival of major American companies in electronics industries, such as General Electric in consumer electronics, Intel, AMD, Motorola and Texas Instruments in semiconductors, and Cisco Systems and Lucent Technologies in IT sectors.

Under these circumstances, major challenges confronted Japanese manufacturers and their Japanese-style management and production system on two fronts. First, the difficulties and the 'hollowing out' of domestic plants in Japan became more serious. They faced a major problem of how to maintain the scale of operations of domestic plants that had underpinned their competitive advantage. Secondly, the superiority of the Japanese system was called into serious question. There emerged the growing trend praising the American-style management, accompanied with an extreme argument that the Japanese model indeed constituted major hindrance for the recovery of competitive edge of Japanese companies. However, many aspects cited for the problems of Japanese companies, such as the practice of lifetime employment and seniority-based wages premised on the 'steadily growing' economy and the 'back-scratching' nature of subcontracting and *keiretsu* affiliations that tended to drag down efficiency, were mostly the limitations and shortcomings of the late 1980s Japanese model.

In the face of these major changes in the economic and management environment in the 1990s, many of Japanese major companies were confronted with re-synthesizing global business systems: production and procurement at optimal locations, allocation of management resources to, and integrated management of, overseas production bases stretched out all over the world, innovation and improvement of management organizations to maintain and enhance competitive edge. They had to transform themselves into global companies, and not limit overseas production to a response to trade friction and the appreciation of the yen. It also meant that Japanese local transplants overseas had to more seriously address than before the challenges to reconcile the Japanese management and production system with specific local conditions, particularly in terms of costs, and making it fit in well with the management environment different from Japanese ones to maintain and enhance their competitive edge. Those movements must affect the 'application' and 'adaptation' patterns in their transplants overseas.

Meanwhile, special factors that worked particularly in the North American market in the 1990s need to be accounted for. The US economy marked the longest-ever expansion, and, coupled with an acceleration of the IT boom in the latter half of the 1990s, the 'new economy' phenomenon prevailed. Though the US trade and current account deficits expanded further since the latter half of the 1990s, the Japan–US trade friction became latent by the general improvement of US corporate earnings and the expansion of employment (and by increased local production by Japanese companies).

In the automobile industries, demand expanded by several million units in the latter half of the 1990s. Market demand increased significantly for many other sectors. American economy experienced general increase of output and a growing labor shortage. This macroeconomic environment affected the management and operations of Japanese local transplants. Especially it should be noted that the augmentation of production volumes in the 1990s helped strengthen the inclinations toward the logic of mass production.

These changes that took place after the previous survey constitute the important focus to analyze the current state and vicissitude of the local transplantation of the Japanese management and production system in North America. As a matter of fact, three major changes have been observed.

First, many Japanese local transplants with long experience of operation in the automobile and electrical machinery industries achieved fairly clear progress in stabilizing management and becoming firmly rooted locally. Automobile production at Japanese local plants (at 1,828,000 units) overtook exports from Japan (at 1,617,000 units) in 1993; voluntary restraints on auto exports to the US market were lifted in 1994; and the Japan–US friction in automobile trade became latent. On the other hand, however, the performance of individual companies varied widely.

Secondly, Japanese manufacturers built new production facilities in the US and increased production at existing plants in North America. These developments were particularly conspicuous in the automobile industry (both in assembly and auto parts). Toyota and Honda constructed new assembly plants. Similar movements were also seen in other industries as well. According to the data on Japanese companies with overseas operations provided by Toyo Keizai, of about 345 cases of Japanese manufacturers setting up operations abroad between 1994 and 2002, a little over 140 cases, or 40 per cent, were by automakers and auto parts makers (including automobile-related firms classified into industries other than the automobile and auto parts industries).

The new entries in these industries particularly stood out at a time when direct investment by Japanese companies in the United States and North America as a whole declined in terms of both value and number from the peak levels of the early 1990s. The decline in direct investment in the United States as a whole can be seen as the consequence of the deterioration of corporate earnings performance due to the collapse of the bubble economy and the prolonged '*Heisei* recession' as well as the shift of manufacturing bases to China. Meanwhile, the yen's sharp appreciation against the dollar in the first half of the 1990s and the remarkably long expansion of the US economy that ensued appear to be the major factors behind new entries and the expansion of existing plants. In addition, the North American Free Trade Agreement (NAFTA) pressured Japanese companies in these sectors to satisfy NAFTA criteria for local content and respond to the abolition and changes in preferential arrangements they previously enjoyed in Maquiladora zones in Mexico.

Thirdly, however, as a whole, many Japanese companies in the electrical machinery and electronics industries withdrew from North America by closing, transferring or selling off their local plants, in connection with the growing shift of production bases to Asia/China, whereas some Japanese companies advanced into the US local production in the IT and semiconductor sectors responding to the IT boom. The major factor of the withdrawals from North America is the increased competition with the Taiwanese – in semiconductors and PC boards, with the Korean – Samsung, LG and other companies in the consumer electric appliances and electronics equipment, and also with China deeper into the 1990s, amid the 'IT boom.' It accelerated the trend toward fabless production and outsourcing. This was a part of the process of 'hollowing out' of the industrial base of US electrical machinery and electronics devices.

Data on the withdrawals/sales of Japanese plants overseas are not so readily available. According to data provided by Toyo Keizai, the electrical machinery and electronics industries account for a relatively large portion of plant closures and sale globally (23 per cent of the total number). In North America, particularly between 1999 and 2002, they accounted for a high 29 per cent of the total number of withdrawals and sell-offs, double the ratio for the chemical industry that ranked second. Among the companies we surveyed, many of electrical machinery and electronics companies withdrew (including Maquiladora zones) between 1989 and the latest survey. In particular, only a single major Japanese semiconductor-manufacturing plant now exists in North America.

Those developments reflect the 1990s changes in the economic and managerial environment surrounding Japanese transplants in North America. However, what should be reaffirmed here is the unchanged underlying trend, i.e. the less competitiveness of the traditional postwar American-style (Ford–Taylor-type) mass production system. This is caused by a broader transformation of global economic structure and therefore continues as an irreversible trend. Rather, this basic trend has even intensified further under the pressure of intensified global 'mega-competition' in the 1990s. This provided the foundation for the superiority of the basic logic of the Japanese management and production system, universalized as the 'lean production system,' and proved to be the major agent of 'Japanization.' The wide adoption of basic logic of the Japanese system for management reorganization incorporating a variety of elements of the Japanese systems has been observed not only in the United States but also in Europe and other regions[2] It is quite likely that the responses of American as well as Japanese companies in various ways to the increased pressures of mega-competition in recent years have been causing changes of the 'hybrid pattern' of Japanese plants in North America.

The above-mentioned two points constitute the focal points of the hybrid model analysis. They provide, on the one hand, the foundation for the validity of the 'hybrid model' analysis, although at the same time calls for a modification of the 'model' itself. The 'hybrid model,' was initially developed on the results of the previous survey in North America. The basic framework of the 'Hybrid Analysis' is constructed on the dynamism where the local 'application' of the Japanese system, which is the basic strategy, adopted by Japanese companies for their overseas local plants, leads to the 'hybrid' as it competes with and is constrained by specific local conditions, local systems and institutions. The American management and production system that once constituted the basis of the overwhelming competitive edge of the US industries and formed the global standard still looms large in the Untied States in particular. The 'application' of the Japanese system is still subject to the constraints by and in competition with strongly-rooted the local various local systems, practices and labor-management relations, among others.

However, since the 1980s, American companies have been pushing forward the transformation and reorganization of the traditional American corporate system to face the major difficulties caused by the completely altered managerial environment. They have pursued innovation of management organizations and business restructuring, outsourcing, greater flexibility of the labor market and labor–management relations, etc. These developments continued to evolve even amid the expanding macroeconomic environment of the 1990s. How these developments helped change the constraints on the transplantation of the Japanese system is a major issue here. At the same time, amid intensified mega-competition and an acceleration of technological innovation, the direction of the innovation of production system is becoming more diversified in response to differences in the characteristics of industrial technologies or in 'architecture' and other product characteristics, or differences in corporate culture. Various types of innovations have appeared – modularization in the automobile industries, IT-based supply chain management and knowledge management, and the 'cell production' method[3] that has been spreading remarkably in the electrical machinery and electronics industries. Thus, it would be necessary to rethink what really is the 'model' of the Japanese system that should be applied locally.

The following section discusses the results of the latest survey of the Japanese transplants a little more specifically to make clear the impacts of the changes in the economic and managerial environment since the 1990s described above.

Overall characteristics of the 'hybrid pattern' in the 2000–2001 survey results

In Table 2.1, the aggregate average 'degree of application' for a total of 37 Japanese transplants in the United States surveyed and evaluated in the latest survey was 3.2, almost identical with the average for a total of 34 such plants surveyed in 1989. This means there is little change in the degree of application in the Untied States even after a decade. Moreover, it is not much different from the general level of the survey results conducted in various regions. The aggregate average degree of application in various regions has been at a level just above '3.' The level in the United States in the latest survey is just below that in

Table 2.1 Comparison between 1989 and 2000–2001: 23 items

	USA (00-01) N-37	*USA (89) N-34*	*Comparison, 89/00-01*	*UK N-20*	*Europe N-36*	*S. Korea & Taiwan N-24*	*ASEAN N-35*	*East Asia N-39*
1 Job classifications	4.1	3.7	0.4	4.4	3.2	4.9	4.5	4.7
2 Multifunctional skill	3.1	2.6	0.5	3.3	2.8	2.9	2.6	2.7
3 Education & training	3.1	2.9	0.8	3.5	3.1	3.4	3.3	3.3
4 Wage system	2.2	2.4	–0.2	2.8	2.8	3.9	3.1	3.5
5 Promotion	2.9	3.1	–0.2	3.4	3.1	3.7	3.1	3.4
6 First-line supervisor	3.2	2.9	0.3	3.4	3.1	3.4	2.9	3.2
7 Equipment	3.9	4.3	–0.4	3.9	3.4	3.5	4.0	3.7
8 Maintenance	3.1	2.6	0.5	3.0	2.8	3.3	3.0	3.2
9 Quality control	3.4	3.4	–0.0	3.6	3.1	3.6	3.2	3.4
10 Process management	3.5	3.0	0.5	3.6	3.2	3.5	3.2	3.4
11 Local content	1.8	2.7	–0.9	1.9	2.8	2.9	3.1	3.0
12 Suppliers	2.9	3.9	–1.0	2.7	2.9	3.5	3.8	3.7
13 Procurement method	3.1	2.5	0.6	2.9	2.8	3.2	2.8	3.0
14 Small group activities	2.6	2.5	0.1	2.7	2.5	3.2	2.9	3.0
15 Information sharing	3.6	3.6	0.0	3.6	2.8	3.5	3.3	3.4
16 Sense of unity	3.7	3.5	0.2	3.7	2.8	3.6	3.3	3.5
17 Hiring policy	3.6	3.4	0.2	3.3	3.1	3.0	3.1	3.0
18 Long-term employment	3.5	3.4	0.1	3.4	3.2	3.3	3.0	3.2
19 Harmonious labor relations	4.2	4.4	–0.2	4.2	3.5	4.0	3.3	3.6
20 Grievance-procedure	3.7	3.3	0.4	3.0	3.1	3.2	3.1	3.1
21 Ratio of Japanese expatriats	2.1	3.7	–1.6	2.4	2.6	1.5	1.6	1.5
22 Delegation of authority	3.1	3.6	–0.5	3.0	3.2	2.7	3.2	2.9
23 Position of local managers	3.1	3.6	–0.5	3.0	3.1	2.7	3.8	3.3
Overall average	3.2	3.3	–0.0	3.3	3.0	3.3	3.2	3.3

Source: from JMNESG database.

Southeast Asia (Thailand, Malaysia and Singapore) (3.3), the same as that in Britain, Korea and Taiwan (3.2), and just over that for Continental Europe. Though a simple comparison may not be warranted due to the difference in the survey time, it is shown that the level of the 'degree of application' of the Japanese management and production system at local plants is almost identical for different regions or countries.

However, the in-depth comparison between the latest survey and the previous survey in North America reveals significant differences in the contents of the 'degree of application.' By and large, we recognize the following two results: (1) the 'degree of application' dropped, reflecting the progress in localization in terms of the 'human' and 'material' aspects, and (2) the 'degree of application' rose in terms of the 'method' aspects of the Japanese system. As a combination of these two developments, the level of the aggregate average degree of application did not change between the two surveys.

Progress in localization of 'human' and 'material' elements

The above means that the changes in the 'hybrid pattern' at Japanese plants in North America over the past 10 years are characterized by the progress in localization in 'Human' aspects and 'Material' aspects (such as production equipment and parts) of the management and production system on one hand, and progress in the local transfer of methods of the Japanese system. On the surface, the local transfer of the Japanese system in the Untied States seems to have moved ahead smoothly toward the 'ideal' pattern.

The progress in localization of 'Human' and 'Material' aspects involves, first, in Table 2.2, the decline in the degree of application of Group VI 'Parent and Subsidiary Relations.' This primarily stems from the decreased ratio of Japanese expatriates and the higher positions of local (American) managers in management organizations. Responsibility for the operation and management of plants has shifted to local managers, relying less on management decisions by Japanese head quarters and more on the broader, strengthened local authority, including local head offices.

This trend is particularly remarkable in the auto industries and at parts makers in particular. In the electronics industry, comparison of the same plants between the 1989 survey, when they were still new, and the latest survey shows that the degree of application of Group VI dropped slightly for electronics assembly but rose for other electronics makers. This reflects that while local plants started operations with

Table 2.2 Comparison between 1989 and 2000–2001: 6 groups

		USA (00-01)	*USA (89)*	*USA 89/00-01*	*UK*	*Continental Europe*	*S. Korea & Taiwan*	*ASEAN*	*East Asia*
GI	Work organization	3.2	2.9	0.3	3.4	3.0	3.7	3.3	3.5
GII	Production management	3.4	3.3	0.1	3.5	3.1	3.5	3.4	3.4
GIII	Procurement	2.6	3.0	–0.4	2.5	2.8	3.2	3.2	3.2
GIV	Group consciousness	3.3	3.2	0.1	3.3	2.7	3.4	3.2	3.3
GV	Labor relations	3.7	3.6	0.1	3.6	3.2	3.4	3.1	3.2
GVI	Parent–subsidiary relations	2.8	3.6	–0.8	2.8	3.0	2.3	2.9	2.6
Overall average		3.2	3.3	–0.0	3.3	3.0	3.3	3.2	3.3

Source: Table 2.1.

more local elements but the degree of the transfer of the Japanese system increased later for survival, as displayed in the rise of the degree of application of the 'method' aspect.

Secondly, the local content ratio for all the plants surveyed rose from the level of just over 60 per cent (2.7 in evaluation points) in the 1989 survey to the level of around 80 per cent (1.4 in evaluation points) in the latest survey. The rise is particularly conspicuous in the automobile industries (auto assembly and auto parts) and also noted in the other electronics industries, but declines in the electronics assembly industries.

In the 1990s, the sustained expansion of the US economy brought about strong earnings for American companies, making latent the trade friction that used to work as a major pressure for a higher local content ratio at the outset of North American operations of many of Japanese companies. Rather, the rise in the local content ratio in the automobile industries can be ascribed, other than construction and expansion of local engine plants, mainly to (1) progress in the establishment of local plants by Japanese auto parts makers, (2) latent pressure from trade friction; and (3) consideration of procurement cost. On the other hand, the decline in the local content ratio in the electrical machinery industry and the higher ratio of procurement from regions other than North America reflect weakened pressure for higher local content due to the absence of competing American major makers in the United States as well as the development of the Asian region including China as a major source of electrical and electronics parts and components amid the IT boom in the 1990s.

The changes in local content ratios in North America were also influenced by NAFTA. The local content ratios for automobiles and television sets were already higher in 1989 than the present NAFTA requirements.[4] The Maquiladora system was integrated into NAFTA in January 2001, and since then Japanese auto parts makers have been actively using Mexico as production bases. This is pushing up the local content ratios for automakers within the NAFTA area. Conversely, in the electronics assembly industries, which heavily depended on Maquila plants for procurement of television chassis and other parts and components, some makers of electrical machinery and electronics parts withdrew from Maquila zones and the Untied States or cut down on the scale of operations. The drop in the local content ratio for Japanese electronics makers reflects this trend.

Thirdly, the progress in localization of production facilities probably reflects chiefly longer years of local operation. Regardless of industry, in the initial years of operation, Japanese companies tend to bring in production equipment that incorporate Japanese know-how and *kaizen* results, together with personnel to manage them, in order to maintain the operation of local plants at the same level as in Japan. The degree of application in the 1989 survey presumably reflected the fact that it included many plants with a relatively short history of local production. In the latest survey, in consideration of this factor, the evaluation criteria were modified to reduce the degree of 'bringing-in' of production equipments. But the degree of 'bringing-in' of production equipments from Japan is still high for the 37 plants in the latest survey. The aggregate average degree of application of 3.9 indicates that almost 60 per cent of production facilities at local plants are the same as at plants in Japan. Many local plants utilize production facilities and production lines that are basically the same as those in Japan, though with some partial modifications using local facilities or incorporating *kaizen* improvements made at local plants. Local plant's reliance on Japan for production facilities is still high. The strong trend of dependence on Japan for production facilities among auto parts makers reflect the fact that many of them set up local plants in the 1990s. In the electrical machinery industry, three was a case where a whole range of production equipment for toner was brought in from Japan. However, the degree of application for electrical machinery assembly, which was low from the beginning (the average degree of application of 3.0 in 1989 meant that Japanese plants had Japanese equipment for half and local equipment for the other half), declined further to show the further progress in localization, probably reflecting the characteristics of Japanese plants in the United States seen in the specialization in the assembly process.

Constraints on the transfer of the Japanese management and production system by US labor-management relations and practices

The progress in localization of 'Human' and 'Material' aspects and the application of the Japanese 'method,' even though there are differences by industry and continued dependence on Japan, seems to show, as an overall trend, the progress in the 'maturing' of Japanese local plants in the United States. However, from the perspective of the 'system transfer' of the Japanese management and production system, the changes in the 'hybrid pattern' over the past 10 years indicate the workings and constraints of the circumstances unique to North America, or the impact of the changes in the economic and managerial environment in the United States and North America.

First, in the work organization and its administration at the shop floor level that constitutes the core of the Japanese-style production and management system, the strong influences of local conditions can be observed, especially the constraints from the work rules and labor practices, as well as labor–management relations in the United States. The influences are particularly prominent in 'promotion' and 'wage system.' Despite some changes in the US labor–management relations since the 1980s through the 'concession bargaining,' the constraints of the traditional American practices are still working in these areas.

Secondly, while the 'application' seems to progress along with the introduction of the Japanese systems and elements in many aspects, it has been fairly broadly observed that the substantive functions of these Japanese systems and elements, in fact, have been rather diluted from the perspective of the basic logic of the Japanese system.

The wage system has been greatly simplified in comparison with the traditional American system, but there was not much progress from 1989 in such areas of the number of job classification and wage grades. If anything, there has been a pullback in some aspects. In automobile assembly, for instance, the 'single status' of the unified wage grade for production line workers is maintained, but it has proved difficult to introduce Japanese-style employee evaluation and assessment. Some companies gave up an attempt to introduce it. Besides semiconductor plants with the distinct non-union high-tech characteristics, it proved extremely difficult to introduce the Japanese-style ability-based grade system linked to employee evaluation and the system has not been fully in place to reward skills and proficiency.[5] Along with the broad framework for job-based wages, the framework for the seniority system has also been maintained. While the traditional strict seniority system, which keeps employees to narrow job fields, job grades and promotion tracks, tended to be eased by making it applicable plant-wide or company-wide, the seniority system itself is an important element in the determination of promotion and job alternation at many plants.

As cases conspicuous in the automobile assembly industry, job rotation, an important means of the formation of multiple skills that serve as the basis for the 'team-based' administration of work organizations in the context of the Japanese system, appears to be becoming nominal. The adoption of the 'single status' helped reduce direct obstacles by job classification, but too much emphasis is being laid on the equalization of work burdens for ergonomic considerations, with the tendency toward 'excessive rotation' like job switches every two hours. To top it all, these job switches are being often administered on the seniority basis.

These phenomena reflect the traditional attempts by the labor to restrain the arbitrariness of the management, and also indicate that traditional American labor–management practices are still deep-rooted in industrial American.[6] In particular, they are conspicuous in unionized workplaces. This trend is apparent at automobile plants unionized by the United Auto Workers (UAW) or plants under the organizing attempts. In the electronics industries, traditional unionized plants tend to have inflexible job assignments under a larger number of job classifications and job-linked wage systems. In industries organized by influential trade unions like auto industries with the union shop system, basic labor-management relations need to be recognized as still within the framework of the postwar 'traditional' type practices. But things are not completely different at Japanese transplants without trade unions. There are certainly under direct and indirect influences by the traditional work rules and labor-management relations. As long as developments over the past decade are concerned, workplace rules in trade union-based labor–management relations in the United States, as a whole, are seen as firmly rooted as widely accepted rules in the US industrial society.

Thus, we can argue that constraints by traditional American labor practices and work rules, particularly in personnel management, at Japanese local plants in the United States basically remain an important element in determining the 'hybrid pattern.' Conversely, the results of the latest survey demonstrate this. The application of the Japanese system is making headway in areas where there are fewer constraints by traditional labor-management practices and work rules, such as 'education and training' and 'quality control,' as well as in areas where American companies may need it commonly and find it easy to accept amid intensified market competition.

Needless to say, in terms of the American industrial system as a whole, the unionization rate had fallen to less than 15 per cent by the 1980s. Thus, traditional labor–management relations, labor practices and work rules in the heavily unionized sectors cannot be described as the mainstream in a strict sense of words. If anything, the major trend should be toward an increase in 'non-union' plants that have relative similarities with the Japanese system, as Kochan *et al.* (1986) have been emphasizing since the 1980s and Jacoby (1997) argues, though a quantitative evaluation of this is difficult. In the semiconductor industry found to have non-union hi-tech characteristics in the 1989 survey, Motorola and other American companies are confirmed in the latest survey to have maintained characteristics similar to the Japanese system, such as the job classification system linked with performance evaluation of production workers and an emphasis on long-term employment.

However, despite the easing of the seniority rules in the unionized sector since the 1980s, changes in the traditional wage–determination formula[7] with COLA and AIF, and the expansion of 'non-union' labor relations and practices, the traditional labor-management practices and work rules, including seniority rules and 'job-linked wages,' are still deep-rooted in the American industrial system. The basic legal framework for American labor-management relations such as the Wagner Act of 1935 and the Taft–Harley Act of 1947 remains intact. Although the so-called 'JIT system of employment' and the expansion of the two-tier wage and lump-sum payment system have been often cited as big changes in the US labor market employment practices and wage systems, in practice these developments should be interpreted as responses to significantly increased pressures of market competition. US companies are maintaining an overall traditional framework for core workers, albeit with certain changes in the non-union direction, while seeking to reduce labor costs that have become fixed expenses in a more market-oriented manner by making wages and employment of peripheral workers more flexible.[8]

Therefore it is necessary to emphasize that the changes in labor–management relations in the United States have not led to the realization of the Japanese-style labor–management system and labor–management relationship as such. We have to assume that, on the shop floor of Japanese local transplants, the materialization of the Japanese labor–management and work practices are still being constrained by American-style labor–management relations, labor–management practices and work rules, as is shown in our results in the survey. Almost all the companies surveyed tended to focus rather on 'labor–management cooperation' and 'a sense of unity' as is shown by the results of the survey. It will be a collateral evidence of the situations.

However, the fact that the US industrial system has a general tendency to tilt toward the non-union system, which share some similarities with the Japanese system, since the 1980s has an important significance for the *system transfer* of the Japanese management and production system at Japanese local plants there. It has created the so-called 'functional equivalents' of the Japanese system and thereby expands the scope for the 'revised application.' In a broader context, this is where another important significance can be found of the changeover of the American management and production system, including labor–management relations, in the 1990s for the local transplantation of the Japanese system.

Expanded scope for 'revised application'

The 'revised application' is the method of 'application' of the Japanese system through the existing local forms and practices when it faces the difficulty in its direct application. By borrowing the local practices and forms readily acceptable by local concerns, this approach seeks the system transfer along the line of the basic logic of the Japanese management and production system (Abo *et al.* 1991: ch. 2). The simplification of traditional job classifications (the so-called 'single status') in the auto industries was originally tried as part of the QWL movements (Kochan *et al.*, 1986: see ch. 6 and others). To a varying degree, the revised application can be seen in various instances of the 'application' of the Japanese system, like efforts to seek the transfer of proficiency and skills formed in Japanese workplaces by compiling them in manuals and introduce an American-type performance evaluation formula in lieu of the Japanese employee evaluation. These examples can be found also in surveys in other regions. Local forms and practices that have functions similar or equivalent to Japanese forms and practices are called 'functional equivalents' by Boyer, who discusses them as one of the most important aspects of 'hybridization' (Boyer *et al.*, 1998: 23–56).

In the United States, the decline in the rate of unionization led to the setback of the traditional union-based framework of labor–management relations and helped encourage the trend toward the expansion of non-union type labor relations and practices, with the traditional seniority system turning lax and traditional wage-determination formula such as COLA and AIF undergoing change and becoming more diversified (Kochan *et al.*, 1998; Freedman, 1989). These changes led to changes in the constraints of local conditions on labor management at Japanese local plants in the United States. If the shifts in the corporate system and labor–management relations in the United States in the 1990s caused various traditional systems to become less rigid and brought about changes in the direction of 'non-union' forms that have commonalty with Japanese forms, it means in a sense that systemic changes corresponding to 'functional equivalents' as described by Boyer are becoming more widespread than before. Consequently, we can argue that the scope is broadening for the 'revised application' for the transfer of the basic logic of the Japanese system.[9]

Since the 1980s, the management environment went through major global changes, including the shortened product cycles and accelerated technological innovation, making the lean production innovation inevitable to implement small lot production of a wide variety of products. The age of 'mature oligopoly' for the US big business and its mass production logic has gone in the long past. In the 1990s, global competition among major companies in automobile, electronics and other sectors, an acceleration of product innovation due to technological change, and other changes in the macroscopic and microscopic business environment further accelerated market competition. Lean production is the inevitable course of events as the production system and production innovation in response to these developments. As demonstrated in the North American survey in 1986–89 and the following surveys in Asian NIEs/ASEAN and Britain/Europe as well as the latest survey in North America, not only overseas plants of Japanese companies but also American and other foreign companies in the automobile, electronics and semiconductor industries are aggressively trying to introduce elements of the Japanese production system, centering on lean production.

The latest survey in North America found notable cases of factory administration through the active introduction of the Japanese system, such as plants of Delphi, Visteon and Samsung in Mexico, where there are no constraints of the traditional American labor–management relations, and American firms' plants such as the GM Lansing factory

(Michigan) and a semiconductor plant of Motorola (Austin, Texas).[10] These moves are seen amid the business environment where the 'mature oligopolistic system' has been replaced by the 'mega-competition' both at home and abroad with the inevitability of lean production.

Meanwhile, after the collapse of the Japanese 'bubble economy' in the late 1980s, problems and limitations of the Japanese enterprise system were discussed in many ways, giving rise to calls for 'reform.' In response, Japanese companies themselves have made various efforts toward systemic reforms, including incorporation of American models of personnel management such as performance-based wages and the 'JIT approach to employment,' etc.

These moves by both Japanese and US companies encourage Japanese companies to adopt the 'revised application' strategy. If Japanese companies are seeking reform of the enterprise system on the American mode, there may be, in a broader sense, a tendency of 'convergence' of the management and production system at Japanese plants in the United States amid the trend of lean production.[11] In this connection, cases of note include: the GM Lansing plant, which is basically based on the NUMMI model, with the combination of the 'verification station' method of quality control, which can be described as the American version of the 'building-in of quality within the work processes' approach, and the line-side *kaizen* laboratory method; the introduction of the Six Sigma quality control system, an American version of Japan's traditional small group activity formula and the TQC method at Japanese electronics plants. In this regard it is worth noting that there is a tendency among electronics assembly plants of Japanese companies to move toward the revised version of the American production system for their survival, based on the American system complemented by elements of the Japanese system.

However, this raises a major problem. Our method of evaluation of the 'degree of application' evaluates the 'degree of application' for each element and subsystem that comprise the Japanese management and production system by gauging the closeness to or remoteness from the Japanese system. For this reason, the 'revised application' that makes use of 'functional equivalents' tends to show the higher 'degree of application' as it incorporates forms and methods with common or similar functions for each item with stronger elements of the Japanese system. This is deeply related to the 'recontextualization' issue addressed by Brannen, *et al.* (1999).[12]

Certainly, in the United States and else where, there are local forms and methods that can perform functions similar to those of Japanese ways in the context of the Japanese system. They are called 'functional equivalents.' Locally, those forms and elements have different functions and significance under different systems and social contexts. For example, Germany's 'tariff system' can be administered in a way similar to that of Japan's ability-based grade system. However, its function and significance in the context of 'social regulations' of 'corporatism' labor–management relations are different from those of the Japanese ability-based grade system. Similarly, the 'work council' could have a function similar to that of Japan's labor–management consultation. But its function and meaning under the corporatism-based 'social regulations' in Europe are different from those of the labor–management consultation in Japan. Yet, those local forms and elements similar to those of the Japanese system may still play similar functions as elements of the Japanese system if they can be adequately placed in the context of the basic logic of the Japanese system. This relationship is the basic nature of the 'functional equivalent.'

This is related to the second biggest problem in the latest survey pointed out previously. As stated earlier, while the latest survey confirmed the progress in the 'application' on the surface, with Japanese forms and elements introduced in many areas throughout the 1990s, it also found extensive developments where the actual functions of these forms and elements are rather lax in light of the basic logic of the Japanese system. In-house JIT guidelines, building-in of quality in processes, and talk about the ST performance falling considerably below the target all suggest the transplanting of 'methods' on the surface, but in reality, they are not functioning exactly as the 'system.' Even at established manufacturing plants, there were cases where buffer stocks were piled up along the production line or the inadequate understanding of parts storage site rules caused a line stop.

One important direct factor behind the lax implementation of the basic logic of the Japanese system may be the fact that a growing number of Japanese companies, by way of the 'revised application,' introduced the 'functionally equivalent' local forms and methods in the United States. In these cases, the first look may give you the impression of the higher 'degree of application.' Actually, however, when looked at as a system, there are cases where Japanese local plants have become the 'American-led hybrid' or the 'revised American system,' instead of the 'Japanese-led hybrid' or the 'revised Japanese system.'

Limitations on local transfers of the 'capability-building system'

The above-mentioned problems, when looked at from a different angle, are inextricably linked to the problem of the inadequate transplanting of the Japanese 'capacity-building' system at local Japanese manufacturing plants amid the growing trend of 'localization' of the 'Human' and 'Material' aspects, including the relative decline of the role of Japanese expatriates. This point becomes even clearer when the basic characteristics of the Japanese system is examined deeper.

The Japanese management and production system, in terms of a theoretical model, is the production system that realizes production of a small lot with variety of products highly efficiently and with good quality, with 'hauling' and 'synchronization' as its basic principles. The management and production system as a whole is formed with the addition of work organization methods and various devices and forms of management methods, both fine-tuned for the realization of the basic logic. It is the system that is sustained through continuous *kaizen* improvement activities and problem-solving activities at points of production. For this nature of meticulously constructed system, there always exists a latent possibility of the whole system being easily undermined depending on the management environment and specific local circumstances if elements and methods of the system are transferred to local plants only on a pro forma basis. This trend is particularly noticeable in the United States.

An analysis of the 'hybrid model' must focus on the extent to which the local American system constrains the realization of the basic logic of the Japanese system. When these constraints are mighty and chew up the basic logic of the Japanese system, it would be no longer 'Japanese.' As a matter of fact, the Japanese and American systems are not made up of totally opposite aspects or elements. But the basic logic of the both systems are quite contrary. Therefore, particularly in the Untied States, the Japanese system could easily convert itself into the American system depending on circumstances. It should be noted that our model is designed as an 'internationally transferred model,' by extracting aspects and elements of the Japanese system that are quite contrary to the American ones. They are particularly susceptible to constraints of the American system and the American management environment when the Japanese system is transferred to local plants.

For example, the IE method of Taylor system itself provides the common foundation for the Japanese and American systems. However, the implementation of the Industrial Engineer (IE) method under the Japanese system features the direct on-site engagement of production workers and first-line supervisors, while the American system takes quite the opposite approach by putting specialized IE divisions in charge. American companies have extensively adopted the method of statistical quality control itself, first developed at a military factory of the US Army during the World War II period. But our model sees the distinct feature of the Japanese system in that such quality control is undertaken as a company-wide system centering on on-site voluntary small group activities.

A slightly different approach may be necessary concerning the wage and treatment system, one of important focal points of the problem. In terms of principles of the market economy, there are, in nature, no direct or corresponding relations between wages and jobs or the results of work. This is the point that the 'contract theory' recently re-formulated. The monetary remuneration becomes related to jobs and performance in order to enhance awareness of commitment and willingness of the workers by the management. However, the linkage between remuneration and incentives and 'results' of jobs can be realized only through forms and conventional rules that reflect historical, cultural and social characteristics.

The wage and treatment system that corresponds to the Japanese on-site 'capability-building' system, which incorporates multifunctional skilled workers and their mutual cooperation and commitment on shop floor, has been developed in Japan as the system combining employee evaluation with the ability-based grade system, traditionally premised on length-of-service-based implicit employment security. On the other hand, in the United States, the traditional wage and treatment system, comprising the job classification system based on detailed job description and job evaluation and associated with promotions linked to the seniority system, 'job-corresponding wages' and the system of 'fringe benefits,' has been institutionalized as the system fit with the logic of the American mass production management while rooted in the socioeconomic characteristics of the market-based economy against the backdrop of its history and socio-economic climate. As the American wage and treatment system is opposite in nature to the Japanese wage and treatment system, transplanting and making workable the Japanese on-site 'capability-building' system at local plants constrained by the management environment and worker consciousness based on persistent American practices would face considerable difficulties. Surely, the labor aspects at American points of production, the scope for the 'revised application' is expanding as elements that can be used as 'functional equivalents' are increasing due to the spreading 'non-union' labor relations and practices. As discussed earlier, however, the changes in labor–management relations in the United States are not of a nature that would help the Japanese system take root in the Untied States. For this reason, the wage and treatment system necessary for the transplantation of the Japanese 'capability-building' system cannot be introduced in disregard of implicit or explicit rules of the American industrial society, thus requiring the 'revised application' making use of 'functional equivalents,' such as the 'single status.'

Crucially important here is what sort of the basic logic of the production system whose context these 'functional equivalents' are placed in. Depending on this, the labor system at Japanese local plants might be part of the revised American system, a system that departed from the traditional system but still is not quite a Japanese one. In this regard, it is important to note that Japanese local plants came under heavy pressure to tilt toward the 'revised American system' in the 1990s in the face of the combination of pressure for increased production volume in the Untied States and the flagging of the Japanese management and production system as a model. Officials at several Japanese companies in the automobile and other industries covered in the latest survey actually pointed out that the Japanese-style operating system and practices became lax and meticulous management was neglected as Japanese local plants experienced production increases beyond their capacity to meet robust market demand brought about by the sustained US economic boom. Calls for the reinforcement of the Japanese system in response to quality problems that occurred at Ford and other American companies can be seen as a reaction to such development. It appears that these problems were hide in continuing expansion of sales amid the booming American economy in the 1990s.

The management and production system at Japanese transplants in the United States can be easily converted to the American one, if the materialization of the basic logic is blocked due to the teeth of its devices being taken out facing the difficulties to put them into practice. Japanese companies' 'capability-building' of their competitive edge depend on the continuous *kaizen* improvements and problem-solving activities in the incessant pursuit of enhanced quality and efficiency. They are sustained by the specific management and production system that incorporates mechanisms that secure workers' active commitments to those activities. It is quite necessary to transfer and establish the Japanese *system* itself locally in order to materialize the basic logic of the Japanese system and thereby prevent the Japanese system becoming a mere facade

As pointed out earlier, in the early years of the operation of Japanese local plants in the United States/North America, many of Japanese companies tried to maintain the operation of local plants somehow at the same levels that their domestic plants achieve by 'bringing-in' of production equipment and machinery with a proven track record in Japan, with the same parts and components as in Japan, coupled with well-experienced personnel who run them well. Sometimes they narrow down the variety of products to be manufactured. Now, going beyond those initial stages after years of local operations, how to establish the 'capability-building' *system* itself at local plants, including that of continuous *kaizen* and problem-solving activities, is the key to successful local production operations amid the mega-competition environment.

Problems with the localization of 'human' elements and human resources development

In this regard, as is notable in the results of the latest survey, the decline in the ratio and absolute number of Japanese expatriates has tended to negatively affect the local transfer and establishment of 'Methods' of the Japanese management and production system. This tendency was unequivocally pointed out in hearings as a matter of fact at Japanese transplants in the latest survey. From the viewpoint of transplanting the 'capability-building' system at Japanese local plants, the decrease in quantity as well as in the ratio of Japanese expatriates does not simply mean the progress in 'localization.'

Thus, one of the major problems confronting Japanese companies in local production in the United States is the development of local human resources. Japanese companies face similar problems in other regions as well. First, they have to develop the local human resources at local plants. Given the present US situation that constraints of local labor practices and work rules remain extensive about the transplantation of the Japanese 'capability-building' system at the shop-floor level, key is the development of local management personnel from top executives to first-line supervisors. Even though the understandings of the lean production methods have become fairly deep in the Untied States, they still have a long way to go, especially if the on-site Japanese labor management methods are included.

Under the general circumstances of the insufficient materialization of the Japanese-style on-site human resources development, which depend on Japanese-style team organizations and the functions of first-line supervisors, including the development of multifunctional skills through on-the-job training, in Japanese transplants overseas, Japanese companies have to rely on the results of capability-building and *kaizen* generated in Japanese mother plants. It means that the source of production innovation ultimately lies in Japanese mother plants. In this case, it is essential to send to local plants personnel from Japan capable of transferring the results of *kaizen* accomplished in Japan, or at qualified local plants in other regions. It is necessary to maintain basic control by the Japanese headquarter. In the short run, the development of the on-site capability-building system using local human resources is incompatible with the dispatching and stationing of Japanese staff. From a long-term perspective, however, it is ultimately essential to send key personnel from Japan to promote the development of human resources, including local managers, and thereby realize the *system* transfer, including the capability-building system. However, there are limitations at the current stage, even at large companies, on the supply of adequate personnel with capabilities and experiences overseas. Thus, there is an urgent need to upgrade and expand the development of qualified personnel for overseas operations both at home and abroad. Furthermore, it is necessary for major Japanese companies with production bases around the world to upgrade and expand the mechanism to share production innovation achievements at those bases and make good use of them for local plant operations in respective regions while taking local conditions into consideration.

Conclusion – the 'hybrid model' analysis and prospect for its evolution

In the United States in the 1990s, the 'functional equivalents' for the Japanese system spread to broaden the scope for the method of 'revised application.' In the meantime, amid the sustained expansion of the US economy, pressures mounted on Japanese local plants for tilting toward the mass production logic of the American system. In this regard, one most important aspect of local transfer of Japanese management and production system comes into focus: That is the *system* transfer of the Japanese system, particularly of the one of the 'capability-building' system, the core of which is the system of continuous *kaizen* improvement and problem-solving activities centering on the points of manufacturing. It became apparently clear that we have to measure more explicitly the extent to which the *system* has been realized locally in order to make full account of the *system* transfer. Actually it is the most central issue regarding international *applicability* (or universality) of the Japanese management and production system overseas.

Table 2.3 Four-perspecrtive evaluation: comparison between 1989 and 2000–2001

	North America (00-01)	*North America (89)*	*North America 89/00-01*	*UK*	*Europe*	*S. Korea & Taiwan*	*ASEAN*	*East Asia*
Human – methods	3.3	3.1	0.2	3.4	2.9	3.5	3.2	3.4
Material – methods	3.2	2.8	0.3	3.2	2.9	3.4	3.0	3.2
Human – results	2.6	3.7	–1.0	2.7	2.9	2.1	2.7	2.4
Material – results	2.8	3.6	–0.8	2.8	3.0	3.3	3.6	3.5

Source: Table 2.1.

So far, our 'hybrid model' analysis has shed light on the *system* transfer of the Japanese-style management and production system through the evaluation of the degree of application particularly in the 'Method' aspect. In particular in the '4-perspective evaluation,' in Table 2.3, we measure the degree of the system transfer of the Japanese system by extracting the respective attributes of the main 'Methods' that comprise the Japanese *system* out of our 23-item and 6-group model and established the evaluation axes of the 'Human Methods' and 'Material Methods.'

However, the local institutional settings and elements that are workable as the 'functional equivalents' usually perform the original functions dictated by the basic logics of local system, coupled with other local elements and factors. When they do not function as expected under the Japanese system due to the constraint by the logic of the local system, even though the incorporation of apparently similar forms of institutions and elements by local Japanese plants gives the impression that the 'application' of the Japanese system is progressing, what appears to be the 'application' is, in reality, more like the 'adaptation' to local conditions and significantly constraining the *system* transfer of the Japanese system.

In order to measure the extent of the local transfer of the Japanese management and production *system* and to clarify its international applicability, it is necessary to specifically verify what significance and actual functions of the local forms and elements adopted at Japanese transplants which are similar to Japanese ones. We need to clarify the context in which they are placed in terms of the basic logic of the production system. Furthermore, regarding Asia, local Japanese plants were measured only for the 'application' aspect for the reason that at the time of the survey, unlike in the United States, modern management and production systems were not firmly established. This gives rise to the problem of different dimension: the low degree of 'application' of Japanese elements, which are evaluated according to the criteria established for the American transfer model, does not immediately mean that local elements got into local Japanese plants by replacing Japanese elements as is in the cases in the United States.

Therefore, it is necessary not only to measure the 'degree of application' in terms of individual aspects and forms of constituent elements of the Japanese system, but also to make clear whether the basic logic of management and production systems at local Japanese plants in the United States is really Japanese or American, and in this connection, it is also necessary to measure the degree of transfer in terms of actual function of respective aspects and elements and then in terms of the *system* as a synthesis of these aspects and elements. It is true that with in the current model, an analysis by mutually linking respective items of the 'Human Methods' and 'Material Methods' of the '4-perspective evaluation' make it possible to specifically elucidate the individual situations of the *system* transfer in individual cases. However, it is not sufficient to look at simply the sum total of the degree of application of individual items indicative of the 'Method' aspects of the Japanese management and production system. To conduct a comprehensive evaluation of the degree of the *system* transfer at Japanese local plants by more explicitly measuring it in numerical terms. We need to go an extra step forward to demonstratively extract, sort out and evaluate various elements that indicate the basic logic of process control and management. The major aspects and elements of them are lumped together as 'operating control' in the current 23-items model. Therefore, it is necessary to reconstruct models, centering on the basic logic of the production system, to measure the *system* transfer in the following two ways: by adding items that indicate the 'methods' of the current '4-perspective evaluation,' that is, items in the 'human method' as human aspects (items of I [Work organization and administration], all items of IV [Group consciousness], [18] Long-term employment, and [20] Grievance procedure) to items of Group V [Labor relations], and in terms of material management, by linking items of the 'material method' ([8] Maintenance, [9] Quality control, [12] Suppliers, and [13] Procurement method.

Then, by realigning evaluation criteria along this line, the evaluation of the degree of the *system* transfer of the Japanese management and production system as a synthesis of the 'degree of application' provided as a result of such evaluation should be coupled with to the current 'hybrid' analysis model. Through a combination with such approach, our 'hybrid model' analysis should become a tool that makes it possible to more stereoscopically analyze and elucidate the overseas transplantation and internal applicability of the Japanese management and production system as well as problems of 'hybridization.'

Notes

1. The survey was conducted for a period of two years on a scale larger than the previous survey in 1986–89. In 2000, a total of 15 research leaders, *partners* and Japanese research partners as well as three American joint researchers and two Mexican research partners, divided into four groups/regions, visited and surveyed a total of 44 mainly Japanese but also American and some Korean plants located in the United States, Canada and Mexico (15 automobile assembly plants, 13 auto parts plants, eight electrical machinery plants, four other electrical machinery plants, three semiconductor plants, and another plant). In 2001, a total of 14 people, including almost all research leaders and partakers, as well as research partners, again divided into four groups/regions, visited and surveyed a total of 37 North American Japanese and American (some Korean) plants and regional head offices (eight automobile assembly plants, including two American ones, 11 auto parts plants, seven electrical machinery plants, four other electrical machinery plants, one semiconductor plants, and six other plants). In parallel with this, plants across Japan were also surveyed to shed light on the present state of management and production systems at domestic plants for the purpose of comparative analysis.
2. The term 'Japanization' was used by Peter Turnbull in 1986 in his case study of Lucas Electrical of Britain, and became widely used after a research done by Nick Oliver and Barry Wilkinson. See Oliver and Wilkinson (1992), and particularly Elger and Smith (1994 Introduction). However, since the transplantation of the Japanese system in the different soils and management environment always entails constraints by specific local conditions, the process is not the straight forward 'Japanization.' Rather, understanding the 'Japanization' as the 'Hybridization' through the interactive dynamism of the 'application' and the 'adaptation' under the impact of the logic of Japanese system reflects the actual state of things more accurately. See Elger and Smith (1994: 36).
3. See Tsuru (2001) and others, particularly Tsuru (2001): ch. 1–3, for an overview of the innovation of production systems until now and the expansion of the cell production method.
4. For rules of origin related to tariff exemptions under NAFTA, see materials provided by the Ministry of Foreign Affairs. http://www.mofa.go.jp/mofaj/area/usa/keizai/nafta.html
5. Shinohara (2003), summing up his research into the work organization reforms and remuneration system reforms in the United States since the 1980s argues that 'the Japanese work organization, interdependently with the characteristics of production control such as JIT and *kanban* formula, is

recognized as the organization that can improve the traditional rigid labor organization and enhance work efficiency' and the wage system is headed toward the introduction of pay-for-skills/knowledge. But he points out that ultimately, 'the line for performance appraisal could not be crossed' and the 'substitute for appraisal' is being introduced to motivate employees. See Shinohara (2003): ch. 1, ch. 2.

6. The hollowing of job rotation or problems with the 'change of function' has been discussed from diverse points of view. See Liker *et al.* (1999: 41–8). In the case of the Lansing plant of General Motors, which was taken up in our survey, Shinohara (2003) points out that the seniority rule was reinforced as something that would constrain the authority of foremen in the conversion of work positions in exchange for the introduction of the 'team concept.' See Shinohara (2003: 139–41). Also, see Shinohara (2003) for many cases where the seniority system, traditional American work rules and workplace practices are all constraining the introduction by American companies of the Japanese work organization and its administration formula (team concept, worker participation, labor-management cooperation, and so on).
7. For example, these can be confirmed in issues in collective bargaining about fringe benefits including lump-sum payments, two-tier wages, cost of living adjustment (COLA) and medical insurance contained in a survey on employers' attitudes by the Bureau of National Affairs (BNA, 1996). See UAW (1996).
8. See discussions in Freedman (1988: 36–8). Dunlop (1988) and Freedman (op.cit.) cite three things as the new phenomena that emerged in labor–management relations in the United States since the 1980s. First, they cite mainly three phenomena regarding wage determination: (a) two-tier wages; (b) expansion of allowance-type 'lump-sum payments' and (c) a major setback for 'automatic' wage determination formulas such as COLA (cost of living adjustment) and AIF (annual improvement factors). Overlapping the last point, the second is the expansion of so-called 'concession bargaining.' The third is the expansion of 'labor–management cooperation' and 'workers' involvement in management.' See Dunlop (1989: 29–30) and Freedman (1998: 35). Dunlop, partly because his arguments were done in the late 1980s, generally tends to underline the temporary nature of these changes. See Kawamura (forthcoming: ch. 6) for basic changes in the labor–management relations and labor market conditions in the United States since the late 1980s, including the points mentioned above.
9. Our hybrid model, in practice, examines the polarity of the Japanese and American systems by approximating it to the 'automobile model.' In the United States, the 'non-union, high-tech model' has rather many things in common with the Japanese model, which was ascertained in the case of semiconductor plants in the 1989 survey. For an in-depth analysis of individual cases, see Abo (1994: ch. 6).
10. There is a broad array of research on these cases. See Elger and Smith (1994) and Liker (1998).
11. The notion of the 'capability-building' system of Japanese manufacturing plants, associated with the 'capability-building' concept of Fujimoto (2003), means a comprehensive system of continuous *kaizen* improvement and

problem-solving activities on the shop floor and organizational and formal elements that make them possible. For 'capability-building competition,' see Fujimoto (2003: esp. ch. 2). The Japanese 'capability-building' system at manufacturing plants almost overlaps the 'innovative production work practice' as described by Florida (Florida, *et al.*, 1998; also see note 9 of introductory chapter). Doeringer *et al.* (2001) calls this the 'efficient organizational regime,' and based on the comparison of actual conditions at Japanese 'hybrid' plants in Europe and elsewhere, observes that although the traditional labor–management relations presented a major obstacle to its transfer to the Untied States, but the weakening of workplace regulations through collective bargaining linked to government regulations is giving rise to labor–management relations that make the adoption of the Japanese 'high performance management practices' easier. See Doeringer (2001: 17–18).

12. Originally, the idea of 'recontextualization' is a concept of anthropology that concerns the change of meaning and function of the same idea and form in the different social and cultural context. But Brannen *et al.* (1999) address this as an issue in the international transfer of the management and production system (118–21). Here, in light of their discussion, we address this issue as the 'transformation of function' in the 'social context' of the logic of the American (Ford–Taylor) mass production system and the basic logic of the Japanese production system.

References

Abo, T. (ed.) (1994) *Hybrid Factory: The Japanese Production System in the United States.* NY: Oxford University Press.

Abo, T., H. Itagaki, K. Kamiyama, T. Kawamura and Kumon, H. (1991) *Amerika ni Ikiru Nihonteki Seisan Shisutemu* (*The Japanese Production System That Thrives in the U.S.*), Toyo Keizai Shinpo -sha.

Brannen, Mary Yoko, Jeffrey K. Licker and W. Mark Fruin (1999) 'Recontextualization and Factory-to-Factory Knowledge Transfer from Japan to the United States: The Case of NSK,' in Liker, Jeffrey K., W. Mark Fruin, Paul S. Adler and Mark Fruin, (ed.), *Remade in America: Transplanting and Transforming Japanese Management Systems,* Oxford University Press, 1999.

Boyer, Rober, Elsie Charron, Ulrich Jurgens and Steven Tolliday, (ed.) (1998) *Between Imitation and Innovation: The Transfer and Hybridization of Productive Models in the International Automobile Industry,* Oxford University Press.

Bureau of National Affairs (1996) *Employer Bargaining Objectives.*

Doeringer, Peter B. Edward Lorenz and David G. Terkla (2001) 'The Transferability of Efficient Organizational Regimes: Evidence From Japanese Multinationals'. (www.bu.edu/econ/ied/neudc/papers/).

Dunlop, John T. (1988) 'Have the 1980's changed U.S. industrial relations?', U.S. Department of Labor, BLS, *Monthly Labor Review*, May 1988.

Elger, Pony and Chris Smith *et al.* (1994) *Global Japanization? The Transnational Transformation of the Labour Process*, Routledge.

Florida, Richard, Dqavis Jenkins and Donald F. Smith (1998) 'The Japanese Transplants in North America: Production Organization, Location, and

Research and Development', in Robert Boyer, Elsie Charron, Ulrich Jurgens and Steven Tolliday, (ed.), *Between Imitation and Innovation: The Transfer and Hybridization of Productive Models in the International Automobile Industry*, Oxford University Press, 1998.

Freedman, Audrey (1988) 'How the 1980s have changed industrial relations,' US. Department of Labor, BLS, *Monthly Labor Review*, May 1988.

Jacoby, Sanford M. (1997) *Modern Manors: Welfare Capitalism Since the New Deal*, Princeton: Princeton University Press.

Kawamura, T. (ed.) (forthcoming) *Hybrid Factories in the United States under the Global Economy*, Oxford University Press.

Kochan, Thomas A., Hary C. Katz and Robert B. McKersie (1986) *The Transformation of American Industrial Relations*, Basic Books, Inc.

Liker, Jeffrey K. (ed.) (1998) *Becoming Lean: Inside Stories of US Manufacturers*, Productivity, Inc.

Liker, Jeffrey K., W. Mark Fruin, Paul S. Adler and Mark Fruin (ed.) (1999) *Remade in America: Transplanting and Transforming Japanese Management Systems*, Oxford University Press.

Oliver, Nick and Barry Wilkinson (1992) *The Japanization of British Industry: New Developments in the 1990s*, Blackwell.

Shinohara, Kenichi (2003) *American Industrial Relations at a Cross Road*, Minerva Publishing Co.

Tsuru, T. (2001) *Seisan Shisutem no Kakushim to Shinka (Innovation and Evolution of Production System)*; Nihon Hyoron-sha.

United Auto Workers (1996) 'What employers want in 1996 bargaining?', http://www.uaw.org/

3

The Japanese Production System in a Changing Environment: Changes in Japanese and American Hybrid Factories in Northern Mexico

Jorge Carrillo

Introduction

The issue of hybridization has once again gained importance in Mexico. The Japanese Production System (JPS), more commonly known in this country as flexible production or lean production, is currently under academic debate. While one approach has viewed the JPS in its more general concept, i.e. as local-capacity building and the creation of different evolutive paths (Alonso *et al.*, 1994, 2000; Buitelar *et al.*, 1999; Lara *et al.*, 2003; Dutrenit and Veracruz, 2004), another continues viewing it as unchanging structures, which intensify labor and impoverish employment. This second approach asks itself whether the *maquiladora* (as the best example of the industrialization model for exports in Mexico) remains a Taylorist/Fordist industry and the introduction of the JPS is merely an example of the precarious reach 'Toyotism' has in Mexico (Wilson, 1992; Martinelli and Schoenberger, 1994; De la Garza, 2004). In other words, the discussion goes beyond the understanding of JPS in and of itself, combining the analysis of productive models with those of growth and industrialization.

And while this is an old debate and much has been written on an international level, the return of JPS's reach in transnational subsidiaries in Mexico is linked to a deeper discussion: does the export model mean development? The controversy is intimately related to the current climate in Mexico: loss of competitiveness and slowing of industrial growth, especially the export *maquiladora industry (EMI) as a whole*, as well as other dynamic sectors (garment, computers, TVs, auto parts and car assemblers). The Mexican manufacturing export crisis has brought with it new critical looks on the '*maquiladora* model' and on the reach of JPS. Most of the controversy centers on how widespread is the second and third generation (in other words JPS's plants and Research and Development (R&D) centers), and the interpretation of JPS itself.

However, very little attention has been given to comparing JPS in Japanese, American, Korean, or German plants. Studies in Mexico have focused mainly on the analysis of productive and product sectors, but little attention has been paid to the differences in terms of where the capital comes from and its respective corporate cultures. Japanese and American companies are of particular interest to Mexico (main sources of Foreign Direct Investment FDI) both as regards JPS implementation and the capacities acquired with it.

Thus, the main purpose of this chapter is to determine JPS's reach and shape in export companies established in Mexico. Electronics and automotive transnationals, both Japanese and American, are analysed through a survey (2002) and company case studies (Carrillo, J. Field work in Tijuana during 1999 and 2001). It is important to mention that the perspective and methodology design by the Japan Multinational Enterprise Study Group (JMNESG), coordinated by Professor Tetsuo Abo, for the evaluation the implementation of JPS in Japanese transplants, has been very useful in different studies in Mexico like theoretical background. Unfortunately, there is no application of either Hybrid evaluation model or the four-perspective evaluation model in this case.

This chapter is structured so that it presents, first, the importance of FDI in Mexico and the new context of competitiveness. Then, it presents the debate surrounding JPS in this country and, finally, the research methodology and results.

The FDI in Mexico, *Maquiladoras* and vehicle industry 'new' challenges

The FDI in Mexico has played a very important role in its economic growth, particularly in manufacturing exports. The 2003 *GAO* report concluded that the US and Mexico share a common interest in the future of the manufacturing industry, and particularly in the *maquiladora*, because of its central role in trade and the economy on both sides of the border region. Through the *maquiladoras*, Mexico has in recent years assumed a prominent position as a US trade partner, only recently becoming the second-largest trade partner after Canada. Of Mexico's exports to the United States 54 per cent (and 40 per cent of its imports) were *maquiladoras*-related in 2002.[1]

Table 3.1 FDI in Mexico ($m)

	Total	*Manufacture*	*Maquila*
1994	11.0	6.2	0.9
1995	9.5	n.d.	1.1
1996	9.2	n.d.	1.4
1997	12.8	n.d.	1.7
1998	11.9	n.d.	2.1
1999	12.7	9.0	2.8
2000	14.9	9.4	3.0
2001	26.7	6.0	2.2
2002	14.5	6.4	2.0
2003	10.7	4.7	2.0
2004	18.9	n.d.	2.5
2005 (Jan.–Sept.)	12.9	n.d.	2.1

Source: Based on Bank of Mexico, SECON, SHCP. Taken from Christman (2006).

Although the role of Mexican exports has not changed, its position certainly has. Investment amounts have decreased considerably in the new millennium. During 2000–2003, it went from being close to US$17 billion down to US$10 billion. Moreover, manufacturing and *maquiladoras'* share in the overall FDI has decreased (Table 3.1). China, on the other hand, has managed to attract a considerable volume of FDI, which represents a value 3.2 times higher than that in Mexico in 2000 and 4.3 times higher in 2002. Several industries with different technologies in China are competing directly with Mexican exports in the US market as Table 3.2 shows.

The 'China issue'

As 2004 Wall Street article clearly point out, while the loss of jobs to China has become a hot political issue in the US, nowhere has China's economic emergence been felt more sharply than in Mexico. During 2000–2003 Mexico lost an estimated 400,000 jobs (probably half to China) and was replaced by China as the No. 2 exporter to the US market, behind Canada. The article mentioned that the lost exports cost Mexico at least US$5.8 billion in 2002 according with Crédit Suisse First Boston. China's rise caught Mexico unprepared. Having signed the NAFTA in 1994, Mexico rode its privileged access to the world's biggest market to become the globe's sixth-biggest exporter by 2000 – placing Mexico and China as the only developing countries in the top ten exporters. Competitiveness with China is an obsession in Mexico – much as the economic rivalry with Japan entered the American consciousness in the 1970s, Mexicans view China as a major

Table 3.2 US imports from Mexico and China (2001, current US$ billions)

	*Mexico**	*China**
Total imports	130.51	102.07
Computers, peripherals and parts	10.36	10.55
Wearing apparel	8.13	8.91
Consumer electronics (excl. TV sets)	2.81	6.23
TV sets, video monitors	5.07	0.26
Automotive wiring harnesses	3.82	n.a.
Telephone and related apparatus	4.39	3.22
Household appliances	1.84	2.85
Base metal products	1.35	1.44
Electric transformers, static converters	1.50	0.92
All other products	91.23	67.95

Note: * Total declared imports, not only maquiladora.
Source: US International Trade Commission, U.S. Department of Commerce. Taken from Christman (2003).

threat. In this sense as jobs move east, plants in Mexico retool to compete (Wall Street Journal, 5 March 2004).

Despite the above, Mexico still has great opportunities for business, even though the losts of competitiveness factors (Christman, 2004). For instance, Mexico stands in third place worldwide as a source for new FDI, only behind China and the United States (2003), compared with ninth place in 2002, in a study carried out among executives of 1,000 multinational firms.[2]

On the other hand, Mexico remains competitive given that it has the three key characteristics that make it a natural outsourcing destination for transnational corporations (TNCs) wanting to penetrate the US market: 1.) complex product specification, 2.) short inventory cycle, and 3.) goods that are a reasonably large in size, which implies that production cost advantages would be offset by shipping costs (Robert Berges, Merrill Lynch, quoted by Christman, 2004).

In order to better understand these opportunities and the challenges faced, a more detailed look into those involved – the *maquiladora* and the automotive sectors – is necessary.

The *Maquiladora* industry

Although the gain or loss of competitiveness is based in first instance on the performance of the firms and in the advance of the JPS, external factors are now making a strong difference. The assembly industry for export in Latin-American countries (Mexico and Central America especially) is at the biggest crossroad in its history. On one hand, it has seen a great competitiveness of auto parts, electronics and garment plants and the diffusion of more complexity, technology, organization and skills (companies with extensive diffusion of JPS) (Carrillo and Hualde, 1998; Buitelaar *et al.*, 1999; Dussel and Xue Dong, 2004) and even of new aspects of centralized coordination that represent qualitative changes (Uriostegui, 2002; Lara and Carrillo, 2003). But on the other hand EMI are suffering the most serious crisis in their history, which has had negative impact on employment, on regional activity and on the reduction of FDI. The new paradox can be expressed in the following way: the biggest implementation of JPS and its industrial upgrading path, is limited by the structural loss of competitive advantages.

Industrial upgrading can be illustrated by television and wire harnesses production. It has evolved from making wooden cabinets (labor-intensive, simple commodities), and assembly activities to flat panels, and digital and high-definition television sets, in the case of electronics; and from simple cables to design and developed modules of ignition sets with high technology (Koido, 1992; Lara, 2001; Carrillo and Hualde, 2006). Also, local inter-firm trade and multi-product plants has been increased. A number of firms, for example Sony, Samsung, Thomson, Philips, Delphi, Visteon and Valeo, have their own R&D, particularly in product design, and they manufacture under their own labels and those of other companies (Original Equipment Manufacture, [OEM] production). As is obvious when comparing wooden cabinets to flat panels, the level of technology involved in the products has risen substantially. Even within some standardized products, however, such as wiring harnesses for auto cars, embodied technology and the rate of technological change is very high (Carrillo and Hinojosa, 2001). Additional evidence of technological evolution and industrial upgrading in the EMI industry is provided by the development of greater decision-making autonomy at the local level (Arias and Dutrenit, 2003). Purchases of equipment, selection of suppliers, changes (improvements) in manufacturing processes, selection of manufacturing technology, product design, and other decisions has become more common (Carrillo *et al.*, 1999; Katz and Stumpo, 2001; Dussel, 2003). The development of greater local autonomy has gone hand-in-glove with increases in quality standards and the use of more skilled labor. Engineers, in particular, have come to play a greater role in *maquiladoras* (Hualde, 2001; Fuchs, 2003; Dutrenit and Vera-Cruz, 2004). Also private and government institutions have been created in order to participated in this process of upgrading (Villavicencio, 2002; Villavicencio and Lara, 2003).

JPS is in the core of this upgrading path – as we will briefly see – but the process has been characterized as a hybrid (Alonso *et al.*, 1994; Carrillo, 1993, 1995).

In the other hand, structural and cyclical downturn can be emphasizes by the dramatic decline in *maquiladora* activity and employment in Mexico. Between October 2000 until December 2003 the number of *maquiladoras*, value added and employment in the northern region has been dramatically suffer. From 300,000 jobs were lost at national level – 60 per cent were at border communities; approximately 890 *maquiladora* factories were close. Half of them have relocated to Asian countries. Among the most important causes of this decline was the economic recession in the United States (Dallas Federal Reserve Bank, 2003), the appreciation of the Mexican currency and the end of the *maquiladora's* duty-free privilege for components imported from outside the region (Gerber and Carrillo, 2003). A preliminary conclusion from a recent study shows that recovery depends basically on Mexico's action (GAO, 2003)

Even though *maquiladora* manufacturing (both auto parts and electronics) is once again picking up – largely due to economic recovery in the United States – there is a growing concern that three-year's crisis could be the beginning of a long-term decline in manufacturing along the border, due to Mexico's relatively high overheads when compared to that of countries like China. Technology change also could imply less needs for skilled people and for volume of employment such as is the case of TV industry, where technology is changing from analog to digital (Kenney, 2003).

It seems clear that relatively expensive labor costs will tend to make low-end manufacturing in Mexico increasingly unattractive. The challenge is to move towards a more sophisticated manufacturing platform, which employs a better trained workforce and takes more advantage of synergies with high tech, information technology and R&D sectors located in US south border cities (called twin cities). Mexican industrial cluster policies are trying actively to support this change.

In this context the analysis of different types of companies according with JPS (or generations in a local conception) it is a good analytical instrument since the companies are being affected in a different way by the economic recession and particularly by the new competitors (China) in relation with labor-intensive industries, but with the level of capabilities of the firm. The evaluation model (application/adaptation–Methods/Results) permits us to go deeper in to the analysis of source and the potential of the changes.

The American and Asian Maquiladoras

The more dynamic sectors (electronics, auto parts, and garments) concentrated 72.8 per cent of *maquiladora* added value and 73.4 per cent of employment in Mexico. FDI participation in those industries has been fundamental and growing – except in the case of the garment industry. In 1999, about 81 per cent of electronics and 100 per cent of auto parts plants received foreign capital investment. These are very dynamic, highly competitive industries with an oligopolistic market[3] based on important transnational corporations such as Delphi, Yazaki, General Electric, Hewlett-Packard, Matsushita, Ford, Sony, Samsung and Thompson. In industries such as televisions sets there are only five leading Asian companies (Sony, Samsung, Matsushita, Sanyo and Sharp) and two European firms (Thomson and Philips); in the case of wire harnesses there are mainly two American (Delphi and Lear) and three Asian companies (especially Yazaki, and then Sumitomo and Wire Products) involved.

Since 1965, EMI's performance has been driven mainly by the American TNCs affiliates (represents 50 per cent of *maquiladoras* foreign plants), as is the case with the US Big Three (62 per cent of vehicle exports). The most important US affiliates have always sought to be near the large markets in interior Mexico and have only kept marginal operations in the border region, however, with the changes in economic policy that began taking place in the mid-1980s, and with NAFTA, the border became a priority area for these companies. As a result of this, the great majority of these marginal operations made a significant turn towards consolidating into competitive, world-class plants. Thus, US companies have come to have a dominant presence in sectors such as electronic components and mechanisms, and auto parts.

Although the sources of FDI in the EMI have been mostly American, Asian firms continue to gain relevance: they grew from 154 to 230 establishments in only 2 years (1997–1999). Out of this flow of Asian investment, the electronics, auto parts, and garment industries stand out. And it has not been only Japan who has penetrated the *maquiladora* program or other export programs, but also other countries, such as NIEs, with salaries twice as high as Mexico's, and even emerging countries with lower wages than Mexico, such as China.

The history of Asian investment in *maquiladoras* begins in the 1980s. Japanese firms were the first to arrive in the 1980s, followed a short time later by the companies from the Asian Dragons (Korea and Taiwan). Finally, after NAFTA, other Asian countries began to arrive (Philippines, and China).

In electronics, companies such as Sony, Matsushita, and Samsung have been a clear example of not only the adoption of JPS but also of the evolution in learning, and the establishment of design, development, and research capabilities. The transformation from conventional TV to digital (*flat panel display*) manufacturing provides a illustration of the capacities achieved by these affiliates and of their potential.

The automobile industry

The pre-NAFTA development of Mexican institutions supporting auto production can be summarized by examining the government series of policy decrees (Layan, 2000; Humphrey and Oeter, 2000) (see Table 3.3).

Although the process began much earlier, regional integration was accelerated with the implementation of the NAFTA in 1994, due to the consolidation of open market changes, especially in the institutions that govern trade (Pries, 2003). The rules of origin contained in NAFTA (62.5 per cent of American content) inspired of further investment projects with the intention of expanding and consolidating their networks of local distributors; furthermore, despite the advantages offered to the original makers, new corporations introduced production facilities in the region (BMW, Mercedes, Honda and Toyota).

Table 3.3 Evolution of the Mexican automotive industry

	Average 1978–82 import substitution policy	*Average 1983–87 export promotion policy*	*Average 1988–94 development of the industry and explosion of exports*	*Average 1995–2000 (NAFTA)*	*Average 2001–2003 (crisis period?)*
Production	477,663	351,589	871,827	1,280,347	1,752,888
Domestic	457,848	295,243	518,555	322,355	462,530
Exports	19,815	56,346	353,271	957,991	1,291,358
% Cars (of total production)	62.0	67.1	75.0	67.1	61.8
% Trucks (of total production)	38.0	33.4	25.0	32.9	38.2
% Imports (of total production)	0.0	0.0	2.8	30.4	30.4
% Exports of Total Production	4.1	16.0	40.5	74.8	75.2
% 'Big Three' (Ford, GM, Chrysler) of total production	48.1	55.5	62.2	65.1	58.6

Source: Based on AMIA.

As important as the emergence of new plants was the fact that existing facilities also increased their production and export levels (Table 3.3). The production of engines reached 2.7 million and vehicles 1.82 million in 2002. The fastest pace of this growth has been within the auto parts sector, especially in those labour-intensive products such as electric wire harnesses and interior systems. For example, Delphi has close to 55 plants and employs more than 70,000 workers in Mexico. In addition to Delphi, other companies including Yazaki, Valeo, Lear, Visteon and Siemens constitute most of the auto industry in Mexico, and they established R & D centers.

Outsourcing and divestment were increasing rapidly in the industry throughout the period as well. The spin-off of Visteon and Delphi changed the rate of integration of Ford and General Motors to much lower percentages. They also imposed extreme competitive pressures on suppliers, opening up contracts to pressure-filled bidding roundtables and demanding continual product improvement, zero-fault performance and technological innovation from suppliers. This rationalization has the effect of increasing production in low wage areas (such as Mexico), as suppliers struggled to impose cost savings by outsourcing even smaller segments of production (Helper and Sako, 1995).

In addition, there has been a shift in the relationship between American automakers and their suppliers in the US, Canada, and Mexico. While in the past this association relied on one-year contracts, higher and more selective levels of integration have replaced this relationship. These involve the interchange of information and engineering, as well as medium and long-run work contracts (between 3 and 5 years, Helper and MacDuffie, 2000). In this context, cooperation relationships may have precedence over price (Raff, 1998), although cost continues to remain a very important factor. As a result, the industry works under the combined pressure of achieving high levels of cooperation, and the search for low operating costs (Cook, 1998).

In spite of the growing *OES* market, the number of tier-one suppliers has been falling, and is expected to continue to do so. Industry executives feel that over the next decade growth in the sector will come from companies that excel at systems integration. Delphi, Lear and Johnson Controls in Mexico are good examples of companies that have achieved great success in this process.

In geographical terms, the Mexican case has been understood, contrary to the US like polycentric region (Pries, 2003). The crisis after the import substitution period benefited cities in northern and central Mexico, as well as border cities. By now, different types of automotive enterprises cover most of the Mexican territory. It can generally be concluded that production specialization and territorial specialization have gone hand in hand. Concurrently, some of the oldest plants were closed. Volkswagen is the only firm that did not disperse geographically. Thus, Northern Mexico rapidly developed in the field of exports during that first stage of the export promotion until the present.

The strategies of the three large American corporations led to a new configuration of production in Mexico, via construction of new plants and restructuring of existing ones so that they could be integrated into the North American production system. From this viewpoint, the Mexican motor industry changed their strategic role of a internal market orientation, toward seeking efficiency in direct investments for exports, which was achieved in great part thanks to industrial relocation in Greenfield zones in the northern and northern-central part of Mexico (Romijn *et al.*, 2000)

The Mexican auto industry has eight OEMs (BMW, Daimler-Chrysler, Ford, GM, Honda, Nissan, VW and Toyota), which in turn have 20 plants in 11 states around Mexico. In 2000 there were 875 auto parts companies, of which 34 per cent are subsidiaries of foreign corporations, and over 1,000 agencies in the distributor segment (Bancomext, 2002).

Since proximity is such an important constraint upon the location of tier-one automotive parts suppliers, this spatial reconfiguration of production in the assembly industry will continue to have sharp impacts on the location of primary parts producers. The increasing two-way trade on both sides of the US border indicates an increasing social division of labor in the manufacturing process. The boom in US imports from Mexico, along with the boom in US exports to Canada (much of which is constituted by Mexican components which are processed and re-exported to assembly plants along the 401 highway) indicates that an increasing share of the production of all North American automobiles and trucks, especially in parts, is occurring in Mexico. Certain highly labour-intensive tasks have been completely transferred to Mexico, as in the case of wiring harnesses assembly.

Ultimately, however, the ongoing southward relocation of parts production at the current rate can only be achieved via a relocation of assembly plants. There exists the possibility of a trajectory of gradual relocation of assembly plants to Mexico, as the existing facilities grow obsolete over a span of 25 years. But this relocation remains a distant possibility, even more distant, given the overvaluation of the Mexican currency; the associated lose of competitive advantages and the emergence of China like an ideal place for assembly intensive labor parts. Although there has been an upswing in investment in Mexico, there has not been a simultaneous drop in investment in United States production facilities. There is thus no indication that existing investments are being allowed to deteriorate in any way or that the pace of investment in the motor vehicle industry is declining in Canada or the United States. Although production growth will continue to occur outside the core, the figures indicate that production inside the core manufacturing area should remain about flat.

As the North American integration has caused the region complementarities and asymmetries to come to the fore of corporate strategic awareness, it has also received mounting criticism from social actors and powerful political forces in the three countries. While the question of wages and labour rights were, and remain a critical issues in this debate, increasingly, the ability to internalize within countries and regions the social and economic benefits of the industry success will increasingly emerge as issues that will require corporate attention. The asymmetries between countries are large enough to expect that the most powerful pressures will come from the US corporate boardrooms and political arenas. Even as Canada and Mexico role in the industry has acquired increasing strategic relevance, both will remain, with their specific differences, peripheral to the US (for example, Lung, 2000, 2004).

In spite of export automotive manufacturing in Mexico being limited to satellite facilities and closely linked to the US market, corporations such as Ford–Hermosillo, Lear, and no doubt Delphi, represent more than just fringe production. At Delphi, 40 per cent of their worldwide business is in Mexico. At Ford–Hermosillo, JPS has been widespread from the outset, and at other companies, it is on a learning curve. But the capacities reached at Delphi, such as R&D and the centralized coordination of functions (a kind of regional headquarters) show a trajectory of industrial upgrading. The Ford Futura project in Hermosillo, the implementation of the 'Ford Production System' and its experimental, quasi-condominium shaped Supply Chain Management system, are additional proof of the confidence foreign investors have in continuing to develop productive, organizational, and human capacities in Mexico (Carrillo and Montiel, 2004).

Evolution of JPS in Mexico: debates and results

Since the mid-1980s, different studies have shown the introduction of JPS into Mexico. The *maquiladoras* are its most studied case, with a very likely second place being the automotive industry (See, for example Grunwald and Flann, 1985; Mertens, 1987; Louv, 1987; González-Aréchiga and Ramírez, 1989; Székely, 1991; Shaiken and Browne, 1991; Koido, 1992; Kenney and Florida, 1993, and 1994; Choi and Kenney, 1997; Kamiyama, 1998). The two main conclusions reached are that there is a generalized spread of JPS, but the process was heterogeneous and segmented; and that the enrichment of work and organization does not translate into the improvement of occupational structures, salaries, and labor stability.

Several typologies have been developed since the implementation of JPS. Some of the most relevants are the folowing: Gereffi ('old & new' *maquilas*), Wilson ('traditional', 'posfordism' 'manufactuer'), Carrillo and Hualde (first, second, third generation). Carrillo (1995) compared Ford–Hermosillo (FH), Ford-Cuautitlán (FC) (brown- field site complex) and Ford-Favesa (FF) (American wire harnesses plant). He found three trajectories: (a) application of American version of JPS (FH), (b) the adaptation of JPS to the labor relations context (FC) and (c) the adaptation to the productive conditions and labor market context (FF). The central debate was, and continues to be: to what extent has JPS spread in all the EMI, and is it systemic or partial? What is most relevant to this work is the generalized conclusion in every case of the high partiality of its implementation, i.e. its degree of hybridization, on the one hand, and on the other the central adoption of its work organization and automation aspects. However, none of the studies has evaluated the adoption or adaptation of JPS. The core concern in many of the studies and typologies developed has been to what extent the Taylorism/Fordism model has truly been changed. Other views asked whether the transplants are learning or reproduction factories? (Kenney *et al.*, 1998). Based on the study of the consumer electronics Japanese *maquiladoras* they considered that, in this case, are most likely 'reproduction factories' and therefore can not be compared with the parent company.

The case of Ford–Hermosillo is interesting because is an experimental model of American type of JPS and represents an important example of the trajectory of hybridization for less industrialized countries. On the one hand, FH has demonstrated the productive success of introducing a transplant based on the Japanese system of flexible production, to a green field site, making certain adaptations to regional socio-labor conditions, with consistent high performance. And on the other, FH has exposed the obstacles that arise for the implantation of this system when labor is insufficiently taken into account. Recently new flexible system have been appear in the vehicle sector, such as 'bank of hours' and outsourcing workers throw employment agencies. Since year 2000, new model has been implemented in all Ford plants in Mexico: the 'Ford Productions System.' This model is more focus in logistics and reducing labor cost 'from the source'. However, the ups and downs of JPS, and their new model adapted, the scenario for the plant is optimistic because the new project recently approved (*Ford Futura*) and the supplier's park that is include. It will bring new investment ($US 1,600 million) a fresh air to the model.

Probably, the two most enriching studies regarding the *maquiladora* adoption of JPS and the trajectories they create have been the Kamiyama study in 1998, and the Alonso *et al.* study in 2000. The first analyzed 12 Japanese *maquiladora* plants in 1989 and 1991, and contrasted them with plants in the US and Asian countries using the Hybrid model and 4-perspective evaluation. And the second contrasted 64 Japanese and American *maquiladoras* visited in 1996, 1998–1999 for the purpose of establishing learning patterns.

The key results of Kamiyama study (1998: 4–7) are the following:

1. The *maquiladoras* have a strong towards the importation of production equipment from Japan.
2. There is a lower degree of 'Human–Results' application than in US transplants.
3. There is a trend to strengthen the application of the 'Human–Methods' aspect of the Japanese production system.
4. The use of cooperative labor relations in the *maquiladoras*.
5. Difficulties in the 'Material–Methods' section.

The Alonso *et al.* (2000) study analyzes learning trajectories, understood as manufacturing evolution. This classification is based on an acknowledgement of the changes that have taken place in this type of operations since the 1960s. Under any standard of classification, the operations that characterized EMIs during the 1970s were extraordinarily simple, and could be reduced to assembling. Socio-technological demands were minimal, and were generally limited to labor supervision and management. Since manufacturing operations that integrated R&D functions in heir subsidiaries, as well as design functions under modalities of integral cooperation between affiliates and parent companies began to arise starting in the mid-1990s, it is worthwhile to ask oneself how you get from one level of manufacturing proficiency to the next.

Since these are operations that emerged as subcontracting of partial operations (sub-assemblies), most of the industrial change along Mexico's northern border is reflected either through gradual manufacturing integration processes, or through the establishment of vertically integrated operations.

The different types of trajectories firms took were established based on the development of ever more advanced processes, or the emergence of continuingly more important roles in coordination tasks with the parent companies, the functional enrichment of their organizational structure, and the institutionalization of qualitative upgrades in operational knowledge of manufacturing, and socio-technological learning levels. This is not, of course, an absolute and error-free indicator. In the end, the functions are merely indicators of the scope of learning that translates into organizational departmentalization in companies.

Five main functions stood out among the generic functions used to analyze plant trajectories: (a) administration, (b) process engineering, (c) product engineering, (d) design, and (e) R&D. This classification responds to the fact that these functions represent a progressive scale in levels of knowledge and manufacturing-related learning, while assuming growing levels of autonomy. Additionally, the presence of these functions is closely related to the characteristics of products (or their diversity), and therefore, to the complexity of implementing the manufacturing processes.

Five production organization levels resulted, representing ascending levels in manufacturing knowledge functions. The Roman numerals represent the distinct critical moments for identifying when a trajectory makes a qualitative upgrading from one level another. In this way, company trajectories were identified as the ascent (or descent) from one level in the organizational model to another. The three levels correspond, in a way, to what has been called the generations of *maquiladoras* in other works (Alonsom and Carrillo, 1996; Carrillo and Hualde 1998). Two production process organization modalities were established for the first stage in the trajectory (I.a. Traditional Assembly, and I.b. Traditional Continuous Manufacturing/Assembly), implying that these are the simplest forms of manufacturing operations. Two organization modalities were identified for the second stage in the trajectory (II.a. Traditional Per-Spec Manufacturing, and II.b. State-of-the-Art Continuous Manufacturing), and only one for the third stage (III. State-of-the-Art Per-Spec Manufacturing).

The following trajectories attempt to illustrate the US experience in Tijuana EMI:[4]

American 1
Product: Solid-state relays.
Type of trajectory: *Total Manufacturer Integration.*
I.a ⇨ I.b. ⇨ .... II.a. ⇨ III

American 2
Product: Sensors, precision potentiometers, precision plates.
Type of trajectory: *Productive Maturation.*
Ia. ⇨ I.b ⇨ .... II.b

American 3
Product: Decorative lamps.

Type of trajectory: *Productive Maturation/Exist Trayetory.*
Ia. ⇨ ... II.a

Japanese 1
Product: Digital and microwave reception packages, ceramics for semiconductors.
Type of trajectory: *Transplant.*
⇨ II.b

Japanese 2
Product: Televisions, key components for TV, video tapes, digital reception equipment.
Type Trajectory: *Upgrade Transplant.*
I.b ⇨ .... II.b

The trajectories of Japanese plants in Tijuana can be basically summed up as processes of transferring operations from other places, particularly from the US These plants are predominantly from the consumer electronics sector, however, they also have an important presence in the areas of electric and electronic components and instruments, office and computer equipment, as well as plastics injection. Since the mid-1980s, many companies have set up operations in the region, expanding considerably during the 1990s. So we are not discussing trajectories with a long history, as is the case with many American companies.

The Asian corporations have not only transferred their operations but have also created local supply clusters in order to arrange their productive chains. These are relocated or even new TNC affiliates with whom they have had previous ties in other operations of the global corporate network. This is a somewhat generalized corporate practice, given that similar processes have been experienced in Malaysia, Thailand, Wales, and Scotland. Thus, in spite of the fact that these trajectories include modern manufacturing processes, the Transfer trajectory has kept the most valuable knowledge functions away from local plants, and although it has created regional supply clusters, this process has increasingly excluded the possibility of developing local or domestic suppliers.

The overall result, as can be appreciated in the trajectories, is that American and Japanese companies have managed to develop significant capacities and functions in their plants, but the American firms have gone further in their trajectories than the Japanese. In that regard, the hypothesis that can be formulated, based on the Kamiyama (1994, 1998) and the Alonso *et al.* (1994) studies, is that the adoption of JPS is greater in American than in Japanese companies, and that the system is more oriented, in the case of the former, towards adaptation, particularly of human–methods; and in the case of the latter, more towards application, particularly of 'Materials–Results.'

Methodology

The data we use comes from the *'Survey of Technological Learning and Industrial Upgrading' (STLIU),* coordinated by the author, which was carried out in 2002 by a team of researchers who interviewed the managers of 298 plants (mostly *maquiladoras*). This methodology is part of the project *'Technological Learning and Industrial Upgrading: Perspectives for the Formation of Innovation Capabilities in the Maquiladoras of Mexico'* financed by the National Council of Science and Technology (CONACYT, No. 35947). The survey had as its original purpose to administer a questionnaire at all of the establishments still active in the sectors of electronics and automotive parts in the cities of Tijuana, Mexicali and Juarez. More than 70 per cent of the plants were interviewed. These sectors were selected for their leading edge in the processes of R&D&D, technology, work organization, training programs, workers' performance and involvement, and because of their tendency to develop industrial clusters around them.

For the analysis of American and Japanese firms we use the information in three different phases. This method of analysis has been development in a previous work (Carrillo and Gomis, 2005) and has been used in different documents (*www.maquiladoras.info*).[5]

Phase 1

We selected a set of multiple variables from the questionnaire in order to elaborated indexes. Table A3.1 in the Appendix presents the survey questions that have been incorporated in the five indexes. The index of relevant dimensions refers to capabilities of the plants. We establish five dimensions or levels of capabilities:

- *Level of decision-making*: local autonomy at plant level for purchases, production, organization, and so on. A *'Human–Methods'* type.
- *Level of vertical integration*: all the different activities that are incorporated in the plant, such as final products, components, assembly, packing, machine shops, production, R&D, prototypes and blueprints, toll making, etc. A *'Material–Methods'* type.
- *Level of innovation*: if the plant is involved in innovation in different areas and how often. A *'Human–Methods'* type.
- *Level of technology*: automation and evaluation of their technology on a global base. A *'Material–Results'* type.
- *Level of certification*: the ISO norms that have been incorporated in the plant. A *'Material–Results'* type.

In all cases, the indexes range is 0–1. The value 1, or any other closet t 1, indicated a high profile in this index. On the contrary, close to 0 means a null performance.

Phase 2

In order to eliminate redundancy and eventually reduced the number of variables, we applied a factor analysis to the initial variables in order to grouping in associated factors. The solution of three factors gives us an acceptable model that explains 71.8 per cent of variability. The composition of three factors in terms of variables include is the following:

- **Factor 1**: level of innovation, level of certification and level of technology.
- **Factor 2**: level of autonomy.
- **Factor 3**: level of vertical integration.

Phase 3

For determining the best model in terms of how many different types are in our sample, we applied the cluster analysis using SPSS Version 10. Our results show six different types of plants:

- ***Type I:*** *low level of technology*. Some degree of autonomy and average level of vertical integration, more of the activities are manual, with not an innovation environment, and without quality international standards. Kind of *first generation maquiladoras*. It seems more *American traditional model*.
- ***Type 2:*** *relatively high level of technology but low vertical integration and especially autonomy*. Type of very specific affiliates highly dependent on parent company necessities. Kind of *first generation maquiladoras* in probable transit to second generation. A clear case of *application type with 'Material–Results.'*
- ***Type 3:*** *high autonomy*. Technology level above the average but poor level of integration. Plants with complex activities, intense use of technology, with acceptable degree of autonomy, but simple organization and poor diversified. Probably *second generation maquiladoras*. Seems more *adaptation type, 'Human–Methods.'*
- ***Type 4:*** *low level of autonomy*. Average technology level but high level of vertical integration. We can consider like *second generation maquiladoras*. Between *application and adaptation type*, maybe more *'Material–Methods.'*
- ***Type 5:*** *the highest level of technology*. But average level of autonomy and under average level of integration. Probably second *generation maquiladoras* in a possible transit to third one. Clear *application type with 'Material–Results'*.
- ***Type 6:*** *all factors are high*. Especially in autonomy and level of technology. Probably kind of *third generation maquiladoras*. Clear case of adaptation type with *'Human–Methods.'*

Summary and results

We start with more general results and then more on to more specific ones. It is important to mention that 'general results' means here more synthetic and more analytical. And for specific we mean more descriptive. We can take the method form general to specific because our previous development of indexes factors and clusters. As mentioned before our method of analysis has been probe in others analysis (see Carrillo and Gomis, 2005).

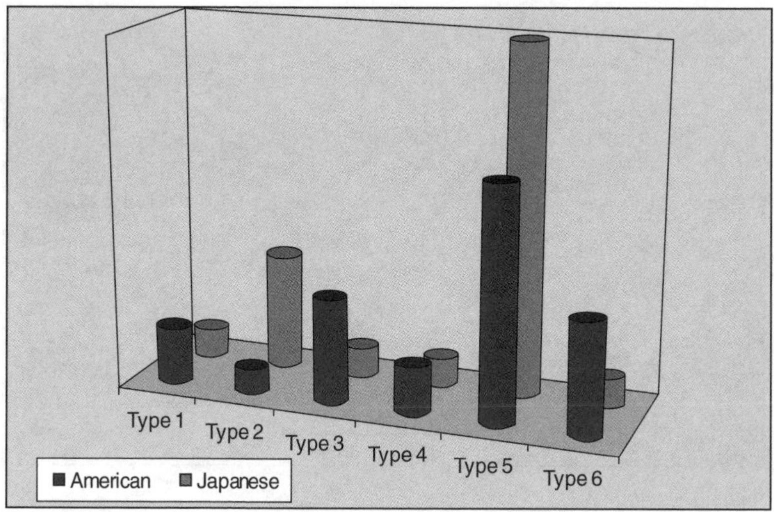

Sources: Based on the survey 'Technological Learning and Industrial Upgrading in *Maquiladora* Plants' COLEF, 2002. Project CONACYT no. 36947-s and 'Technological Learning and Industrial Upgrading. Perspectives for Building Innovation Capabilities in Northern Border *Maquiladoras*,' COLEF/FLACSO/UAM.

Figure 3.1 Mexico: types of plants: TNCs and affiliates

The general results of our sample of Japanese and American transnational affiliates (*n*=53) shows that there are relevant differences among American and Japanese companies. The analysis of six types of plants (or hybrid models based on cluster analysis) is shown in Figure 3.1. First, Americans plants have a more segmented structure but a less polarized one than Japanese plants. Secondly, the global evaluation is higher in US firms than in Japanese companies, but their participation is lower in higher segments (59 peer cent in Types 5 and 6 versus 65 per cent, respectively). In any case, two types are the most important for Japanese companies (T5 with 60 per cent and T2 with 20 per cent), meanwhile in American companies Types 5, 6 and 3 are the most relevant (78 per cent for all three). Therefore, we can interpret that both Japanese and American firms follow and preferred the application model of JPS with material–results type. However, Japanese companies are closer than American companies to the application model of JPS with material results, while US firms preferred the adaptation model with 'Human Methods.' Perhaps the most salient result is Japanese affiliates are less hybrid than Americans, if we take all plants are considered together.

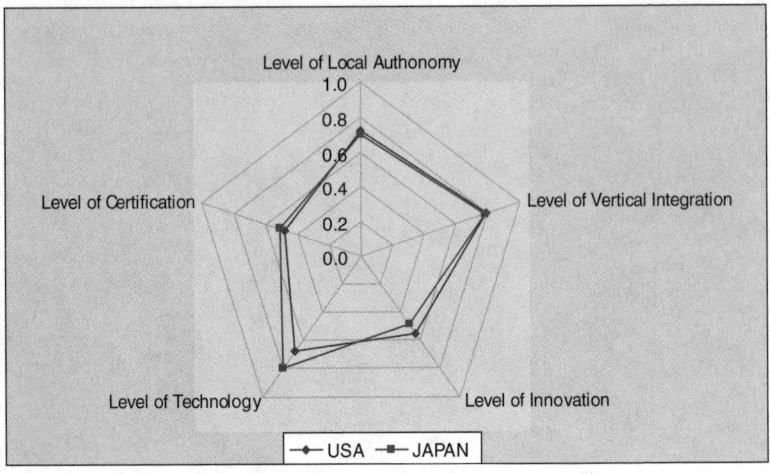

Source: See Figure 3.1.

Figure 3.2 Mexico: capabilities in American and Japanese TNCs

Although the composition of American firms seems to be more oriented to a complex type, that of Japanese firms is more segmented. In any case, at this stage a final conclusion cannot be reached, even though however, the variable types of firms is the stronger indicator of internal capabilities and the kind of mix.

The results related with the indexes by sector, that is the level of internal capabilities, shows also important differences among these two set of firms. As Figure 3.2 indicates, American TNCs and affiliates have a higher level of innovation (human–method) while Japanese firms have a higher level of technology (material–result). The others dimensions of capabilities (autonomy, vertical integration and certification) are quite similar. In other words Figure 3.2 describes how Japanese affiliates are more oriented to the technology level, while Americans are oriented to the innovation level. The high percentages in each level are significant: this can be interpreted as a closeness to japanese production system.

If we compare American and Japanese TNCs affiliates as far as their electronics and auto parts industries are concerned we see more significant differences. Figure 3.3 it shows that in the case of auto parts firms the Americans affiliates are more oriented to innovation than Japanese competitors, and also they have a higher level of autonomy. It highlights the low level of autonomy and especially innovation in Japanese auto parts plants. On the contrary, Japanese auto parts

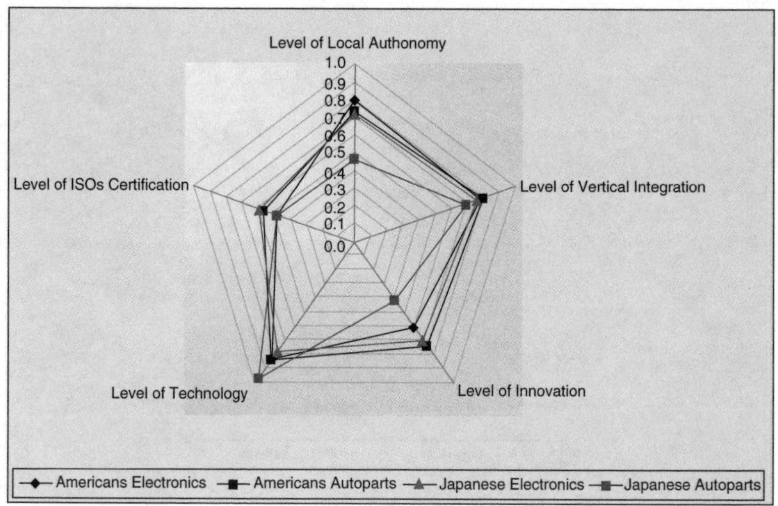

Source: See Figure 3.1.

Figure 3.3 Mexico: capabilities in American and Japanese TNCs by sector

maquilas have a higher level of technology. In the case of electronics firms from USA and Japan the differences are less evident. The only difference that it highlights is the higher innovation in Japanese electronic plants related to Americans. However, the level of technology of the both investments is very high, but Japanese auto parts has the highest level in all indixes.

On looking more closely at the Autonomy level (Figure 3.4) it is evident that, in all cases, American firms have a more plant decision-making capability than Japanese companies, especially in the manufacture of products, and purchases of materials and components.

Table 3.4 provides us a comparison between other key variables. The American plants manufacture a greater number of products and models than Japanese companies, and have a greater percentage of automation. In relation to labor aspects, the American firms use, on the average, more people than Japanese affiliates, and dedicate a more finance in training, education, R&D and environment aspects than Japanese factories.

On the other hand, Japanese firms have developed more electronics trade (e-business) than Americans (Table 3.4). An important indicator of this is the presence of logistics information systems such as *ERP*. A total of 64 per cent of the Japanese plants have ERP and only 33 per cent of the American plants. In relation to labor aspects, the Japanese

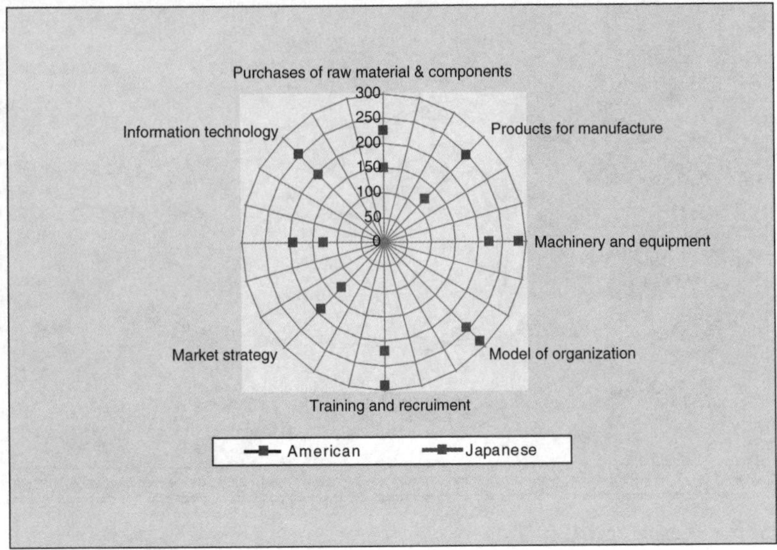

Source: See Figure 3.1.

Figure 3.4 Autonomy: local decision-making – TNCs and affiliates (%)

affiliates have a higher unionization rate (33 per cent vs 23 per cent), because Japanese companies prefer to avoid future contingencies signing labor agreements with 'protections unions.' Also, their labor turnover rates are higher than in the Americans companies. Due to their technological orientation, the Japanese plants spend relatively more on investment of equipment than the Americans, and being of a non-NAFTA country Japan incurs higher customs expenses.

Finally, although most of the companies carry out diverse activities inside the plants, important differences exist among American and Japanese firms (Table 3.5). Nipon companies develop relatively more manufacture of final products (OEM products), fabrication of tools, and elaboration of prototypes and blue prints, than American enterprises.

Table 3.5 illustrates low American firms are much more optimistic than Japanese in terms of the forecast of growth in specific activities. The expectation of growth for activity in next three years figured very high by in the responses of the American managers. In the technological aspect, the Japanese plants are clearly more automated than the Americans. Lastly, and related to labor issues, the Japanese TNCS affiliates pay consistently lower wages than their American competitors, in each of the occupational segments.

Table 3.4 Mexico: main characteristics I. American and Japanese TNCs and affiliates

	TNCs (%)	
	American	*Japanese*
Industry		
Electronics	42.1%	40.0%
Auto parts	57.9%	60.0%
Location		
Tijuana	21.1%	26.7%
Mexicali	0.0%	6.7%
Ciudad Juarez	78.9%	66.7%
Production (averages)		
No. of products	171	11
Sales, 2001 (millions)	79	n.a.
Sales by internet (%)	11.6	18.3
Purchase by internet (%)	5.7	15.6
Automation (%)	48.7	32.3
With ERP	33.3%	63.6%
Labor (averages)		
With union	22.9%	33.3%
Turnover, 2001	5.8	9.4
Turnover, 2002	2.6	5.2
Employment, 2001	1547	920
People with university degrees (%)	17.6	17.7
Expenses 2001 (%) (averages)		
Training and education	5.3	2.9
Technical assistance and technology	7.2	6.1
Customs and government bureaucracy	7.3	12.9
Infrastructure investment	10.5	9.3
R&D	5.8	0.0
Equipment investment	5.4	13.5
Environment aspects	6.2	2.8

Source: Figure 3.1.

General conclusions

The first conclusion to draw is that to compare the results of our survey with those of the Japan Multinational Enterprise Study Group, a common interpretation is required. In this sense the interpretation of the indixes that were created previously in connection with the four-perspective evaluation model from JMESG could be described as follows.

Table 3.5 Mexico: main characteristics II. American and Japanese TNCs and affiliates

	TNCs (%)	
	American	*Japanese*
Activities inside the plant		
Manufacture of final product	63	100
Fabrication of components	61	20
Fabrication of tools	34	73
Fabrication of machinery and equipment	16	20
Assembly of finished products	76	60
Assembly of parts, components and subassemblies	100	47
Packing	76	100
Automatic insertion of components	53	80
Plastic Injection	34	27
Machine shops	58	67
Product design	13	27
R&D	26	53
Product test	79	93
Elaboration of prototypes and blue prints	50	80
Increase in the next three years		
Market share	71.1	33.3
No. of activities and departments	36.8	26.7
No. of clients	60.5	66.7
No. of suppliers	68.4	33.3
Volume of production and/or no. of products	68.4	73.3
Productive complex	50.0	20.0
Level of automation	63.2	60.0
Level of quality	94.7	73.3
Product technology	73.7	40.0
Level of engineering	81.6	33.3
Technology information	81.6	40.0
Management capability	84.2	33.3
Activities that has been increase the automation		
Job position	61.8	86.7
Quality inspection in labor process	73.5	86.7
Material flow	55.9	60.0
Production sequence	82.4	86.7
Information systems and process control	94.1	93.3
Automation in general	73.5	80.0
Wages by week (Mexican pesos)		
Operators	983	644
Technicians	1836	1506
Engineers	5652	3388

Source: Figure 3.1.

Levels of innovation, vertical integration and especially autonomy, are related with methods. Autonomy and innovation are more dependent and associated with human–methods. Vertical integration is more related to material–methods. On the other hand, the level of certification and technology is more a result. ISO norms related quality and environment standards are quasi-mandatory for plants if they want to compete on a global base, nevertheless, great efforts and resources must to be applied by each plant. Usually the companies hire consulting firms and/or parent company assistance for this task. Consequently, we feel the level of certification to be more like a 'Human–Results'. Technology depends on machinery and equipment and in this sense is more material–results.

Taking in to consideration the above, in relation to the evolution of JPS in Japanese transplants in Mexico and based on 2002 survey and company visits (2001–2003) we can conclude that the most salient results from the studies of Kamiyama have followed the same tendency but deep, except for a one case. The resulting trajectories from Alonso *et al.* (1994) have been change. Let us conclude and argue.

* * *

An initial conclusion for both American and Japanese affiliates, is that there is a wide range in levels of capabilities that us have been analyzed, especially in those of technology and vertical integration. In comparison terms, it appears there is a preference by Japanese affiliates to bring JPS to Mexican facilities through results more than methods. On the contrary, American TNCs are implementing the JPS by focusing more on methods.

Secondly, importing of production equipment from Japan on the part of the *maquiladoras* has been increasing. A general explanation of this process is the high competitiveness of the machinery industry in Japan, especially automated machines. The process of importing equipment from Japan has changed in two ways: (1) when companies change the origin of capital and then change their preferences by buying equipment and machinery from their home country; and when companies have more local decision-making autonomy and can then use the internet and company intranet in order to search for the best technology available. The survey results support this trend.

Thirdly, the *maquiladora* has been decreasing the 'human–results' application. This trend has been increasing in American firms (electronics, auto parts and OEM vehicle assemblers). Currently, there are no foreigners working at Ford–Hermosillo. At GM Silao, there is a very low number of US personnel. At the Japanese *maquiladora* companies, however, the Japanese do remain in the top positions, although in their numbers have been decreasing. Mexican managers have earned being considered as 'world-class management' especially in American companies

Fourthly, the *maquiladora* has been strengthening the application of the 'Human–Methods.' The analysis of the five factors shows how those oriented towards 'Human–Methods' have gained strength, that is, (a) the participation of company personnel in local decision-making; (b) vertical integration, that is, the productive capacity to carry out different activities within the plants; and (c) innovation processes.

Fifthly, the cooperative labor relation in the *maquiladoras* has been increasing. Official protection unions have expanded. *Maquiladoras* and OEMs such as Toyota–Tijuana want to sign contracts with these unions to avoid future problems, since in Mexico only one union is allowed to be the titleholder or ownership of a labor agreement within a company. Labor contracts are very flexible and inactive on the shop floors, and seek to protect the companies, not the workers. Even new forms of labor flexibility are being developed in Mexico, specifically, 'banks of hours' in the automotive sector, and employment agencies in the electronics and auto parts transplants.

Sixthly, the existence of fewer problems in the 'Material–Methods' section. A quality control, maintenance and procurement method has been introduced. The global standards of quality control such as ISO's 9000 certificates have been widespread in the EMI, especially in Japanese and American TNCs. Some ISO (or QS) certificates have been implemented in 60 per cent of the 298 plants, although only between 19 and 23 per cent have ISO 9002 in electronic and auto parts plants. In the sample of 53 Japanese and American TNCs we found a very high performance (55 per cent of total, 58 per cent in American TNCs and 47 per cent in Japanese). Maintenance has been less developed, but procurement methods such as supply chain management are common in EMI. The internet trade ratio with suppliers and customers, and the implementation of ERPs clearly shows this trend. The case of Ford–Hermosillo also shows this important tendency in quality, and SCM.

Finally, Japanese and especially American firm *maquiladoras* in Mexico have less mass result-oriented patterns and more methods-oriented patterns, as Abo (1997: 228) concluded and predicted for Japanese transplants in US. But in the export industry very different compositions of factors and levels exist in the plants. We found six different combination. Therefore, there is a wide range of hybrid models. The trajectories to taken in arriving at each one are also variable, but the three patterns of generations that we have described in previous work are still useful for understanding these trajectories. Apparently the American transnational corporations (such as Delphi, Visteon and Ford–Hermosillo) have been able to upgrade in such a way that Japanese affiliates (such as Sony and Matsushita) have not achieved. The 'Human–Methods' process has a key role. However, the Japanese and American transplants in Mexico continue improving the adoption of the JPS. Important adaptations to the local conditions (*glocalization*) are being taken account, such as 'protection unions,' the wide use of male labor force, the engineers and managers *like a driven forces* and the absence of Mexican suppliers to support this industrial process.

Appendix

Table A3.1 Index and variables

Index	*Variables*
Level of vertical integration	2.4. In this plant it is carried out the... p2_4_1. Manufacture of the final product p2_4_2. Production of components p2_4_3. Tool making p2_4_4. Fabrication of machinery and equipment p2_4_5. Assemble of finished products p2_4_6. Assemble of parts, components or subassemblies p2_4_7. Packaging p2_4_8. Automatic insertion of components p2_4_9. Plastic injection p2_4_10. Machines shops p2_4_11. Design of products p2_4_12. Research and development p2_4_13. Product Testing p2_4_14. Elaboration of prototypes and blue prints
Level of technology	3_2. How do you evaluate, in terms of years of backwardness, the technology used in this plant in connection with that is used in your field at world level? 3_3. Percentage of production process that is automated?

Table A3.1 Continued

Index	*Variables*
Level of innovation	4_1. How frequent and important the technological innovations are in this plant?. (frequent and important, frequent and not important, occasionally and important, occasionally and not important, hardly ever)
	4_2. With what frequency – frequently, occasionally, hardly ever – have they existed in this plant technological innovations?
	4_2_1. In the machinery and equipments?
	4_2_2. In the production process?
	4_2_3. In the products?
	4_2_4. In the information systems?
Level of autonomy	2_11. The level of intervention of the employees of this plant null, low important or high important in the following areas of decision taking process:
	2_11_1. Purchases and raw material selection
	2_11_2. The products that produced
	2_11_3. The machinery use
	2_11_4. The organizational model
	2_11_5. Training and recruitment
	2_11_6. Sales and marketing strategy
	2_11_7. Investment and finance strategy
	2_11_8. Information technology systems
Level of certification	3.12. Mention if this plants has certified, not certified or the certification is in processes in the following:
	3_12_1. ISO 9001
	3_12_2. ISO 9002
	3_12_3. ISO 14001
	3_12_4. ISO 14002
	3_12_5. QS 9000

Source: Base on the survey 'Technological Learning and Industrial Upgrading in *Maquiladora* Plants' COLEF, 2002. Project CONACYT no. 36947-scend. 'Technological Learning and Industrial Upgrading. Perspectives for Building Innovation Capabilities in Northern Border *Maquiladoras*,' COLEF/FLACSO/UAM.

Notes

1. Despite EMI's importance, it makes little sense to try to differentiate it from the rest of the manufacturing exports in Mexico, taking into account that while 50% of the exports are from EMI, about another 30% come from similar productive models (Dussel, 2003).
2. A.T. Kerney Consultants, Direct Foreign Investment Confidence Index, 2003, quoted by Christman (2004).
3. There is also a trend towards a greater concentration in few companies in both auto parts, due to modular production systems (Sturgeon and Florida, 1999: 68), and televisions, due to strong inter-company competition (Carrillo *et al.*, 1999). It is also happening to a certain degree in final automotive assembly plants (Sturgeon and Florida, 1999: 72).
4. They were not expanded upon due to space constraints See Alonso *et al.* (1999).
5. For a more explanation of the survey and applications of the analysis visit our website: www.maquiladoras.in

References

Abo, T. (ed.) (1994) *Hybrid Factory*. New York, Oxford University Press.

Abo T. (1997) 'The Electronics Assembly Industry', in H. Itagaki (ed.) The Japanese Production System. Hybrid Factories in East Asia, Macmillan Press, London, pp. 206–30.

Alonso, J., Carrillo, J. (1996) 'Gobernación Económica y Cambio Industrial en la Frontera Norte de México: Un Análisis de Trayectorias Locales de Aprendizaje', en *Revista Eure*, no. 67, Santiago, Chile, diciembre, pp. 45–64.

Alonso, J., Carrillo, J, Contreras, O. (1994) 'Mercados laborales y condiciones de trabajo en la transición de la industria maquiladora'. Paper International Seminar 'Las Maquiladoras en México: Presente y Futuro del Desarrollo Industrial', El Colegio de la Frontera Norte and International Institute for Labour Studies ILO, Tijuana, May 23–5.

Alonso, J., Carrillo, J., Contreras, O. (2000) Trayectorias tecnológicas en empresas maquiladoras asiáticas y americanas en México. *Serie Desarrollo Productivo*, no. 72, División de Desarrollo Productivo y Empresarial, Santiago de Chile: Naciones Unidas (CEPAL-ECLAC). Agosto.

Arias, A., Dutrenit, G. (2003) Acumulación de Capacidades Tecnológicas Locales de Empresas Globales en México: El Caso del Centro Técnico de Delphi Corp, Ponencia Congreso Anual ALTEC 'Conocimiento, Innovación y Competitividad: Los Desafios de la Globalización'. México, October 22–4.

BANCOMEXT (2002) La industria automotriz en Mexico, Banco Nacional de Comercio Exterior, Mexico (power point presentation).

Buitelaar, R., Ramón, P. and Urrutia, R. (1999) Centroamérica, México y República Dominicana: Maquila y Transformación Productiva, Cuadernos de la CEPAL 85, Santiago de Chile, Naciones Unidas.

Carrillo, J. (Coordinador) (1993) *Condiciones de empleo y capacitación en las maquiladoras de exportación en México*, Secretaria del Trabajo y Previsión Social y El Colegio de la Frontera Norte, Tijuana.

Carrillo, J. (1995) 'Flexible Production in the Auto Sector: Industral Reorganization at Ford-Mexico', in *World Development*, vol. 23, no. 1, Pergamon, Oxford, pp. 87–101.

Carrillo, Jorge and Redi Gomis (2005) 'Generaciones de maquiladoras: un primer acercamiento a su medición' *Frontera Norte*, vol. 17, no. 33, enero-junio, pp. 25–51.

Carrillo, J., Gomis, R. (2004) 'Medición de las generaciones de maquiladoras', in Frontera Norte, El Colegio de la Frontera Norte, Tijuana (in evaluation).

Carrillo, J., Hinojosa, R. (2001) 'Cableando el Norte de México: La evolución de la industria maquiladora de arneses', en *Región y Sociedad*, vol. XIII, no. 21, Hermosillo, enero-junio, pp. 79–116.

Carrillo, J. and Hualde, A. (1998) 'Third Generation Maquiladoras?. The Delphi-General Motors Case', in *Journal of Borderlands Studies*, vol. XIII, no. 1, Spring, San Diego, pp. 79–97.

Carrillo, Jorge and Alfredo Hualde (2006) 'De la TV de cinescopio a la TV digital: trayectoria evolutiva o imposición del mercado', in Carrillo, Barajas (eds). Escalamiento industrial y aprendizaje en las maquiladoras fronterizas. Resultados de investigación, COLEF, Tijuana (in press).

Carrillo, J. and Hualde, A. (2004) 'De la TV de cinescopio a la TV digital: trayectoria evolutiva o imposición del mercado', in Carrillo, Barajas (eds) *Escalamiento industrial y aprendizaje en las maquiladoras fronterizas. Resultados de investigación*, COLEF, Tijuana.

Carrillo, J. and Lara, A. (2003) 'Maquiladoras de cuarta generación y coordinación centralizada' en *Cuadernos del CENDES* no. 54, sep-dic, pp. 121–48.

Carrillo, J. and Montiel, Y. (2004) 'American versión of Japanese Production System: The plants of Ford-Hermosillo and Delphi Automotive System-Ciudad Juárez', en Tetsuji Kawamura (ed.) Gurobaru Keizaika no Amerika Nikkei Koujo (Japanese Transplants in North America Under Global Economy). Toyokeizai-shinpo sha, Tokyo, (forthcoming).

Carrillo, J., Mortimore, M. and Alonso, J. (1999) Competitividad y Mercados de Trabajo Empresas de Autopartes y de Televisores en México, Plaza y Valdéz: UACJ y UAM.

Christman, John (2006) *Maquiladora Industry Outlook*, Global Insight, January.

Christman, J. (2004) *Maquiladora Industry Outlook*, Global Insight, January.

Christman, J. (2003) *Maquiladora Industry Outlook*, Global Insight, March.

Choi, D. and Kenney, M. (1997) 'The Globalization of Korean Industry: Korean Maquiladoras in México', *en Frontera Norte*, vol. 9, no. 17, enero-junio, pp. 5–22.

Cook, M.L. (1998) *Trade union strategies under NAFTA:The Unit States automotive sector*, Cornell University.

Dallas Federal Reserve Bank (2003) Conference Maquiladora Down Turn: Cyclical or Structural Factors?, Isla del Padre, November 21, http://www.dallasfed.org/news/research/2003/03maquiladora.html

De la Garza, E. (2004) La Polémica de la Maquila en México: nuevas evidencias, paper presented at Latin American Studies Association (LASA), Las Vegas, October 8.

Dussel, E. (2003) 'Ser maquila o no ser maquila, ¿es ésa la pregunta?', in *Comercio Exterior*, Mexico, vol. 53, no. 4, pp. 328–36, April.

Dussel, E. and Xue Dong, Liu (2004) Oportunidades y retos economicos de China para Mexico y centroamérica, CEPAL, LC/MEX/L.633, Mexico, September 27.

Dutrenit, G. and Veracruz, A. (2004) La IED y las caapacidades de innovación desarrollo locales: Leccines del estudio de los casos de la maquila automotriz y eletrónica en Ciudad Juárez, CEPAL, LC/MEX/L.604, México.

Fuchs, M. (2003) 'Learning in Automobile Components Supply Companies: The Maquiladora of Ciudad Juárez, Mexico'. In Lo, Schamp *Knowledge, Learning, and Regional Development*, Berlin.

General Accounting Office (GAO) (2003) International Trade. Mexico's Maquiladora Decline Afeects US México Border Communities and Trade; Recovery Depends in Part on Mexico's Actions. *Report to Congressional Requesters*, United Status, July.

Gerber, J. and Carrillo, J. (2003) 'Competitiveness Characteristics of the Electronics Maquiladora on Mexico's Northern Border', Annual Conference Association of Borderlands Scholars (ABS). Las Vegas, April, 9–11.

González-Aréchiga, B.Y. and Ramírez, J.C. (1989) 'La Inversión Asiática en Baja California: Un Caso Diferente de Especialización Regional', paper presented at *Seminario Reconversión Industrial, Inversión Extranjera y Territorio*, UAM y CIDE, Mexico.

Grunwald J. and Flann K. (1985) *The Global Factory*, Washington, The Brookings Institution.

Helper, S. and MacDuffie, J.P. (2000) 'E-volving the auto industry: E-commerce effects on consumer and supplier relationships', Paper prepared for *E-Business and the changing terms of competition: a view from within the sectors*, Haas School of Business, UC Berkeley, 24 April.

Helper, S. and Sako, M. (1995) 'Supplier Relations in Japan and the United States: Are They Converging?' *Sloan Management Review*, 36, no. 3, Spring, pp. 77–84.

Hualde, A. (2001) *Aprendizaje industrial en la frontera norte de México: La articulación entre el sistema educativo y el sistema productivo maquilador*, Ed. Colegio de la Frontera Norte/Plaza y Valdes, Mexico.

Humphrey, J. and Oeter, A. (2000) 'Motor Industry Policies in Emerging Markets: Globalisation and the Promotion of Domestic Industry', in J. Humphrey, Y. Lecler and M. Salerno (eds) *Global strategies and local realities*, London: Macmillan, 42–71.

Kamiyama, K. (1994) 'Japanese Maquiladoras in the United States and the Asian Countries, a Comparative Study', Paper presented at Seminar 'The Maquiladoras in México. Present and Future Prospects of Industrial Development', El Colegio de la Frontera Norte, Tijuana, April.

Kamiyama, K. (1998) Comparative study of Japanese Maquiladoras with Plants in the United States and Asian Countries, Josai University, Bulletin, The Department of Economics, March.

Katz, Jorge and Gabriel Stumpo (2001) Regímenes competitivos sectoriales, productividad y competitividad internacional, Serie Desarrollo Productivo no. 103, CEPAL/ECLAC, Santiago, July.

Kenney, M. and Florida, R. (1993) *Beyond mass production: The Japanese System and it's transfer to United States*, Oxford University Press, NY.

Kenney, M. (2003) 'The Shifting Value Chain: The Television Industry in North America' In Martin Kenney with Richard Florida (eds) *Locating Global Advantage*, Stanford University Press, Stanford.

Kenney, M. and Florida, R. (1994) 'Japanese Maquiladoras Production Organization and Global Commodity Chains', in *World Development*, vol. 22, no. 1, USA.

Kenney, M., W.R. Goe, O. Contreras, J. Romero and M. Bustos (1998) 'Learning Factories or Reproduction Factories?: Labor-Management Relations in the Japanese Consumer Electronics Maquiladoras in Mexico' *Work and Occupations*, vol. 25, no. 3, pp. 269–304.

Koido, A. (1992) *Between Two Forces of Restructuring: US-Japanese Competition and the Transformation of Mexico's Maquiladora Industry*, PHD Dissertation, The Johns Hopkins University, Baltimore.

Lara, A. (2001) 'Convergencia tecnológica y nacimiento de las maquiladoras de tercera generación: el caso de Delphi-Juárez', en *Región y Sociedad*, El Colegio de Sonora, vol. XIII, no. 21, enero-junio, pp. 47–77.

Lara, A. and Carrillo, J. (2003) 'Technological Globalization and intra-company coordination in the automotive sector: The case of Delphi–México', *International Journal of Automotive Technology and Managment*, vol. 3, no. 1/2, pp. 101–21.

Lara, A., Trujano, G. and García, A. (2003) *Producción Modular y Escalamiento Teccnológico en la Industria Automotriz: Un estudio de caso,* UAM–Xochimilco, Mexico.

Layan, J.B. (2000) 'The integration of Peripheral Markets: a Comparision of Spain and Mexico', in J. Humphrey, Y. Lecler and M. Salerno (eds) *Global strategies and local realities*, London, Macmillan, 122–48.

Louv, R. (1987) 'The Maquiladora Program in Tri-National Perspective' In *The Maquiladora Program in Trinational Perspective: Mexico, Japan, and the United States*, Border Issues series 2, SDSU Institute for Regional Studies of the Californias, pp. 119–22.

Lung, Y. (2000) 'Is the Rise of Emerging Countries as Automobile Producers an Irreversible Phenomenon?', in J. Humphrey, Y. Lecler and M. Salerno (eds) *Global Strategies and Local Realities,* London: Macmillan Press, pp. 16–41.

Lung, Y. (2004) 'The Changing Geography of the European Automobile System', *International Journal of Automotive Technology and Management* (forthcoming).

Martinelli, Mario and Schoenberger, Erika (1994) 'Los monopolios están bien, gracias. Elementos de reflexión sobre la acumulación flexible', in Georges Benko and Alain Lipietz, *Las regiones q ue ganan,* Editions Alfonso el Magnanim, Valencia, pp. 159–85.

Mertens, L. (1987) 'El surgimiento de un nuevo tipo de trabajador en la industria de alta tecnología. El caso de la electrónica', en Esthela Gutiérrez Garza, *Reestructuración Productiva y Clase Obrera,* Siglo XXI, México.

Pries, L. (2003) 'Volkswagen: Accelerating from a Multinational to a Transnational Automobile Company', in M. Freyssenet, K. Shimizu and G. Volpato (eds) *Globalization or Regionalization ot the European Car Industry?,* Basingstocke: Palgrave-Macmillan, 51–72.

Raff, D. (1998) 'Models, trajectories and the evolution of production systems: lesson from the American automobile industry in the years between the wars', in Freyssenet *et al.* (1998) *One Best Way? Trajectories and industrial models of the world's automobile producers*, Oxford: Oxford University Press, pp. 49–60.

Romijn, H., Van Assouw, R., Mortimore, M., Carrillo, J., Lall, S. and Poapongsakorn, N. (2000) 'TNCs, industrial restructuring and competitiveness in the automotive industry in NAFTA, MERCOSUR and ASEAN', in *Interregional Project on the Impact of Transnational Corporations of Industrial Restructuring in Developing Countries*, Geneve, UNCTAD, pp. 117–70.

Shaiken, H. and Browne, H. (1991) 'Japanese work organization in Mexico', en Gabriel Székely (comp.) *Manufacturing across borders and oceans: Japan, the United States and Mexico*, Center of the USA-Mexican Studies, University of California, San Diego, pp. 25–50.

Sturgeon, T. and Florida, R. (1999) *The World that Changed the Machine: Globalization and Jobs in the Automotive Industry*, Final Report to the Alfred P. Sloan Foundation, Cambridge: Massachusetts Institute of Technology.

Székely, G. (1991) *Manufacturing across borders and oceans: Japan, the United States and Mexico*, (comp.) Center of the USA Mexican Studies, University of California, San Diego.

Uriostegui, A.R. (2002) Del Ensamble Simple de Componentes al Producto Final: El caso de Philips México. Tesis de maestría, Universidad Autónoma Metropolitana, Unidad Xochimilco; México.

Villavicencio, D. (2002) La configuración del Entorno Institucional de las Maquiladoras y las nuevas formas de interacción binacional, Paper presenta at Seminario del Proyecto Aprendizaje Tecnológico y Escalamiento Industrial: Perspectivas para la Formación de Capacidades de Innovación en la Maquiladora de México, UAM, México, November 5–7.

Villavicencio, D, and Lara, A. (2003) Technological learning and industrial upgrading in Maquiladoras: Towards a new path of industrialization?, Document for Project Conacyt 35947, Mexico.

Wilson, P. (1992) *Exporters and Local Development. Mexico's New Maquiladoras*. Austin, University of Texas Press.

The Wall Street Journal (2004) 'Jobs move east, plants in Mexico retool to compete', 5 March.

4

Hybrid Factories in East Asia in 1992–93 and After

Hiroshi Itagaki

This chapter is designed to look into the status of application of the Japanese system in East Asian countries in comparison with the situation in the United States and Europe. In doing so, East Asia is divided into Korea and Taiwan, the two newly industrializing economies (NIEs) with the more advanced state of industrialization, and the three members of the Association of Southeast Asian Nations (ASEAN), who have experienced remarkable economic development in recent years[1] for analysis. Though Singapore may well be grouped together with Korea and Taiwan for several reasons, this analysis puts it in the ASEAN group given the geographical and historical conditions as well as locational grouping in our research. This chapter is based on the results of the 1992–93 research, meaning the data are relatively old. However, have been carrying out follow-up research on Japanese plants in the region, and information on this indicates little change in the way these plants are managed, though some in the region now have different strategic importance and some have been closed down amid structural change in the global economy including the remarkable development of the Chinese economy. So, as long as the state of hybridization of operating plants in the region is concerned, the data from the 1992–93 research can still be considered fundamentally not out of date.

Hybrid plants in Korea and Taiwan

An outline of plants surveyed in Korea and Taiwan

The number of plants surveyed in Korea and Taiwan was 25, as shown in Table 4.1 (the survey in 1992). Characteristically, of the surveyed plants, joint venture plants with local companies numbered 18, accounting for more than two-thirds of the total. Next, by nationality

Table 4.1 Surveyed Japanese plants in Taiwan and Korea

	Automobile assembly	*Automobile components*	*Electronics assembly*	*Electronics components*	*Total*
No. of plants	5	7	6	7	25
Ownership (%)					
90–100[1]	0	1	3	4	7
50–less than 90	0	3	2	3	7
less than 50	5	3	1	0	9
Nationality of top manager					
Japanese	1	4	3	5	13
Local	4	3	3	2	12
No. of employees					
1–499	0	5	1	0	6
500–999	1	1	1	3	6
1,000–1,900	1	1	1	3	6
2,000–2,999	1	0	2	0	3
3,000–	2	0	1	1	4
Start of operation[2] in or					
before 1960s	0	0	3	2	5
1970s	1	4	2	4	11
1980–85	2	0	1	0	3
1986 onwards	2	3	0	1	6

Notes: [1] Including cases where Japanese parent companies own the majority and all other owners are Japanese trading companies or Japanese banks;
[2] years of acquisition or equity participation.
Source: Data is based on author's interview and as at the day surveyed.

of presidents or other chief executives for local operations, almost half of the surveyed plants were headed by Japanese top executives and the other half by local non-Japanese top executives, indicating a considerable degree of the localization of management, unlike the situation in the United States. By size of workforce, small plants with workers of less than 500 and large-scale plants with workers of more than 3,000 are almost evenly distributed in all three industry sectors other than the auto parts industry, which is dominated by small plants. While there are 18 plants that came on stream by the 1970s and thus have a relative long duration of operations, there also are five plants that started production after the second half of the 1980s, thus forming a mixture of plants with long and short operating experiences.

As indicated by Table 4.1, the degree of application at plants in Korea and Taiwan shows a very similar pattern overall, except for a few items. There are few distinct differences between industry sectors that can be observed in the United States. These characteristics allow an examination of plants in both Korea and Taiwan and in all the four industries together.

High degree of application at formal systems

The most important characteristic of Korea and Taiwan, when compared with other regions, can be found in that the degree of application in the 'human method' (at 3.5) is significantly higher than the degree of application in the 'human result' (at 2.1). Moreover, it should be noted that the degree of application in the 'Work Organization and Administration' group, which may be described as the core of human elements, is, at 3.7, definitely higher than other regions. In other words, it can be argued that the Japanese system has been transferred with the priority given both to the application of the human method as and core elements.

The progress in the application of the human method in Korea and Taiwan has been possible due to fewer obvious formal obstacles to the transplantation of the Japanese system than in the United States or Europe. It is largely because Korea and Taiwan started industrialization later than the Untied States or Europe and thus had no firmly established Korean or Taiwanese systems that would have blocked the inroad of foreign manufacturing systems when Japanese companies entered their markets. In this connection, it is important to note that Japanese manufacturers advanced into Korea and Taiwan in parallel with the process of rapid industrialization of Korea and Taiwan since the 1960s while giving no small influence on that process. The fact should not be ignored that Korea and Taiwan had from the beginning similar aspects with Japan in terms of the composition of work organizations and the way workers are treated. Because of these backgrounds, it is safe to say that Japanese companies were able to bring their own styles of operations into Korea and Taiwan without too much effort, or sometimes unknowingly.

This point is highlighted in the job classification and the wage system. Similarly with Japan, in Korea and Taiwan, the concept of jobs is not as firmly established as in the United States or Europe, and thus there exists no formal demarcation between jobs. Therefore, they have person-centered wage systems similar to that of Japan, which are based on seniority, educational qualifications and posts, rather than jobs.

Specifically, the wage system can be described as follows, though, needless to say, there could be a variety of differences among companies.

Table 4.2 Hybrid evaluations of Japanese affiliates plants in Taiwan and Korea

	Average	*Korea*	*Taiwan*	*Auto assembly*	*Auto parts*	*Elec. assembly*	*Elec. parts*
I Work organization and administration	3.7	3.6	3.7	3.9	3.7	3.8	3.6
(1) Job classification	4.9	4.9	4.9	5.0	4.8	4.8	5.0
(2) Multifunctional skills	2.9	2.5	3.1	3.8	3.3	2.5	2.4
(3) Education and training	3.4	3.5	3.3	3.6	3.3	3.3	3.3
(4) Wage system	3.9	3.9	3.9	4.4	3.7	4.0	3.9
(5) Promotion	3.7	3.4	3.9	3.4	3.7	4.3	3.7
(6) Supervisor	3.4	3.3	3.4	3.4	3.2	3.8	3.3
II Production control	3.5	3.5	3.5	3.6	3.2	3.7	3.6
(7) Equipment	3.5	3.6	3.5	3.6	3.0	3.2	4.1
(8) Maintenance	3.3	3.1	3.4	3.2	3.2	3.8	3.1
(9) Quality Control	3.6	3.6	3.6	3.8	3.3	4.0	3.6
(10) Process Management	3.5	3.6	3.5	3.8	3.2	3.7	3.7
III Procurement	3.2	3.4	3.1	3.0	3.1	3.1	3.7
(11) Local content	2.9	3.3	2.7	2.4	3.0	2.7	3.4
(12) Suppliers	3.5	3.9	3.3	3.0	3.5	3.2	4.3
(13) Procurement method	3.2	3.1	3.3	3.6	2.8	3.5	3.3
IV Group consciousness	3.4	3.3	3.5	3.9	3.4	3.4	3.4
(14) Small group activities	3.2	3.0	3.3	4.0	3.3	2.8	3.1
(15) Information sharing	3.5	3.4	3.5	3.8	3.2	3.7	3.6
(16) Sense of unity	3.6	3.5	3.7	4.0	3.7	3.8	3.6
V Labour relations	3.4	3.3	3.4	3.6	3.0	3.8	3.4
(17) Hiring policy	3.0	3.1	3.0	3.0	2.7	3.5	3.3
(18) Long-term employment	3.3	3.3	3.3	3.6	3.0	3.7	3.3
(19) Harmonious labour relations	4.0	3.5	4.2	4.2	3.5	4.5	4.0
(20) Grievance procedure	3.2	3.1	3.2	3.4	2.8	3.5	3.1
VI Parent–subsidiary relations	2.3	3.1	3.2	2.2	2.4	2.1	2.6
(21) Ratio of Japanese expatriate	1.5	1.3	1.6	1.6	2.0	1.2	1.3

Table 4.2 Continued

	Average	*Korea*	*Taiwan*	*Auto assembly*	*Auto parts*	*Elec. assembly*	*Elec. parts*
(22) Delegation of power	2.7	2.6	2.8	2.4	2.5	2.8	3.3
(23) Position of local manager	2.7	2.6	2.8	2.4	2.5	2.8	3.3
Average of 23 items	3.3	3.3	3.4	3.5	3.2	3.4	3.4

Source: From author's data base.

The basic pay is determined under the wage table comprising grades and numbers. Educational backgrounds, such as whether a workers started after finishing junior high school, after finishing high school, or as university graduates, determine the starting class, and pay raises are given according to the annual rise in numbers. There are usually four to six grades up to the level of overseers on the shop floor, called group leaders or foremen, and employees go up the ladder of grades by seniority and appraisal. From overseers on the shop floor and above, grades correspond to job titles such as section chief, division chief and department chief. Usually, the basic pay accounts for 70 to 80 per cent of the total wage, with the rest consisting of various benefits. Almost all companies conduct employee performance evaluation, and the results of evaluation are reflected in the wage, including for production line jobs. There are two ways to reflect this: one is to expand or narrow the margin of annual wage increase against the standard margin depending on performance and the other is to accelerate the climb on the ladder of pay numbers when the assessed performance is favorable. Points in performance evaluation seem to be largely similar to those in Japan. Thus, as the job classification and the wage system, the preconditions for the Japanese system, are already in place in Korea and Taiwan, the degree of applications for items in the Work Organization are generally higher than other regions.

Backed up by the application of core elements in the 'human method,' the degree of application in the 'material method' (3.4) in Korea and Taiwan also is the highest among all regions, an indication that production of a variety of products at a single plant, or so-called large-item-small-volume production, is being carried out relatively smoothly. Automobile assembly plants in Taiwan are producing several basic types of vehicles, and a variety of large and small models, with one plant turning out large buses and trucks under the same roof. As for electric machinery assembly and parts production, several plants in Taiwan not only produce a large number of models for color television sets or other products, as they are called mini-Matsushitas or mini-TDKs, but also manufacture several kinds of products that in Japan are produced at respective specialized factories located across the country.

Gaps between forms and actual operations

However, there are important constraints and limitations regarding the high degree of application at formal levels in Korea and Taiwan. If expressed straightforwardly these limitations can be described as the gaps between the application at formal levels and the application in actual operations of plants. The gap is best demonstrated by the gap in the degree of application between the job classification and wage system, and multifunctional skills. Though the job classification and the wage system, the preconditions for multifunctional skills, are in place, the degree of application for the item of multifunctional sills itself remains low at 2.9. But there are big discrepancies among industries. Even in Japan, there is a difference in the item for multifunctional skills between the auto assembly industry where there is a high degree of necessity for multifunctional skills even at the level of ordinary workers and the electric machinery sector where there is less need to require multifunctional skills by all means of female workers and other production-line workers. But, even in the auto assembly and auto parts sectors aggressively seeking multifunctional skills, a variety of constraints were cited, including the difficulty in job rotation.

Quality control is another important example that shows the gap between forms or methods, and actual operations. Many plants are making efforts to realize the so-called building-in of quality, with workers themselves working with full attention given to securing good quality, checking defects that arose in the preceding process and implementing *kaizen* improvements when problems arise. Consequently, there are Japanese plants in Korea and Taiwan that boast of the defective fraction and the level of quality that are identical with plants in Japan. However, several plants have higher in-process defective fractions than plants in Japan. In other words, in terms of method, these plants have a system for the building-in of quality on the shop floor but the system is not underpinned by actual performance.

Where does this gap between forms or methods, and actual operations come from? First, the biggest reason is the low retention of workers. Usually, the annual turnover rate is 20–30 per cent, though it varies by region or the state of the economy. The high turnover rate stems in part from the high proportion of new recruits who leak, but the bigger problem for companies is the high leaving rate of young engineers and maintenance workers. Managers at more than a few plants complain that they come and go so quickly as if manufacturing plants were just offering training schools for them. The high turnover rate almost without fail restricts the breadth and depth of job proficiency, causing a gap between forms and actual conditions. Furthermore, the social gaps, centering on educational backgrounds, are brought into companies to stand in the way of promotions, affecting the retention of employees and further the degree of their participation in management. This point cannot be ignored.

Several plants cited inadequate inter-departmental cooperation as problematic in quality control. This has to do with inadequate exchanges of information or feedbacks between preceding and follow-on processes, between production lines and parts reception or quality control divisions. These are the facts that are not limited to Korea and Taiwan but can be observed at many other local Japanese plants. Since this forms the fundamental aspect of the Japanese system, it can be viewed as the critical problem for Japanese companies. As described later, this is one of important factors that explain the high proportion of Japanese expatriates at Japanese local plants relative to American or European companies.

The point that should be underlined at the same time is that the gaps between forms and actual operations are the gaps that are observed only in comparison with Japanese plants at home. It should not be forgotten that Japanese plants in Korea and Taiwan have high levels of production efficiency and quality when compared with Japanese local plants in other regions of the world.

Low ratio of Japanese expatriates

What makes Japanese plants in Korea and Taiwan considerably different from other regions, except for ASEAN, is the low ratio of Japanese expatriates to the total number of personnel. Japanese plants are being operated basically by local mangers, and many Japanese companies, centering on those in the auto assembly and electric machinery assembly industries, are trying to limit the roles of Japanese expatriates to staff or advisers, keeping them away from management lines. Thus, Japanese plants in Korea and Taiwan are featured by the low degree of application of the human result, or, the high degree of localization of management.

There seem to be multiple factors for this, including the fact that many are joint venture plants with local companies and a majority of plants began operating long years ago. Still, the biggest factor is that local managers have the fairly deep level of, not just superficial, understanding of the Japanese system. Furthermore, not only top executives but also not a few middle-management personnel, can understand Japanese language and communicate directly with Japan, and this certainly helps facilitate the smooth penetration of the Japanese system and make local management with only a limited number of Japanese expatriates feasible.

However, there still are not a few plants where a small number of Japanese retain real power, and it is also necessary to consider that even after the launch of local plants, when a large number of Japanese personnel come to assist, there are always Japanese personnel who come to local plants for a brief stay regularly, or as helping hands at times of trouble and the launch of new products.

Thailand, Malaysia and Singapore

An outline of plants surveyed in the ASEAN region

A total of 35 Japanese local plants were surveyed in the three ASEAN states of Thailand, Malaysia and Singapore (the 1993 survey, Table 4.3). By type of ownership, 16 plants are more than 90 per cent, or virtually single-handedly, owned by Japanese companies (including those with partial equity stakes held by Japanese trading firms and banks), 8 plants are joint ventures with a majority stake by Japanese companies, and 11 plants are joint ventures where Japanese companies have a minority stake. Though joint venture plants account for more than half the surveyed plants, Japanese top executives are at the helm of an overwhelming 32 plants. Moreover, the three companies headed by non-Japanese local executives include Malaysia's state-owned auto assembly plant where Japanese companies made capital participation, which cannot be considered as a Japanese-affiliated company. In other words, Japanese are serving as chief executive officers at almost all companies that can be considered Japanese-affiliated. This is where they are quite different from Japanese plants in Korea and Taiwan. As for the number of employees, plants with the workforce of between 1,000 and 2,000 form the largest group, but plants with less than 500 workers and those with more than 3,000 workers are broadly and rather evenly deployed.

Table 4.3 Surveyed Japanese plants in three ASEAN countries

	Automobile assembly	*Automobile components*	*Electronics assembly*	*Electronics component*	*Total*
No. of plants	8	6	10	11	35
Ownership (%)					
90–100[1]	2	1	3	10	16
50–less than 90	1	2	4	1	8
less than 50	5	3	3	0	11
Nationality of top manager					
Japanese	5	6	10	11	32
Local	3	0	0	0	3
No. of employees					
1–499	0	2	0	2	4
500–999	3	2	3	1	9
1,000–1,900	1	1	5	4	11
2,000–2,999	1	0	2	2	5
3,000–	3	1	0	2	6
Start of operation[2]					
in or before 1960s	4	1	2	0	7
1970s	0	1	2	2	5
1980–85	3	2	1	1	7
1986 onwards	1	2	5	8	16

Notes: [1] Including cases where Japanese parent companies own the majority and all other owners are Japanese trading companies or Japanese banks;
[2] years of acquisition or equity participation.
Source: Data is based on author's interview and as of the day surveyed.

Plants in the three ASEAN nations are diverse in the time of launch. But broadly speaking, they are divided into one group that were established by the 1970s and the other group that began production since the second half of the 1980s. The group of early comers in Thailand and Malaysia are mostly plants that were set up during the period when the host countries adopted the import-substituting industrialization policy and provide the local markets with small quantities of a variety of products. In auto assembly, these plants turn out a variety of large and small models. In electric machinery assembly, there are mini-Matsushita-type plants that manufacture a range of products from so-called white goods to color TVs and thus are similar in nature to some Japanese plants operating in Taiwan. On the other hand, most of electric machinery assembly and electric parts plants that started operation in the 1980s are either plants dedicated to exports or plants with high export ratios. In electric machinery assembly, in particular, they are specialized mass-production plants focusing on a small number of products such as color TVs, video cassette recorders and air conditioners. Japanese plants in the three ASEAN countries are characterized by this polarization between older plants catering to the domestic markets and new plants for export markets. However, as described later, auto assembly plants in Thailand are gaining a higher level of capacity including export competitiveness after going through the economic crisis, rapidly growing out of the mold of old, conventional-type plants.

Person-centered wage systems with big differentials

In looking at Japanese local plants in the ASEAN region, points to be examined other than the social climate in respective countries include: in Thailand and Malaysia, how the industrialization process as late-comers is affecting the transfer of the Japanese system, and in Singapore and Malaysia, whether their experiences as British colonies

Table 4.4 Hybrid evaluations of Japanese affiliates plants in three ASEAN countries

	Average	*Malaysia*	*Thailand*	*Singapore*	*Auto assy*	*Auto parts*	*Elec. assy*	*Elec. parts*
I Work organization and administration	3.3	3.2	3.3	3.1	3.4	3.3	3.2	3.2
(1) Job classification	4.5	4.3	4.9	3.8	4.8	4.7	4.2	4.6
(2) Multi-functional skills	2.6	2.6	2.6	2.5	3.1	2.5	2.5	2.3
(3) Education and training	3.3	3.0	3.4	3.5	3.4	3.2	3.1	3.4
(4) Wage system	3.1	3.1	3.1	2.8	3.1	3.2	2.8	3.2
(5) Promotion	3.1	3.3	3.0	3.0	3.0	3.2	3.4	3.0
(6) Supervisor	2.9	2.9	2.9	3.3	2.9	3.0	2.9	3.0
II Production control	3.4	3.4	3.2	3.8	2.9	3.3	3.4	3.7
(7) Equipment	4.0	4.1	3.7	4.8	3.0	4.2	3.8	4.7
(8) Maintenance	3.0	2.9	3.0	3.5	2.8	2.8	3.2	3.2
(9) Quality control	3.2	3.3	3.0	3.5	2.8	3.3	3.4	3.3
(10) Process management	3.2	3.1	3.2	3.5	3.0	3.0	3.2	3.5

Table 4.4 Continued

	Average	*Malaysia*	*Thailand*	*Singapore*	*Auto assy*	*Auto parts*	*Elec. assy*	*Elec. parts*
III Procurement	3.2	3.4	3.1	3.5	3.1	3.2	3.1	3.5
(11) Local content	3.1	3.2	3.0	3.5	3.0	3.8	2.7	3.3
(12) Suppliers	3.8	3.9	3.8	3.8	3.8	3.7	3.8	4.0
(13) Procurement method	2.8	3.0	2.5	3.3	2.5	2.2	3.1	3.1
IV Group consciousness	3.2	3.2	3.1	3.3	2.9	3.1	3.3	3.2
(14) Small group activities	2.9	2.9	2.8	3.0	2.9	2.7	3.0	2.8
(15) Information sharing	3.3	3.4	3.3	3.3	3.3	3.2	3.5	3.3
(16) Sense of unity	3.3	3.3	3.3	3.8	2.6	3.5	3.5	3.5
V Labour relations	3.1	3.1	3.3	2.8	3.2	3.0	3.1	3.2
(17) Hiring policy	3.1	2.9	3.3	2.5	2.9	3.0	3.2	3.1
(18) Long-term employment	3.0	2.9	3.3	2.5	3.1	2.8	3.0	3.1
(19) Harmonious labor relations	3.3	3.3	3.3	3.3	3.9	3.0	3.0	3.4
(20) Grievance procedure	3.1	3.0	3.3	3.0	3.0	3.0	3.1	3.3
VI Parent–subsidiary relations	2.9	2.8	2.8	3.3	2.4	2.7	3.0	3.2
(21) Ratio of Japanese expatriate	1.6	1.7	1.3	2.5	1.3	1.7	1.6	1.6
(22) Delegation of power	3.2	3.0	3.4	3.0	2.8	2.7	3.2	3.7
(23) Position of local manager	3.9	3.8	3.8	4.3	3.3	3.7	4.1	4.2
Average of 23 items	3.2	3.2	3.2	3.3	3.0	3.1	3.2	3.3

Notes: Auto assy = Auto assembly; Elec. Assy = Electronics assembly
Source: From author's data base.

and the influences of American companies that entered these countries before Japanese firms are presenting obstacles to the application of the Japanese system.

To present conclusions on these points beforehand, it may be safely said that there are no such obstacles, and even if there are, they should not be so strong. This can be seen explicitly in the wage system. Japanese local plants in the ASEAN region, including those in Singapore and Malaysia, adopt wage systems that are based on the length of service, educational backgrounds and age, instead of jobs, and also incorporate performance evaluation. There exist some plants that adopt job-based wages for ordinary workers or those that do not appraise employee performance. But it appears that they are not so eager to introduce Japanese-type systems, rather than they are being prevented from introducing them even when they wish to do so because of the hindrances of the existing systems. In other words, unlike in the United States, it can be said that there are no strong formal obstacles to the transplanting of the Japanese system in the ASEAN region, including Singapore and Malaysia.

Looking at the wage systems in concrete terms, even though there are a small number of plants that adopt wage-by-job systems, most plants have wage systems with several tiers of grades and educational backgrounds determine which grade to start from. Even within the same grade, wages vary due to annual pay raises, the length of experiences and age for each worker. These wage systems are essentially the same in nature as our person-centered wage systems, and in that respect, are similar to those in Korea and Taiwan. The major difference can be found in that wage differentials between grades and job titles are far larger than in Korea and Taiwan, to say nothing of Japan. While the wage gap between ordinary workers and section chiefs is roughly three to four times in Japan, it expands to more than 10 times in Thailand and Malaysia. Generally speaking, the social gaps centering on educational backgrounds are explicit and large, and these gaps are apparently reflected within Japanese local plants. At the time of the survey, about two-thirds of the subject plants had the system of performance appraisal for production-line workers and reflecting the results in wages. So, the level of the penetration of these methods can be considered fairly high, though not as high as in Korea or Taiwan.

Tendency toward static jobs

The low degree of application in the human method and its core, the 'Work Organization and Administration' relative to Korea and Taiwan (Table 4.2) despite low obstacles at formal levels stems firstly from the fact that Japanese companies are restraining themselves from bringing in the Japanese system. This is clearly shown in the area of multifunctional skills. The evaluation point for job rotation is 2.6, the lowest among regions along with North America at the time of the 1989 survey. In the ASEAN regions, there are many instances where Japanese companies choose to narrow the scope of work for employees or not to implement job rotations. The same can be said about quality control. In the area of quality control, there is a stronger tendency than in Korea and Taiwan, to say nothing of Japan, to conduct regular work and quality checks by division of labor. There do exist plants that have identical quality control methods with domestic Japanese plants, regular workers do not usually get involved in quality control and the common practice is to separately assign a large number of employees for product inspections and quality control in order to ensure the good quality of products. The limited scope of work for individual workers and the separation of regular work from quality checks are the practices commonly found in Singapore, Thailand and Malaysia.

The biggest reason behind this tendency is the short history of industrialization in ASEAN countries (except for Singapore). In other words, top priority should be given at the moment to having less experienced employees, including managers, accurately perform the range of assigned work duties, with the stage of seeking flexible plant management by having workers acquire multifunctional skills still far off. Among factors on the part of the host societies that make the application of the Japanese system difficult are the high mobility of employees who change jobs frequently in pursuit of higher wages, however small the margin of increase, and the social gaps far larger than in Korea and Taiwan (symbolized by huge wage gaps between job levels and job titles).

Plant management led by Japanese

Another outstanding discrepancy can be seen unambiguously between ASEAN plants and plants in Taiwan and Korea in the application of the human result. As earlier mentioned, the ratio of Japanese expatriates to the total number of personnel indicates little difference between Taiwan and Korea, and ASEAN. At issue is the localization of plant managers. As pointed out earlier, first of all, almost all Japanese local plants are headed by Japanese nationals as chief executive officers, and this is decisively different from the situation in Korea and Taiwan. Next, Japanese expatriates, rather than taking up roles as advisers or staff, are included in the direct chain of command at the high level of management and also play important roles in respective positions that form the basis of plant management, including manufacturing, production technology, production control, quality control, procurement, accounting and treasury, and sales. In short, Japanese local plants in the ASEAN region are characterized by the management leadership by Japanese who may be small in number but command authority.

There could be many factors that make the ASEAN plants different from those in Korea and Taiwan in terms of the localization of managers. In Thailand and Malaysia, it is easily understandable that part of the problem is the shortage of qualified human resources stemming from the short history of industrialization. Another big factor may be the differing degree and depth of understanding for the Japanese system. The differences in the degree of understanding themselves are affected by a number of conditions, including the differing cultural and historical closeness to Japan when compared with Korea and Taiwan, the stronger European or American influences in education and other areas on people with higher educational backgrounds, communication gap problems resulting from the need to communicate in English. At Japanese local plants dedicated to exports, many said the overall feeling is that it is essential to have Japanese expatriates because these plants have to deal with Japan offices and conduct business with the whole world. This point also reflects the inadequate social accumulation of human resources and relative lack of experience, the relatively inadequate level of understanding of the Japanese system and several other factors. At the same time, however, it should not be ignored that Japanese companies themselves have yet to develop a well-organized system for managing a global network of their production and sales footholds and are still highly dependent on the human factor of Japanese expatriates.

Comparison by type of plant

Finally, the comparison is made between long-running plants catering to the domestic markets and new plants dedicated to export markets. For old, conventional plants, there are some cases where the internal promotion system and the practice of having workers acquire multi-functional skills gradually came to be established during long years of operational experiences. The relatively limited size of plants, and somewhat paradoxically, the less-demanding domestic markets in terms of the quality of products probably made the penetration of these Japanese practices easier. On the other hand, many of the export-dedicated plants with new equipment, which are large in scale in terms of the number of working and investment made, do not give much importance to internal promotion, appoint managers with high educational backgrounds, and making the demarcation of jobs clearer. These plants with advanced equipment are thus being run in a top–down fashion by Japanese expatriates and some locally hired engineers. Many of these new plants place considerable emphasis on the hiring of qualified human resources, education and training of local employees, centering on the dispatching to Japan, and the development of local suppliers. Thus, when these efforts pay off, the degree of application of the Japanese system should increase at these plants in the future.[2]

Japanese local plants in the Asian economic crisis

The Asian economic crisis, triggered by the currency crisis in Thailand in July 1997, significantly affected foreign companies operating in the region, including Japanese companies. After the crisis, the economies of the region got back on the road to recovery faster than initially expected, and automobile and other industries primarily geared to the respective domestic markets, most severely damaged in the economic crisis, were able to return to normal production operations also sooner than expected. Yet, it is still of significance to study how the economic crisis had affected foreign companies operating in the region and how Japanese companies responded to the crisis to examine future prospects for Japanese companies operating in Asia and also to foresee the future of the Asian economy. Further, the observation of corporate behaviors in the crisis phase should give a glimpse of management characteristics of Japanese companies.[3]

Comparison between Japanese and US Direct Investment

Figures 4.1 and 4.2 show direct investment by Japan and the United States in the four ASEAN countries (ASEN 4, thereinafter referred to simply as ASEAN) and Korea around the currency and economic crises on an international balance of payments basis. As the figures show, the Japanese and US investment behaviors were sharply in contrast. Particularly interesting were the patterns of investment in Thailand, Indonesia and Malaysia. In 1997, when the currencies of the ASEAN nations were un-pegged with the US dollar and went into a free fall against the dollar, leading to the financial crisis and then the broader economic crisis, direct investment by Japan increased substantially from the pre-crisis 1996 level. Increases in investment were particularly notable in Thailand and Malaysia, where Japanese companies operate a large number of full-scale production plants. It is hardly thinkable that Japanese companies made aggressive fresh investment in a situation

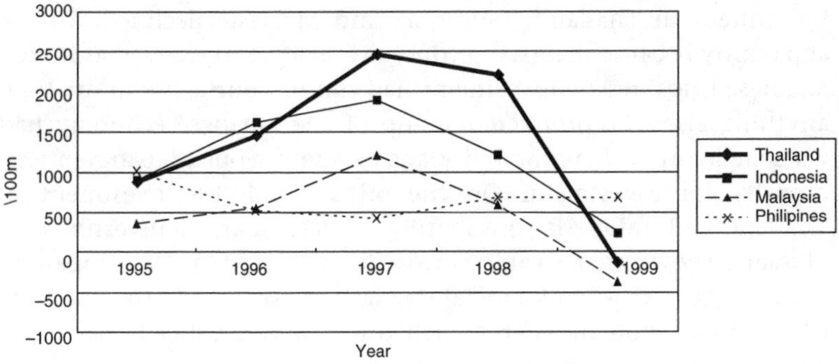

Source: Ministry of Finance, *Statistics Monthly*.

Figure 4.1 FDI of Japan to ASEAN 4 countries: capital outflow

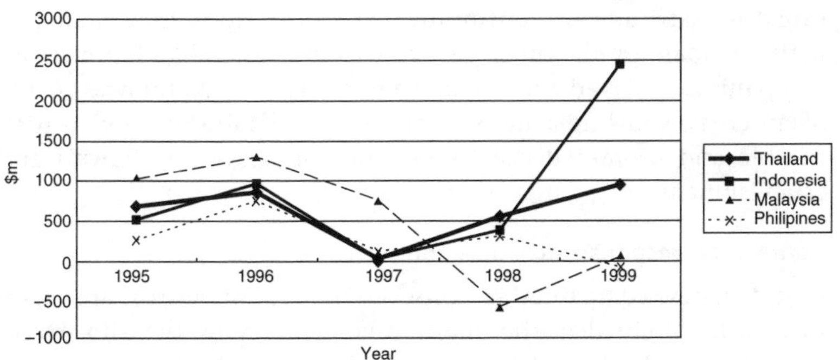

Source: US Department of Commerce, *Survey of Current Business*.

Figure 4.2 FDI of US to ASEAN 4 countries: capital outflow

where the currency crisis turned into the broader economic crisis. Therefore, it appears that the substantial increases in investment in 1997 primarily reflect capital increases and lending in order to prop up and rescue local subsidiaries amid the deteriorating operating environment. Meanwhile, US direct investment in the four ASEAN countries posted sharp declines in 1997. Particularly noteworthy was US investment in Thailand and Malaysia turning negative, or registering a net outflow of capital. This indicates that contrary to Japanese companies that went to the rescue of local subsidies by investment more, many American companies, in the face of the deteriorating business climate, either withheld new investment or withdrew from the region.

Investment behaviors of Japanese and American companies in 1998 and 1999 were again in sharp contrast. In those years, Japanese investment in Thailand, Indonesia and Malaysia declined. This is apparently because the Asian economies had yet to recover, although Japanese firms' rescue investment had run its course, and more than anything else, the protracted slump of the Japanese economy had worsened corporate profitability and severely sapped Japanese firms' capacity for investment. On the other hand, US investment in Thailand and Indonesia rose sharply. In particular, US investment in Thailand showed remarkable growth. This shows that US companies, backed by the growing financial strength at home amid the booming US economy, bought assets which prices were drastically decreased because of the currency and stock market crash.

The investment behavior of Japanese and US companies from 1997 to 1999 underscored the differences in their management styles. In the case of Japanese companies, their investment behavior indicate their attitude of continuing with operations they launched without abandoning them easily. On the other hand, American companies displayed their management style in its fullness in the Asian crisis, showing acute sensitivity to profitability coupled with flexible and prompt decisions on both business withdrawals and establishments.

Companies' responses to the economic crisis

First, Japanese companies' responses to the economic crisis are examined as highlighted in the questionnaire survey by the Ministry of International Trade and Industry (MITI) (now, the Ministry of the Economy, Trade and Industry) conducted immediately after the economic crisis.[4] What is most notable in the survey results is that only a very limited number of companies withdrew from operations in the region in the face of a crisis of that magnitude. According to the MITI survey covering the head offices in Japan, only 3 per cent of companies with business bases in the NIEs and the ASEAN region closed shop and withdrew. For good or for bad, this indicates Japanese companies' orientation toward long-term continuity and their commitment to not withdrawing so easily from operations once they are established. The second point of note is the modality of employment adjustments. About 30 per cent of Japanese business bases in ASEAN carried out employment adjustments, but less than 10 per cent of these bases actually dismissed regular workers. The principal means of employment adjustments was the discharge of seasonal workers and temporary employees. Furthermore, a majority of Japanese business bases in ASEAN showed little change in the number of employees, while over

10 per cent of Japanese companies actually increased employment. Japanese companies' common practices of not to cut the employment of regular workers as much as possible appears to have been maintained not only in Japan but also at ASEAN and other overseas bases. The third point that deserves special attention is the fact that a certain percentage of Japanese bases responded to the crisis by moving from domestic to export markets, making shifts in export markets, and increasing shipments for parent companies to take in. They may represent an extreme measure taken under the pressure of necessity for the sake of the survival of local subsidiaries, but, as a consequence produced the effect of deepening and expanding in-house division of labor in the Asian region, including Japan. Interesting in terms of financial aspects is the considerably high ratio of local operational bases that had received debt guarantees and capital infusions from parent companies. These steps, together with their purchases of products made by subsidiaries, signify parent companies' determination to sustain the local production footholds and also give credence to the earlier assumption that the increased investments in 1997 represented investments for the rescue of local subsidiaries. Two specific cases are described below.

The first case is Toyota Motor Corporation Just before the onslaught of the economic crisis, Toyota launched new assembly plants in Thailand, Indonesia and the Philippines, one after another to replace old factories there. Toyota is one of the most significantly affected companies in the automobile sector and it was hit seriously by the economic crisis. Toyota's responses are reviewed through the example of its subsidiary in Indonesia, which this author visited in the midst of the crisis. The Indonesian subsidiary was hard suffered significantly by the rise in the break-even point due to the launch of the new plant and the shrinking market as a result of the economic crisis. Its sales were halved from 3.2 billion rupiahs in 1997 to an estimated 1.6 billion rupiahs in 1998, and production plummeted from 98,000 units in 1997 to 16,000 units in 1998, less than one-fifth of the preceding year's level. When this author visited the subsidiary in August 1998, the old plant was operating at an average rate 10 days a month, while the new plant was in operation for four days a month each for auto body manufacturing and coating painting. It may be assumed that the old plant's average operating rate of 10 days a month was not much different from the operating rate of the new plant for each of processes like coating and auto body production, because only a single process was in operation at any given time in order to save on power charges. The sudden shrinkage of the domestic market pushed up the export ratio from 3 per cent prior to the economic crisis to 30 per cent. As for export destination, the Indonesian subsidiary shipped finished vehicles of the Asia Car to Brunei and Oceania and complete knocked down (CKD) products of the Asia Car to Malaysia, Taiwan and the Philippines, and also began supplying engines to Japan.

The subsidiary dismissed most term workers as the plant operating rate fell to an extremely low level (however, some 40 term workers at the new plant were not dismissed as they had skills essential for its operation), but it did not dismiss any of regular workers. When the production lines were halted, half of the regular workers reported to work to receive education and training with the other half standing by at home. Employees standing by at home were paid full wages plus expenses for the table. But it also used the very Japanese means of soliciting voluntary retirees from among middle-aged employees aged 45 or older. Early retirees were provided with generous retirement allowances in amounts allowing them to live on interest alone. In 1998, it sent 130 workers to Japan for training. More seriously damaged by the economic crisis were local parts suppliers. The Toyota subsidiary supported local suppliers who had been looked after over a long period of years with advanced payments and other means, taking measures to prevent their bankruptcies as much as possible. These post-crisis measures are largely similar to those taken by the associate plants in Thailand and elsewhere. While these materials and human maintenance costs could be considered to be fairly heavy, they may be viewed as long-term investment with a view to the plant's performance enhancement in the future.

The second case for examination is the Malaysian subsidiary of Alps Electric Co. This subsidiary, 100 per cent owned by Alps Electric, began operating in the suburbs of Kuala Lumpur in 1989. As Japanese electric machinery makers launched or expanded local production in Malaysia one after another since the second half of the 1980s, its plant also kept on expanding since the launch of operation. At the 1995–96 peak, it employed over 6,000 workers, including its second factory built in 1994.

However, as Japanese electric machinery manufacturers shifted production of low-end models to China, Alps Electric, the parent company, also constructed plants in China successively, and some of products at the Malaysian plant were transferred to the Chinese plants. For some products, the Malaysian plant was used a way-stop point before a full shift of production from Japan to China. At the end of the day, the transfer of production of some products to China gave rise to the need to cut back the payrolls at the Malaysian plant to a little over 5,000. But the workforce reduction was achieved through hiring restraints rather than dismissals due to the high turnover rate.

The Malaysian plant is both directly and indirectly dedicated to export markets, but it still suffered heavily from the currency crisis. While it heavily depends on the supply of parts and materials from Japan (it pays in yen for the procurement from Japan), its customers, Japanese electric machinery makers in Malaysia (it receives their payments in ringgit), which quote their exports in US dollars, accepted only price increases of no more than 10 per cent. According to the company, there were no Japanese electric machinery makers that withdrew from Malaysia due to the economic crisis.

The outstanding feature of the Malaysian plant is its aggressive push for production innovation, including the introduction of the cell method for one-man assembly and mini-lines for a small number of workers, coupled with the removal of conveyor lines. Usually, production innovation is first carried out at domestic plants in Japan and new methods of production are then transplanted at local plants overseas. However, the Malaysian plant of Alps Electric is now a model plant of production innovation by introducing innovation ahead of plants in Japan and carrying it out more thoroughly than Japanese domestic plants. As a consequence, the Malaysian plant achieved the doubling or even trebling of productivity even while being engaged in small-lot production.

In order to implement production innovation, the plant made aggressive efforts in the area of multifunctional skills and also sent over 200 regular workers as well as manager-class personnel to Japan. Even greater efforts were carried out to invite instructors from Japan to the Malaysian plant. Some of these non-expatriate Japanese personnel stay in Malaysia for as long as six months, and others made repeated field trips to Malaysia, to provide local workers with guidance and instructions. Through these measures, the Malaysian plant was able to enhance its capacity even in the middle of the economic crisis.

Implications

The implications that can be derived from the overall behavior of Japanese local plants and from specific cases of individual plants are as follows.

First, Japanese manufacturers' commitments to long-term, continuous operations of plants once they are established and not to suspend them easily are evident both at home and overseas. At the same time, Japanese companies' basic stance of trying to avoid employment adjustment of regular workers as much as possible is commonly seen not only at domestic plants but also at a fairly large number of local plants in Asia. There are companies that combine the two basic tenets of management described above and strive to improve manufacturing processes and the quality of products even amid the business environment of the economic crisis by taking on shouldering considerable costs in terms of both time and money. This management approach of Japanese manufacturing companies both at home and abroad is largely responsible for squeezing profitability amid a prolonged period of the business slump. However, as a result of these efforts, Japanese plants in Asia acquired the potential to remarkably enhance the performance in terms of both efficiency and quality after they tided over the economic crisis. In the long run, this should lead to the stronger competitiveness of Japanese local plants. Furthermore, the modality of these Japanese plants should help encourage a new phase of development of the East Asian economy through the more fundamental transfer of technology in such areas as methods and know-how of production and production control. However, there is the impenetrable problem beyond the scope of individual companies' responses. It is the Asian region's heavy dependence on the US dollar. The latest currency crisis and the economic crisis demonstrated the risks of the linkage between local currencies and the US dollar and further of the reliance on the US dollar. Going forward, the major issue will be how to ensure the monetary stability in the region and ways to rectify the region's excessive dependence on the US dollar, including the internationalization of the yen. As mentioned earlier, a lot of Japanese companies are not making particular efforts to increase the utilization of the yen at the level of individual firms, though they do hope to see the yen's internationalization. The biggest reason for this is the yen's unstable exchange rates against the US dollar. Policy responses such as the use of a currency basket need to be considered.

ASEAN after the economic crisis

The biggest factor that could influence the future of Japanese local plants in the ASEAN region and economic development of the ASEAN countries will be developments regarding the rapidly growing Chinese economy. The dominant view, at least temporarily, was that the industrialization of China would significantly degrade the economic status of ASEAN. Recently, however, views have emerged to revalue the strength of ASEAN anew.[5] The ensuing sections address this issue while examining the region as the destination of investment by Japanese companies, because foreign companies have an extremely large role to play for the economic development of either ASEAN or China.

Strengths and limitations as destination of investment

First, the strengths and limitations of ASEAN as the destination of investment by Japanese and other foreign companies are considered.[6]

The first point of examination is the quality and quantity of labor. In this regard, it cannot be denied that China has an advantage over ASEAN. For manual labor, an inexhaustible pool of young labor can be utilized in southern China by taking advantage of the rural registry system. Even for business managers and engineers, China can provide high-quality human resources in abundance centering on urban areas. However, constraints are beginning to emerge on the quantitative supply of manual labor in Shanghai and other urban areas, while China's rapid economic development is making the market for highly educated personnel fairly restricted. While simple comparison is not appropriate given the different job levels of employment, there are companies that provide engineers and accounting personnel in China with salaries several times higher than in ASEAN countries. Thus, for the ASEAN region, ways to enhance the level of education for the category of highly educated employees should be key to countering China.

The second point concerns the procurement of parts and materials. In this respect, China's advantage lies in the fact that it has the foundation of heavy industries already in place in the course of the country's socialist construction, and China has developed thick layers of suppliers of parts and materials in terms of quantity, if not quality. Moreover, as clearly shown in the problems of copied products in recent years, they are strikingly capable of absorbing new technologies. In this area, ASEAN countries are substantially handicapped due to their relatively short history of industrialization. But it is still possible for them to catch up. In ASEAN countries, the entry of foreign-capital suppliers, or joint ventures between foreign and local companies can strengthen the base for suppliers. In fact, a fairly thick layer of suppliers has been developed in Thailand's auto industry through such means.

The third point has to do with infrastructure and networks of physical distribution. In this respect, China has the big problem to resolve. Going forward, to what extent China can resolve the bottlenecks in the physical distribution network, often referred to as the 'Dark Continent,' will significantly affect investment activities by foreign companies.

The fourth point is the market scale. Generally speaking, China is considered to have a major advantage given its huge population. On top of the sheer size of its population, China now has a fairly large number of wealthy people centering on urban areas. However, ASEAN also has a good chance of creating a fairly large market through the ASEAN Free Trade Agreement (AFTA), and there is also an option to incorporate the Chinese market itself by concluding a free trade agreement (FTA) with China.[7] Besides, the ratio of wealthy people willing to purchase Japanese brands in the market is much higher in ASEAN than in China. In other words, it can be stated that ASEAN is larger than China in terms of the scale of the market for foreign companies, including Japanese, not the overall size of the domestic market. Particularly for automakers, electronics companies and other Japanese firms, the ASEAN market is very attractive because of its strong orientation toward Japanese brands.

The fifth point is the policy environment. In this respect, despite considerable improvements seen recently, China still lags far behind ASEAN in terms of uncertainty about the future course of policy developments. Furthermore, as seen in the spread of the severe acute respiratory syndrome (SARS) and its responses to it, China presents far greater political and social risks than ASEAN. Moreover, Japanese companies have faced and will face 'anti-Japan' sentiment among Chinese people, demonstrated by the consumer strike of Japanese goods in April in 2005, though this movement did not continue so long at that time. The significance of direct investment in ASEAN countries from the viewpoint of the diversification of risk will likely be sustained in the years to come.

The sixth point is the importance for Japanese companies of securing the free hand in management. In this respect, this author believes ASEAN has a tremendous advantage over China. In China, a fairly large number of foreign companies chose joint ventures because the establishment of joint firms with Chinese interests is mandatory in auto assembly and some other industries, and also because, even when it is not required, they have to deal with the complicated distribution mechanism and the opaque policy environment. The biggest problems involved in the formation of joint ventures are Chinese joint venture partners' orientation toward short-term gains and their close ties with governmental organizations. There is the risk that Japanese companies which find the source of their competitive advantage in long-term continuity cannot fully play out their strengths under the constraints of management behaviors of joint venture partners. In ASEAN, on the other hand, there are very few investment restrictions, and in numerous instances, Japanese companies can still exert their own initiatives even at joint ventures. For Japanese firms as well as for ASEAN countries that have achieved industrialization at the initiatives of foreign companies, this may be where they can compete with China.

Finally, though overlapping the earlier discussions, Japanese companies already have an accumulation of investment made in ASEAN countries over the years. The in-house accumulation of technologies and know-how, local employees who have acquired them, the existence of the extensive network of Japanese suppliers, and local suppliers which got stronger through transactions with Japanese companies over the years, are major assets for Japanese companies operating in ASEAN.

Auto industry in Thailand

The above points are expounded here using the auto industry in Thailand as an example. The Thai auto industry has achieved remarkable development in recent years, with Bangkok coming to be called Detroit of Asia. Its growth has been led by foreign companies, led by Japanese firms. Furthermore, the Thai auto industry has been growing not only quantitatively but also qualitatively as indicated by its rising export competitiveness.

The case in point is Toyota Motor, cited earlier in this chapter. In August 2004, Toyota started production of the global strategic vehicle (Innovative International Multi-purpose Vehicle, IMV) based on its pickup truck model in Thailand. The IMV, the company's strategic vehicle for sales mainly on emerging markets such as Asia, Oceania, Latin America and the Middle East, has been developed as a model that can be exported to regions other than Asia following the Asian economic crisis. For the time being, Toyota plans to concentrate assembly operations for the vehicle in Thailand, with about half of an annual output of 280,000 units earmarked for exports. Most of Toyota's overseas plants have so far turned out vehicles primarily for sales on their respective home markets. In that sense, Thailand is one of the very few overseas production footholds designated by Toyota specifically as an export base. The IMV features the high local ASEAN content of 90 per cent, an increase from 60 per cent, which also helped lower production costs substantially. In the background of the successful launch of the

IMV are the facts that, first, the AFTA made possible integrated production of key parts and components at production bases within the ASEAN region, and second, Denso Corp. and other Japanese auto parts makers provided the full local procurement backup for the Toyota project by making investments equivalent in scale to Toyota's cumulative investment in Thailand.[8]

Toyota is not an isolated case. Honda Motor is already shipping small passenger cars from its Thai production base to the Japanese market. General Motors and Ford, both of the United States, also position their Thai plants as export footholds. Isuzu Motors of Japan is providing full support to GM and Mazda Motor to Ford in both areas of production models and plant operations.[9] The significant leap forward of production plants in Thailand, as demonstrated by enhanced export competitiveness, has been brought about, as already explained, by an accumulation of investment over the years, strenuous efforts to expand exports amid the Asian economic crisis, and education and training of local employees centering on quality control.

Notes

1. Itagaki (1997).
2. In terms of the transformation of Matsushita's plants in Malaysia from 1993 to 2000, see Abo (2004).
3. Itagaki (2000).
4. MITI (1999a, b).
5. One example of these views is 'The Return of Asia,' (*Nikkei Business*, 19 Apr. 2004).
6. On this score, Kimura *et al.* (2002), particularly its epilogue, is highly thought-provoking.
7. However, this may prove to be the double-edged sword for ASEAN countries as it also smooth the way for Chinese companies to move into the ASEAN region.
8. *The Nihon Keizai Shimbun*, 26 Aug. 2004, morning edition.
9. Op.cit., *Nikkei Business*, 19 Apr. 2004.

References

Abo, Tetsuo (2004) 'A Shortened Path to Transplant the Japanese Management System', in S. Strzelczak, (ed.) *Economic and Managerial Developments in Asia and Europe: Comparative Studies*, Kramist.

Itagaki, Hiroshi (2000) *Keizai Kikika no Ajia niokeru Nikkei Kojo*, Musashi Daigaku Ronshu, vol. 40, no. 3/4.

Itagaki, Hiroshi (ed.) (1997) *The Japanese Production System: Hybrid Factories in East Asia*, Macmillan Press.

JETRO (1998) *Sekai to Nihon no Boeki: Ajia Tsuka Kiki no Eikyo to Sekai Boeki.*
Kimura, Fukunari, Maruya, Toyojiro & Ishikawa, Koichi (2002) *Higashi Ajia Kokusai Bungyo to Chugoko*, JETRO.
MITI (1999a) *Keizai Kozo Hikaku Chosa.*
MITI (1999b) *Ajia Tsuka Kiki Iko no Nikkei Kigyo ni Kansuru Chosa Kenkyu.*
UNCTAD (1998) *World Investment Report.*

5

Hybrid Factories in China: Japanese Production Systems in 'the world's factory'

Kunio Kamiyama

Expansion of the Chinese economy and the significance of the research

The Third Plenary Session of the Eleventh Central Committee of the Communist Party of China, held on 18–20 December 1978, marked the starting point of China's subsequent reform and openness policy. For 20 years since then, China's economy has exhibited outstanding growth, maintaining favorable development even today. In those years, the world witnessed the Tiananmen Square incident in 1989 and the country's traditional political wrangles between right and left, which inevitably had impacts on its economy. Nonetheless, since 1992 when Deng Xiaoping delivered talks during his trip to southern China, the reform and the openness policy has been firmly fixed as an increasingly clear-cut direction in which the country is heading.

Let us confirm China's economic growth during this period by looking at the output of several products. Steel production, for example, grew from 31.78 million tons in 1978 to 66.35 million tons in 1990, and then to 182.37 million tons in 2002. Production of household refrigerators also grew drastically during the same period, from 28,000 to 4,630,600 and then to 15,988,700. Similarly, car production increased dramatically from 149,100 to factory 514,000 and then to 3,251,000 (*China Industrial Economic Statistical Yearbook 2003*). As a result of such development, China has grown out of a stage in which it was perceived as an economically backward and poor developing country and has since become a country drawing much attention due to the magnitude of its economy.

It is true that China's gross national income has grown remarkably to become the world's sixth largest in 2002, reaching US$1.2095 trillion.

In terms of purchase power parity, the country is allegedly the second largest economic power next to the United States. However, it is also true that its per capita income of the same year remained at a low level of US$940, slightly less than a thousand (World Bank 2004). This is the very reason that necessitates for solutions to such problems as unemployment and the expanding gap between the rich and the poor, and such solutions need to solve these problems while still maintaining growth. On the other hand, it is also true that the presence of such an expansive population is in a way contributing to maintaining the low wage level of the country. According to a recent newspaper report in the Zhu Jiang delta area in Guangdong, there is a serious shortage of migrant workers from rural areas(*Asahi Shimbun*, 2004),[1] indicating a new trend in China's seemingly inexhaustible manpower supply structure. Hopefully, this may trigger economic development in rural communities, easing such problems as the widening gap between the rich and the poor and a rising jobless rate, the most serious problems China has ever faced since the country adopted the reform and the openness policy.

As such, Chinese economic development, encompassing over 1 billion Chinese people, is an ongoing process the world has never experienced in its history, and the impact it is having upon the world economy is also becoming considerable. The process is also unprecedented in that the country is pursuing a market economy under a political system of one-party rule by the Communist Party of China. Against this backdrop, some researchers have been repeatedly speaking of the China Breakdown Model; others are advocating the China Threat Model, which came into fashion in Japan during the post-1990 prolonged recession. In recent years amid the trend of the economic recovery in Japan, the China as a Beneficial Importer Model has emerged. As such, perspectives on the country vary a great deal, depending on which aspect of Chinese development is highlighted. Since China at present is changing so rapidly and each of its provinces has its own particular features, it is hard to develop a simple model for the country. Furthermore, unlike the Central and Eastern European countries that are moving away from socialist planned economies to market economies that uphold non-socialist liberalism, it is hard to grasp in which direction China is moving during its period of transition.

This chapter has not been designed to analyze and evaluate the entire picture of the complex Chinese economy. Rather, its purpose is to focus upon Japanese firms operating in China and present the results obtained from the findings of a field study by the Japanese

Multinational Enterprise Study Group (JMNESG) conducted in China during August and September 2002. Factories in China are currently undergoing a dramatic transformation from a state-ownership phase, where production quotas specified under a planned economy had to be filled, to a market economy; however, practices vary a great deal from one factory to another, retaining in varying degrees a legacy from the time of state-ownership. Provincial differences are also great. Furthermore, China has tried to make changes very rapidly in its legal and institutional fields as well as in its economic practices. Therefore, the task of this report is to analyze factories in China having such complex aspects based on the findings of our field survey in 2002 of Japanese automobile manufacturers and electronics industries. As an analytic framework, we have adopted the model developed by the JMNESG as a basis.

The Japanese Multinational Enterprise Study Group (JMNESG), starting with a field study in the United States in 1986, has conducted similar group surveys twice in North America, in Korea and Taiwan, ASEAN, the United Kingdom, continental Europe, South America and in other places. As for China, team members conducted research on an individual basis with differing emphases, and for the first time in 2002, a team survey was carried out. After the team survey, many of the members, including the author, returned to China for further studies.

As introduced in the following section, the factories analyzed are located throughout China: in Beijing, Shanghai, Dalian, Tianjin, Guangzhou, Dongguan, Shenzhen, Chongqing, Chengdu and Zhengzhou. This includes almost all the major locations in China where Japanese enterprises are engaged in local production. According to a survey by Toyo Keizai Shinpo-sha (2004), as many as 3,476 companies had been locally incorporated in China by 2003 out of which 551 are in the electronics industry and 180 are auto and auto parts companies (Toyo Keizai Shinpo-sha 2004). Given these numbers, this research does not attempt to cover all the local factories affiliated with Japanese electronics and auto enterprises. However, in the light of the diversity of the provinces covered and the number of samples, this research may be considered to illustrate to some extent trends associated with local manufacturers affiliated with the Japanese auto and electronics industries. This research, along with the surveys of Japanese factories that JMNESG conducted in other parts of the world, can be of significance because it provides materials for analyzing the various characteristics Japanese factories demonstrate in their local production.

Let us briefly compare this survey and analysis with the earlier studies in the same arena. There are numerous studies concerning Chinese enterprises that include Japanese-affiliated firms. Speaking only of the studies that include factory-level analyses, there are many including these studies done by JMNESG team members: Hao Yanshu on color TV factories,[2] Yuan Zhi Jia's analysis of semiconductor factories,[3] the studies by Tadashi Matsuzaki and others that provide a detailed analysis of Chinese electronic and steel enterprises,[4] Chunli Lee's analysis of Chinese auto factories,[5] and a study by Mitsuhiro Seki that presents detailed analysis of each of the Chinese provinces. Many of these earlier studies presented detailed analyses on various aspects of Chinese factories, from which much was learned. Having surveyed only a limited number of factories, these studies do not portray a holistical picture of Japanese factories operating in China, and they do not compare auto and electronics companies. In contrast, the research presented in this chapter illustrates the overall characteristics of Japanese auto and electronics factories in China. We shall review the outline of the surveyed factories in the following section.

Outline of surveyed factories

Three groups were organized for the survey and the groups carried out two-week-long field studies from the second half of August to the first half of September 2002, visiting 32 places and 27 factories (including a Chinese motorcycle manufacturer and 26 Japanese-affiliated factories). In addition, team members visited two offices of Japanese auto assembly manufacturers in Beijing, an office of a Japanese electronic manufacturer in Shaghai, and the Institute of Japanese Studies of the Chinese Academy of Social Sciences, and Fudan University Center for Japanese Studies. Although some team members conducted additional surveys of some other factories, these have been excluded from the analysis for this report. The Japanese factories visited are predominantly in the auto and electronics industries, including four auto assembly factories, eight auto parts factories, 13 electronics and electronics-related factories.[7] The remaining factory produces zippers. Of these factories, factories belonging to the auto and electronics industries were targeted. However, parts factory, though of interest, was excluded from the analysis because it is essentially a branch of a factory in Tianjin that manufactures wire harnesses for automobiles. Consequently, a total 24 factories were analyzed including 11 auto assembly and auto parts plants and 13 electronics plants.

An outline of these 24 factories is shown in Table 5.1. This group of factories includes those that became operational in the 1980s as well as a factory that was still test operating for a fully fledged production scheduled beginning at the end of 2002. A few are wholly-owned Japanese companies like AE, but the majority are joint venture operations with China. In the cases of plants BI and BL, the management of the factory is left in Japanese hands, but in some provinces, some businesses are engaged in consignment production in which production is carried out in factories that have no capital relationship with the Japanese parent company whatsoever. This practice is particularly evident in southern China. The factories in southern China seem to be operated in such a distinctive manner that we have classified the five factories, BI-BM, as southern China factories for the purpose of analysis. According to the report of the Japan–China Investment Promotion Organization, there are usually two types of consignment processing; namely, materials processing and imports processing. However, in Guangdong there is a different form of consignment processing from that in other provinces. The term 'consignment processing' is likely to generate an image of a method that commissions production to an already existing Chinese production plant, but this applies only in eastern China and northern China. In Guangdong, it actually means management of a factory by foreign capital (*'Seminar:Consignment processing management in Guangdong,'* by Japan–China Investment Promotion Organization, January 2002, p.2).

Before delving into an analysis of the degree of application of a Japanese-style production system, this chapter comments on the relationship between the Hybrid Factory Model and the Chinese management environment.

Evaluating applicability by the Asian standard and Chinese environmental conditions

Often it is pointed out that the Chinese economy has been in a transitional period since the country adopted the reform and the openness policy. As stated earlier, although the socialist political system has been inexorably kept intact, China's planned economy has been virtually phased out as market economy features have penetrated into the country. The factories we have analyzed are also undergoing a transformation from state-owned factories where maximum effort was made to fulfill designated production quotas to management entities that practice various reforms as state-owned enterprises in a market economy.

Table 5.1 Outline of surveyed plants as of 2002

Plant name	*Start of operation*	*No. of employee (Japanese employees)*	*Location*	*Production items*
Auto Assembly				
AA	2002.10	1107(17)	Tianjin	Passenger cars
AB	1999.12	650(11)	Chengdu	Coasters
AC	1993.2 (started as JV)	1700(3)	Zhengdong	Pickup trucks
AD	1985 (started as JV)	2600(3)	Chongqing	Commercial vehicles
Auto Parts				
AE	1989.11	3200(9)	Tianjin	Wire harnesses
AF	1997.12(started as JV)	175(6)	Tianjin	Air conditioners, Radiaters
AG	1998.11	48(4)	Tianjin	ECU, fuel pumps, A/C amps, meters
AH	1995.10(started as JV)	1492(6)	Tianjin	Seat, trim, roof lining etc.
AI	2000.4	737(4)	Tianjin	Parts for brake, parts for clutch
AJ	1994.9	347(5)	Tianjin	rubber parts(door seal etc.), resin parts
AK	2001.2 (started as JV)	78(1)	Zhengdong	Seats
Electronics				
BA	1989.7	4000(8)	Beijing	Color picture tubes
BB	1994.3	841(15)	Beijing	Semiconductors
BC	1995.1	4208(54)	Shanghai	Ballbearings
BD	1999.12	958(33)	Shanghai	Semiconductors
BE	1988	8681(6)	Dalian	Direct current mini-motors
NF	1993	1850(12)	Dalian	Parts for picture tubes, parts for mini-motors, industrial-use mortors
NG	1996	2089(6)	Dalian	Color television, projection television, DVD
BH	1995.10	470(3)	Dalian	Car audio & related parts
BI	1994	4500(5)	Dongguan	Motors etc.

Table 5.1 Continued

Plant name	*Start of operation*	*No. of employee (Japanese employees)*	*Location*	*Production items*
BJ	1993.8	783(8)	Guangzhou	Motors
BK	1993.4	3400(12)	Guangzhou	Video heads, micro printers, remote control switches, etc.
BL	1983.8	3814(10)	Shenzhen	Coils, ceramic filters, dieletic filters, etc.
BM	1994.3	(30)	Shenzhen	Assembly of single-lens reflex cameras, digital cameras

Source: Plant information provided by the management of the plants.

Furthermore, genuinely private enterprises are increasing their share of China's economy. Nonetheless, it still remains to be seen where the Chinese economy is headed. In this respect, it should be emphasized that a different analytical approach is needed for China than for Russia and the Central and Eastern European transitional economies. Furthermore, China is unique in that it is going through rapid legal institutional changes. The country, having a great expanse of land, still retains the legacy from its history of provincially based local state corporatism. As such, the current status of the management and operation of the factories in China is complex and multifaceted.

Reflecting such characteristics of the present phase of the Chinese economy, the management and operation of factories in China is also strikingly diverse and complex. Apart from a limited number of wholly-owned subsidiaries such as AE, the Japanese enterprises visited as part of this study are predominantly joint venture operations with varying stakes that range from a majority to a minority fraction of equities. Consequently, there are also variations resulting from equity ratios. In addition, what is particularly characteristic to southern China is the fairly widespread practice of a Japanese subsidiary in Hong Kong or elsewhere commissioning processing to a local company but leaving the management of the factory to the Japanese company. This is a point worth noting in reviewing the local production of Japanese multinationals companies in China.

As pointed out earlier, Japanese factories in China are indeed multifaceted, and for analyzing them, the Asian standard for application evaluation system was adopted (Itagaki, 1997). This framework of application– adaptation analysis was originally developed as a method to analyze the factories of Japanese multinationals that moved into the United States in the late 1980s (Abo, *et al.*, 1991). At that time, a hybrid factory evaluation model was formulated that places the Japanese production system on the application side of the scale and the American production system on the adaptation side, and the target factory is analyzes by its position between the two. However, since many Asian countries have only a short history of industrialization, production systems are not necessarily firmly established and perfected. This is why the Asian standard for application evalution system was adopted to measure the degree of attainment of the Japanese production system.

China, following the establishment of the People's Republic of China in 1949, initially adopted a Soviet-style system with the assistance of the Soviet Union, switching to a policy of self-reliance after the decline in Sino-Soviet relations. Thus, a certain level of industrialization was achieved. Since the adoption of the reform and the openness policy at the end of the 1970s, factories in China, especially when they are in alliance with foreign capital, have been influenced by the different systems of Japan, Europe, and the United States. So, even if a typical Chinese production system existed, it would be difficult to perceive it as a kind of universal system. Accordingly, the Asian standard was adopted as the primary approach of this research, though the standard has some deficiencies which will be described here.

The weaknesses of the Asian application evaluation system are largely found in Group V, Labor Relations. Regarding 'hiring methods,' initiatives for hiring personnel are sometimes taken by the partner enterprise (or the parent company thereof) in factories practicing consigned processing and also in joint venture operations, and this renders it difficult to evaluate the hiring method of the target factory. It is true that the consigned processing system is not a phenomenon specific to China, but in China, particularly in southern China, the system is utilized so widely that it could not be treated simply as an exception, which is problematic.

As for long-term employment, Chinese state-owned factories originally adopted a lifetime employment system, a system more rigid than the system in Japan. However, since July 1994 when the Labor Law was enacted, China's employment system went through sweeping reforms. The Labor Law provides that a labor contract shall be concluded to establish labor relations (Article 16), thereby obligating firms in China to implement a labor contract system. The labor contract must be in writing, specifying its term, job descriptions, protections of labor and conditions of labor, compensation of labor, labor discipline, conditions of terminating the labor contract, and responsibility for the violation of the labor contract (Article 19). Employment periods for workers are classified into 3 types: term, no fixed term, and a term when a certain job is completed (Article 20). It thus became general practice that companies, including those affiliated with foreign capital, establish labor terms under the labor contract system. Labor Law, however, does not provide for the term of labor contracts, and in some provinces, the labor contract system applicable for the province is established within the framework of the Labor Law. For example, the City of Shanghai, erected its Labor Contract Ordinance in May 2002. Also, there is a regulation that workers who have served the same employer for ten consecutive years or longer are required to sign labor contracts with no fixed term. It still remains a great task to establish a clear-cut understanding of such a labor contract system in relation to long-term employment. Furthermore, such a situation where systems vary from one company or province to another was not included in the assumptions used to develop the Asian standard.

A big problem with harmonious labor relations and grievance procedures is how to position the Chinese labor unions and party organizations. Chinese labor unions are greatly different from Japanese unions in that they are obligated by law as their mission to defend socialist political system (people's democratic dictatorship), to participate in the work of the state and the society, and to mobilize workers and employees (who are the union members) to actively participate in the economic development of the country (Chishima, 2003, p.1). Their activities are directly controlled by the leadership of the party organization, and party executives are often acting also as executives of labor unions and enterprises. As long as corporate development is desirable for the Chinese state under one party rule, labor unions must exert themselves to that end. This feature has been difficult to address within the Asian application evaluation system. In a broader sense, this is a question of how to position China's 'socialist market economy' in relation to the Japanese production system. Tentatively, the Asian system has been applied to the roles labor unions are playing with the companies; however, further clarification is needed in this respect.

The problem that Chinese management conditions are not easily addressed by the analytical framework is evident in items other than in Group V, Labor Relations. For example, in the case of a consignment processing system, can there be parent-subsidiary relationship between the Japanese home office and the local company engaged in production by consignment? This is just one of the many problems that have to be addressed. Given the limitations imposed by such problems, the 24 target factories have been evaluated by stretching the Asian standard, which measures the extent the Japanese production system is attained in local factories. The results of this evaluation are shown in Table 5.2. In the following section, the application degrees in the Chinese factories shown in Table 5.2 will be analyzed.

Six-group, 23-item hybrid evaluation

The application levels of the 24 subject factories of those visited in the 2002 survey are shown in Table 5.2. As can be seen in Table 5.3, the overall average of the application degree is 3.2, which is identical with

Table 5.2 Application evaluation of surveyed plants in China as of 2002

Industry	*All industries*	*Automobile*	*Assembly*	*Parts*	*Electronics*	*Southeast China*
No. of plants	24	11	4	7	13	6
I Work organisation and administration	3.5	3.5	3.8	3.3	3.5	3.2
1. Job classification	4.4	4.2	4.3	4.1	4.5	4.6
2. Multifunctional skills	3.0	3.4	3.3	3.4	2.7	2.4
3. Education and training	3.5	3.6	4.0	3.4	3.3	2.6
4. Wage system	3.4	3.3	4.0	2.9	3.5	3.2
5. Promotion	3.4	3.3	3.5	3.1	3.5	3.2
6. First-line supervisor	3.3	3.2	3.8	2.9	3.3	3.2
II Production control	3.3	3.0	3.1	3.0	3.6	3.4
7. Equipment	3.8	3.1	3.0	3.1	4.3	4.0
8. Maintenance	3.1	3.1	3.3	3.0	3.1	2.8
9. Quality control	3.2	3.0	3.0	3.0	3.4	3.4
10. Process management	3.3	2.9	3.0	2.9	3.5	3.2
III Procurement	3.0	2.5	2.4	2.5	3.5	3.2
11. Local content	3.0	2.1	1.8	2.3	3.8	3.4
12. Suppliers	3.3	2.5	2.5	2.6	3.9	3.2
13. Procurement method	2.8	2.8	3.0	2.7	2.8	3.0
IV Group consciousness	3.0	3.0	3.3	2.9	3.1	2.8
14. Small-group activities	2.6	2.5	2.8	2.3	2.8	2.6
15. Information sharing	3.1	3.3	3.5	3.1	3.0	2.6
16. Sense of unity	3.4	3.4	3.8	3.1	3.4	3.0

Table 5.2 Continued

Industry	*All industries*	*Automobile*	*Assembly*	*Parts*	*Electronics*	*Southeast China*
V Labour relations	3.1	3.3	3.8	3.0	3.0	2.8
17. Hiring policy	2.9	3.1	3.5	2.9	2.7	2.2
18. Long-term employment	3.0	3.3	4.0	2.9	2.8	2.4
19. Harmonious labour relations	3.7	3.9	4.5	3.6	3.5	3.6
20. Grievance procedures	3.0	2.9	3.0	2.9	3.0	3.0
VI Parent–subsidiary relations	2.7	2.5	2.0	2.7	2.8	2.7
21. Ratio of Japanese expatriates	1.8	1.8	1.5	2.0	1.7	1.8
22. Delegation of authority	3.0	2.7	2.3	3.0	3.2	2.8
23. Position of local managers	3.2	2.8	2.3	3.1	3.5	3.4
Average of 23 items	3.2	3.0	3.2	3.0	3.3	3.0

Source: Based on author's data.

Table 5.3 Four perspective evaluation scores for automotive assembly and auto parts by region

Region *Year visited*	*China 2002*	*North America 2000–2001*	*North America 1989*	*United Kingdom 1997*	*Continental Europe 1998*	*Korea & Taiwan 1992*	*ASEAN 1993*
No. of plants	*24*	*37*	*34*	*20*	*36*	*24*	*35*
I Work organization and administration	3.5	3.2	2.9	3.4	3.0	3.7	3.3
II Production control	3.3	3.4	3.3	3.5	3.1	3.5	3.4
III Procurement	3.0	2.6	3.0	2.5	2.8	3.2	3.2
IV Group consciousness	3.0	3.3	3.2	3.3	2.7	3.4	3.2
V Labor relations	3.1	3.7	3.6	3.6	3.2	3.4	3.1
VI Parent–subsidiary relations	2.7	2.8	3.6	2.8	3.0	2.3	2.9
Average	3.2	3.2	3.3	3.3	3.0	3.3	3.2
Human method	3.3	3.3	3.1	3.4	2.9	3.5	3.2
Human results	2.5	2.6	3.7	2.7	2.9	2.1	2.7
Material method	3.0	3.2	2.8	3.2	2.9	3.4	3.0
Material results	3.3	2.8	3.6	2.8	3.0	3.3	3.6

Source: Based on author's estimates.

that of North America from the survey in 2000–2001. No significant difference can be observed from those for the other major regions of the world studied.

In a groupwise comparison with the other regions, the application degree of 3.5 of Group I, Work organization and administration, though lower than that for Korea/Taiwan in 1992, is characteristically higher than those for other regions. In contrast, the score of Group VI, Parent–subsidiary relations, is 2.7 points, conspicuously lower than that other regions, though again higher than that for Korea/Taiwan. Group V, Labor relations, which as described earlier is hard to evaluate using the Asian system, shows the lowest application degree of 3.1, equivalent with that of ASEAN(South-eastern Asia) in 1993. The score of IV, Group consciousness, is lower than those for other regions except for Continental Europe. The score of Group II, Production control, at 3.3, exceeds that for Continental Europe in 1998 but is about the same level with or slightly lower than those for other regions. The score of Group III, Procurement, is identical with that of North America in 1989, higher than the other results of the survey in Europe and the United States and lower than those for Korea/Taiwan and ASEAN. The result of the groupwise analysis indicates that China has some common ground with Korea/Taiwan and ASEAN, which means China's manufacturing can be interpreted as having Asian characteristics.

In Table 5.1, significant differences between the automobile and electronics industries can be observed. The overall average of the application degree was 3.2, and the score of electronics plants is 3.3 whereas in auto factories it is 3.0. This is because all the auto-related factories other than AE are joint ventures, and therefore the influence from partner companies is apparently stronger than in electronics factories, which are likely to pose restrictions upon the application of a Japanese production system. It is noteworthy that in electronics factories in southern China, the application level is lower than those in other provinces.

Let us break down the scores by six groups and 23 items to analyze the interesting characteristics that emerge therefrom. The average application degree of Group I, Work organization and administration, is the highest of all the groups. Of Group I, the score of 'job classifications' is the highest at 4.4, while that of 'multifunctional skills' is the lowest (3.0) within the group. Unlike European countries and the United States, virtually no strict job classification was present in China, and Chinese multifunctional skill development has not yet reached a satisfactory level. This phenomenon was also observed in Korea/Taiwan and ASEAN and can be perceived as an Asian trait. However, it is interesting to note that auto and electronics factories contrast sharply with each other in the application of 'multifunctional skills.' In the case of auto industries, both auto assembly and auto parts factories are enthusiastically encouraging workers to have multifunctional skills, whereas many of the electronics factories are rather weak in such a pursuit. This difference is linked with the inclination toward 'long-term employment.' In most of the auto-related factories, long-term employment is considered desirable, and in many factories the labor contract term is almost automatically renewed if the employer wishes so. The 0.3-point difference between auto and electronics in 'education and training' could also be a reflection of the difference in the inclination toward training employees on a long-term basis.

As for the other three items in Group I, the application degrees of electronics factories slightly exceed those of auto-related factories. What's notable in 'wage system' is the big 1.1-point difference between the scores for auto assembly and auto parts, and this is the factor that contributed to lowering the overall application degree of the auto factories. This is because the legacy of the egalitarian wage system from the time of state-owned factories was strongly present in some auto parts factories. The scores of 'promotion' and 'first-line supervisor' reflect the fact that even in electronics factories that do not aspire to long-term employment as a whole, efforts are being made to secure and nurture quality personnel for group leaders or higher positions.

In Group II, Production control, the score of electronics factories is conspicuously higher (3.6) when compared with the score of auto factories (3.0). The major reason for this is found in the difference of application degree of 'equipment.' In many of the electronics factories, equipment is brought from Japan directly as is, whereas in auto factories, localization is pursued to some extent. The score of 'quality control' of electronics factories is also higher by 0.4 point than that of auto factories. The difference is relevant with Group III, Procurement. The application score of 'local content' is 2.1 and 3.8 for auto and electronics factories respectively, whereas the score of 'suppliers' is 2.5 for auto factories and 3.9 for electronics factories. In the case of electronics factories, most of the functional components are brought over from Japan and other overseas factories, while Chinese factories are strongly inclined to take charge of labor-intensive processes where they implement a thorough quality control. However, as a result of a powerful nationalization policy established by the Chinese government(though to a lesser degree now compared with before), non-labor-intensive processes are also being implemented in Chinese auto-related industries. As such, quality control systems are not fully in place for all the complex processes of auto manufacturing, and this is reflected in the lower application score for the auto industry. This is another factor that explains the difference of the applications degrees between the industries.

There is no significant difference in Group IV, Group consciousness, between the auto and electronics industries. The score of this group, as stated earlier, is notably lower than those for other regions of the world, and this is primarily because of the larger number of joint venture operations in China compared with other places. The structure of a joint venture operation impedes the inclination toword 'information sharing' and for nurturing a 'sense of unity.' In this respect, however, auto assembly factories perform more strongly in those areas.

In Group V, Labor relations, there is a conspicuously high application score of auto assembly factories. Accordingly, the score of auto factories is about 0.3 point higher than that of electronics. As for Labor Relations, the application level is lower than that for other regions, though equivalent with that for ASEAN. However, a conclusion concerning the items of the group needs to be made after further scrutiny of Chinese environmental conditions.

The application score of Group VI, Parent–subsidiary relations, is 2.7 points for all the factories, reflecting the large number of joint venture operations, and the score is again higher for electronics (2.8) than for auto (2.5) by about 0.3 point. Underlying this difference is the fact that in auto assembly enterprises (unlike in other industries) the management and operation of local companies is not completely entrusted in Japanese hands because of the vested interest on the part of the Chinese authorities including the central government in developing a domestic auto industry.

So far, this paper has analyzed part of the actual conditions of the local management and operation of Japanese enterprises, which vary from one industry or province to another. These variations are not shown by the overall average application score of 3.2 for all the entire surveyed factories. Finally, applying a four-perspective evaluation as a key angle, I shall summarize the characteristics of the target Japanese auto and electronics factories.

Low application of 'Human Result' in auto, and high application of 'Material Result' in Electronics Factories – four-perspective evaluation

Table 5.3 indicates the provincial comparison of the application degrees in a four-perspective evaluation of the 24 target factories in China and other regions of the world. The application scores of 'Human Method' (operating systems and procedures related to employees) and 'Material Result' (equipment and parts imported from Japan) are both slightly high at 3.3, while the score of 'Human Result' (operating systems and procedures related to materials) is a low 2.5 and the score of 'Material Method' is between the two at 3.0. Comparing the scores with those of other regions, the score of 'Human Method' (the influence of Japanese expatriates on the local company) is also found to be high for other regions, indicating that the score for China is not at a particularly high level. Meanwhile, the score of 'Material Result' for China was as high as those for Korea/Taiwan and ASEAN, since the score for North America, previously high in 1989, declined to 2.8 in the recent survey in 2000–2001. The score of 'Human Result' is characteristically lower than other regions except for Korea/Taiwan, where the score is exceptionally low. There is no particularly prominent characteristic about the score of 'Material Method' as compared with other regions.

As can be seen, it is hard to find any conspicuous characteristics of Chinese factories as a whole in comparison with the other regions of the world. However, Table 5.4, which illustrates comparisons between the auto and electronics industries within China, reveals some interesting features. The biggest feature is the willingness of the local company towards adoptind 'Result' aspects of a Japanese production system between the auto and electronics industries. The score of 'Human Result' is 2.3 for auto versus 2.6 for electronics. The difference in the 'Material Result' aspects is even larger; the score for electronics is as high as 4.0 as opposed to 2.6 for auto. As such, the auto industry has a weak intention toward importing Japanese personnel and materials, whereas the electronics industry strongly intends to rely upon Japanese expertise in the form of personnel and materials. In particular, the electronics industry is conspicuously strong in applying 'Material Result' aspects. Auto's weak inclination in the 'Result' items is particularly distinct in 'Human' aspects, and this is even more prominent with the auto assembly industry.

In contrast, there is no outstanding difference between the two industries in the 'Method' application in both the 'Human' and

Table 5.4 Four perspective evaluation scores by industry in China as of 2002

Industry	*All Industries*	*Automobile*			*Electronics*	
			Assembly	*Parts*		*Southeast China*
No. of plant	24	11	4	7	13	5
Human method	3.3	3.3	3.6	3.1	3.3	3.0
Human results	2.5	2.3	1.9	2.6	2.6	2.6
Material method	3.0	3.0	3.1	2.9	3.1	3.1
Material results	3.3	2.6	2.4	2.7	4.0	3.5

Source: Based on author's estimate.

'Material' aspects. However, a scrutiny of the application of 'Human Method' characteristically reveals a 0.3 point higher score for auto assembly (3.6) than that for all the factories (3.3). No big difference is observed in the application of 'Material Method,' and one can conclude that auto assembly factories have a strong inclination toward applying 'Method' aspects, primarily 'Human Method' aspects. In the meantime, the 'Method' application of auto parts factories is even weaker than that for electronics factories, both in 'Human' and 'Material' aspects. This result in some factories retaining the influence of the legacy of state ownership. In relation to this, an interesting story comes from an auto parts factory in Tianjin (not included in this survey), in which a Japanese firm has a majority stake, as with plant AJ. The author visited this factory site in 2001 and 2004. In 2001 only one factory was in operation at the site, whereas by 2004 a second factory had also begun auto parts operation. The Japanese general manager of the factory said that in the first factory, where employees were carried over from the Chinese partner company, Japanese *kaizen* activities have never been successfully implemented, whereas in the second factory newly hired employees are promoting *kaizen* activities with strong enthusiasm.

In general, Japanese auto assembly factories in China, rather than directly bringing over equipment and components from Japan or relying upon Japanese expatriates in promoting local production, are exerting efforts to implement Japanese 'Methods' as practiced in Japan in their local operation. In this respect, it seems that in the majority of the auto parts factories, the legacy of state ownership still remains. Even though measures such as throughgoing employee's training are being taken to challenge this legacy, this is not evident in the overall application scores. Meanwhile, electronics factories are characteristically engaged in local production strongly oriented toward the application of 'Material Result' by bringing over equipment and components directly.

Conclusion

As we have seen so far, the analysis of Japanese factories in China using the Asian application evaluation system indicates that the overall application degree is comparable with those for other regions. Moreover, the application of a Japanese production system is more dependent on 'Method' aspects with regards to personnel. However, in 'Material' aspects, this dependence relies more on 'Result' than on 'Method.' In order to categorically determine what this means, Chinese management conditions have to be reviewed in greater detail. For the future, it will be necessary to focus on 'Method' rather than 'Result' in 'Material' aspects as well. When the current competitive advantage in wage cost diminishes, process control that corresponds to the increasingly sophisticated level of technology will be needed, and this in turn will call for a new employee management method. To portray the future of the Chinese electronics and auto industries, the complex and multifaceted Chinese business conditions have to be fully analyzed by province, industry, enterprise, forms of joint ventures, and other aspects.

Notes

1. This shortage of migrant workers has widely been reported in China. It is said that the amount of the shortage is around two million only in the Pearl River Delta alone (*The Daily NNA*, No.2065, 30 Aug. 2004).
2. Hao, Y. (1999).
3. Yuan, Z. J.(2001)
4. Matsuzaki, T. (1996).
5. Lee, C. (1997).
6. For example, see Seki(2000).
7. Since this last category includes one camera manufacturer and another factory that manufactures a variety of electronic products and parts including semiconductors, all the factories in the category will subsequently be referred to as just 'electronics' for the sake of convenience.

References

Abo, T., Itagaki, H., Kamiyama, K., Kawamura, T. and Kumon, H. (1991) *Amerika ni Ikiru Nihon-teki Keiei-Seisan Shisutemu,* Toyo Keizai Shinpo Sha. *(Japanese Management and Production System Enlivened in the United States).*

Asahi Shimbun (2004) 20 August, 2004. *China Industrial Economic Statistical Yearbook* (2003).

Chishima, A. (2003) Chinese Labor Organizations and Labor Relations, Organization and Function of Labor Unions, Productivity & Labor Information Center.

Hao, Y. (1999) Cyugoku no Keizai Hatten to Nihon-teki Seisan Shisutemu, Mineruva Shobo. (Chinese Economic Growth and the Japanese Production System).

Itagaki, H. (ed.) (1997) *The Japanese Production System: Hybrid Factories in East Asia,* Macmillan Press.

Kamiyama, K./JMNESG (eds) (2005) Kyodai-ka Suru Cyugoku Keizai to Nikkei Haiburiddo Kojo, Jitsugyo no Nihon Sha. (Toward Gigantic Chinese Economy and Japanese Hybrid Factories).

Lee, C. (1997) Gendai Cyugoku no Jidosha Sangyo, Shin Zan Sha. (Contemporary Chinese Automobile Industry).

Matsuzaki, T. (ed.) (1996) Cyugoku no Denshi-Tekko Sangyo, Hosei Daigaku Shuppan Kyoku (Electronics and Steel Industries in China).

Seki, M. (2000) Nihon Kigyo Cyugoku Shin Syutsu no Shin Jidai: Dairen, Shin Hyoron. (New Era of Japanese Companies Advancing in China/Dalian).

Toyo Keizai Shinpo-sha (2004) *Kaigai Shinshutsu Kigyo Soram, Kunibetsu-hen (2004) Comprehensive List of Japanese Companies Operating Abroad: By Country).*

World Bank (2004) *World Development Report.*

Yuan, Z.J. (2001) Cyugoku ni Ikiru Nichi-Bei Seisan Shisutemu, Tokyo Daigaku Shuppan Kai (The Japanese Production System that Thrives in China).

6
Hybrid Factories with Functional Equivalent in Europe

Hiroshi Kumon

Purpose of the research

The purpose of the chapter is to clarify the transferability of the Japanese management and production system into Europe. The prediction on the basis of the findings of the research in North America and Asia is that the Japanese system is potentially transferable into Europe. The question, however is to identify through on-site inspections what is transferable and what is not, and what hybrid patterns have been formed in this region. The findings of the survey in North America and Asia is that the transfer of the system and hybrid patterns are regulated by two factors, namely, the system application strategy of the Japanese multinational enterprises and the local managerial environment. For that matter, corporate investment strategy, too, is in a way determined in the comparative relationships with the local environmental factors.

In the next section, I shall therefore deal with the unique factors of the managerial environment in Europe, regulations by the member countries and the European Commission and their impact upon the Japanese corporations as well as the compatibility of local labor environment with the Japanese system. In the subsequent section I shall describe the characteristics of the hybrid patterns in Europe. First, the characters of the local factories are discussed, based on which application–adaptation relation should be clarified in comparison with those in North America and in Asia. Next, I shall illustrate the hybrid patterns in Europe, country by country.

At this point, let us look at the existing studies concerning this theme and describe their relationships with this study.[1] First, I shall review the studies concerning the transferability of the Japanese system in the context of the change of basic viewpoints, which can be divided into three periods. During the first period, till the first half of the 1980s, conflicting views existed concerning the international transferability of the Japanese system. A group of studies claimed that international transfer was difficult, and that for such a transfer, the management system in Japan itself had to be reformed (Tsurumi, 1976; Yoshino, 1976; Dohse *et al.*, 1985). Another view considered that such a transfer was feasible (Takamiya, 1981; Schonberger, 1982; Trevor, 1983; Kujawa, 1986). The second period was from the latter half of the 1980s to the beginning of the 1990s, during which the views supporting the international transferability of the system came to the mainstream position, involving three studies with differing nuances. One regarded the Japanese system as an alternative model to the mass production, thus having international universality (Womack *et al.*, 1990; Kenney and Florida, 1993). The second is the study concerning Japanization of the British industry (Oliver and Wilkinson, 1992). The third is the study by the Japanese Multinational Enterprise Study Group (JMNESG) concerning the transferability of the Japanese system as a result of its hybridization (Abo, 1994). In the third period after the second half of the 1990s, studies that affirm the transferability through hybridization and/or transformation of the Japanese system became the mainstream (Boyer *et al.*, 1998, Liker *et al.*, 1999). Out of all the research, the study that considers the Japanese system as internationally transferable but requiring certain modification prevailed. This study, which integrates application–adaptation hybrid of the Japanese system as a basic viewpoint, is in complementary relationship with many other studies that have converged into the discussion of hybridization.

Secondly, let me introduce a study in Europe that points out functional equivalent with regards to the mutual relationship between the application of the Japanese system and the environmental factors in Europe. Oliver and Wilkinson assert that the core conditions of the Japanese production system can be created in Britain – the conditions are not exactly the same but functionally equivalent with those in Japan and they called this process Japanization (1992: 14). They pointed out that the method Japanese firms adopt to secure cooperation from workers is similar with the human resources management (HRM) and that the HRM movement that already existed was functional equivalent (1992:175). Boyer presented hybridization as a theory of international transfer of an productive model. And in the process of transferring a production system, he assumed three elements of imitation, discovery of functional equivalent and innovation, claiming that when the local socio-economic environment is different from that in the home country, there is either a discovery of functional equivalent or creation of innovation (Boyer *et al.*, 1998). There is an interesting phenomenon in Europe, where adaptation to the constituent elements of the local system becomes an application of the Japanese system. In Europe there is a well-established production system. Integration of the elements of the European system into the Japanese system is adaptation in a formal sense. However, there are some European environmental factors, the adaptation to which is in fact application of the Japanese system in terms of function. Therefore, the concept of functional equivalent will be incorporated into the analysis. In this chapter, functional equivalence is used in the sense that it is a formal adaptation but also a functional application of the Japanese system.

Japanese industries' cautious approach to Europe and the characteristics of the labor environment

Restrained production strategy of Japanese multinationals: their response to regulation and market integration

Europe ranks third, following North America and Asia, among the world regions that have attracted Japan's FDI (Foreign Direct Investment). In the cumulative amount invested by the manufacturing industry (1951–2001), North America accounts for 42.3 per cent, Asia 26.7 per cent and Europe 19.4 per cent. Investment in Europe by Japanese manufacturers was in two waves. The first wave came toward the end of the 1980s, when Japanese companies moved into the European market hoping to secure a foothold prior to the market integration in 1992. The second wave came ten years later at the end of the 1990s, when Japanese multinationals ventured into Europe afresh amid the booming merger and acquisition worldwide. The industries our research has been dealing with, electronics assembly, electronics parts, auto assembly and auto parts manufacturers generally moved into Europe with this trend.[2]

The European market in view of Japan's FDI is characterized by the tight regulation imposed upon Japanese industries by the European authorities in both aspects of export of finished products and FDI. This created a difficulty for Japanese firms in determining the location and the size of their factories in Europe. First, in terms of the form of operation, in consideration of the cooperation with the host government and local companies, they chose a joint venture or restrained operations to avoid outright competition against local companies. Secondly, in terms of the size and the operation of the factories to be constructed, due to the limitation of the market size obtained through trade by then, the plants were of medium to small size, and because of the strict local content regulation, the factories, notwithstanding their smaller size, were required to accommodate local contents.

The United States also demanded from the Japanese government various self-imposed export regulations upon the export of automobiles and electronics products. However, the United States did not inflict strict regulations upon Japan's direct investment and the operations of factories. Rather, the country welcomed such investments. Japan–US trade frictions were solved generally by Japan's self-imposed quantitative export restraint. Japan–US trade frictions eventually culminated to the point where the United States, indicating specific quantitative targets, demanded Japan to buy US products on a preferential basis (for semiconductors and automobiles) but were settled by Japan's taking the case to WTO. To the strategic trade policy of the United States that capitalizes on its political clout, Japan responded by utilizing WTO. On the other hand, the United States solicited local production by Japanese industries and state governments in particular induced them by offering various enticements. No particularly strict regulation was placed upon the operation of the Japanese subsidiaries.

Europe was different. Europe regulated not only trade but also local production by Japanese subsidiaries. In the 21st century, when Europe has come to respond to the stormy waves of international competition by market integration and the formation and expansion of the European Union, Europe became more generous and some countries even welcomed Japan's direct investment, whereas in the 1980s and 1990s, the local production by Japanese subsidiaries was not free. The Japanese automobile and electric and electronic companies we have surveyed ventured into Europe at this juncture when the regulation in Europe changed from the regulation by individual countries to that by the European Commission. The timing of the on-site inspection (1997, 1998) coincided with the period when deregulation and expanded EU membership was projected.

Let us review the European history of regulation of trade and local production in automobile and electronics industries. In the automobile industry, the export of Japanese cars to Europe gradually expanded in the 1970s. As a countermeasure to the increasing import of Japanese cars, five EC countries (UK, France, Spain, Portugal and Italy) and Germany, respectively, introduced quantitative import limitations, for example, the United Kingdom, 10 per cent of its car market, France 3 per cent, Spain 1 per cent, and Portugal 14 per cent. As its result, the shares of Japanese cars in 1989 were 11.1 per cent in Britain, 2.8 per cent in France, 1.4 per cent in Italy, 1.8 per cent in Spain and Portugal, 15.1 per cent in Germany and 24.8 per cent in other EC countries (Mason, 1997: 55–57). In the same year, 1,230,000 Japanese cars were sold in the EC market, with the market share of about 10 per cent.

Import regulation by the EC countries prompted Japanese multinationals to undertake local production. Britain's Thatcher Administration invited Japanese firms by offering enticement. Japanese industries chose the United Kingdom as a site location not only for the British market but also as a basis of operations for exporting to the EC market. Nissan (1984), Honda (joint venture with Rover, 1985), Isuzu (JV with G.M., 1987) and Toyota (1989) made a decision, chronologically in that order, to move into the country and all began their production prior to the market integration in 1992. Japanese companies thus adopted a strategy to choose the United Kingdom as a production base from which exports are directed to the market in continental Europe. After this, export from the UK became a point of issue in regulating Japanese cars in the EC market.

According to EC's Single European Act (SEA), the member countries, by the end of 1992, were supposed to remove restrictions on the product transfer within the integrated market. At this point, EC's regulation changed hands from individual governments to the European Commission. Automakers in 1991 formed a transnational industry group, Association of European Automobile Constructors (ACEA). As European auto companies were not competitive enough to face squarely the Japanese firms, they demanded regulating Japanese cars even after the start of the integrated market. European Commission sat with Japan's MITI in Japan–Europe automobile trade negotiations with their demand of continuing regulation of Japan's export to Europe and with a vague principle of locally produced car regulation.

The point of contention in the negotiation was the regulation of import cars and locally operating Japanese manufacturers. In August 1990, a draft agreement was reached between the two. The draft agreement introduced 5–7 year transition period starting 1993, during which regulation upon Japanese cars would continue. The European Commission assumed that the share of Japanese cars within the EC would increase to 21 per cent in 1997/1999 from 10 per cent in 1989.

Four production vehicle makers in Europe, namely, Fiat, Renault, Peugeot and VW, hardest hit by the increase of Japanese cars, rejected the draft agreement by the Commission. Three of them, Fiat, Renault and VW, in February 1991, organized ACEA, which was later joined by Peugeot and other automakers. ACEA demanded minimum seven-year transition period and the inclusion of locally produced cars into the total volume control. Country-wise, four Latin countries (France, Italy, Spain and Portugal) supported ACEA's demands, while Germany opposed to blatant regulation of locally produced cars, and the United Kingdom clearly dissented from regulating such cars. The European Commission thus had to negotiate with the MITI having conflicting opinions unsolved.

In June 1991, an agreement was reached between the European Commission and the MITI that practically approved the position of the four Latin countries. The agreement, somewhat difficult to understand, first provides that the transition period continues until the end of 1999, during which Japan monitors export volume to Europe, and the export volume as of end-1999 was projected to be the level of 1,230,000. Secondly, before January 1993, regulation by individual countries based on Article 115 of Treaty of Rome will be abolished and the projection level of imported Japanese cars and their shares in five countries as of 1999 shall be set as follows: France 150,000 cars (5.3 per cent), Italy 138,000 (5.3 per cent), Spain 79,000 (5.3 per cent), United Kingdom 190,000 (7.0 per cent) and Portugal 23,000 (8.4 per cent). Thirdly, European Commission shall not impose limitations and regulation in writing upon locally produced cars and new investments. However, Japan agreed to inform to the Japanese auto industry the concern held by the European Commission that the sales of locally produced Japanese cars could cause turmoil in the market and undermine the efforts to acquire international competitiveness on the part of European companies (Mason, 1997: 67–70). The MITI thus practically admitted to the regulation of local production by (1) monitoring export volume directed toward Europe; (2) effectively admitting to the import ceiling by individual countries; and (3) conveying to the Japanese industry the concern held by Europe toward the expansion of local production by Japanese companies. Consequently, notwithstanding the exclusion of the regulation of local investment in words, the Japanese auto industry was faced with a situation in which they had to strategize local production and direct investment with no support coming from the MITI.

Next, let us review the electric and electronics industry. Primary regulators include individual countries, the European Commission and private companies. In this industry, different regulations are inflicted upon CTV (Color Television), VCR (Videocassette Recorders) and CD (Compact Disc) Players respectively. I shall review CTV as a typical case. A variety of regulations exist with regard to export, local production and investment, which led the Japanese industry to adopt a restrained form of local production as well as a relatively small size of factories. First, let us look at the trade regulations. (1) There is a trade barrier from the 1970s. Unlike in Japan and the United States, PAL (Phase Alternating Line) system became the mainstream in Europe. Telefunken, the license holder of the system, in exchange for licensing Japanese companies, demanded restriction of export from Japan and confining the Japanese export to of small, less-than-20 inch CTV; (2) and the European Commission introduced a 14 per cent custom duty. There were also import regulations by member countries. France and Italy had an import quota system, while Britain had a 10 per cent share regulation.

Secondly, we will look into the regulation of direct investment. As a countermeasure to the import restriction, the Japanese industry opted for local production. However, this, too, was on a short leash because of many regulations. Japanese investment was focused in the United Kingdom. The British government, from 1977 to 1985, banned Japanese companies from investing in new site locations and demanded high local content. Japanese companies accepted the condition of joint ventures with existing enterprises as a form of investment in local production. Later they were switched to 100 per cent Japanese ownership, but at the time of start-up, Japanese chose a joint venture. Also, as a condition of licensing PAL system, 50 per cent or more export of the production by Japanese subsidiaries in Britain was restricted and this regulation was also applied to the Japanese factories in Europe outside the UK (Cawson *et al.*, 1990: 244–5). As an indicator of the result of those regulations and European industry protection efforts, I will look at the production capacity of major manufacturers. At the end of the 1980s, Philips, Thomson, Nokia had a capacity of producing two to three million level of CTVs, whereas Sony, the top Japanese manufacturer, was able to produce only 850,000 CTVs (Mason, 1997: 88)

Japanese firms' penetration strategy in Europe was, because of the trade and investment regulation by the local governments and the European Commission, to launch local production in a restrained manner and to plan the expansion through a wait-and-see approach. From such a low-key approach toward local production, what kind of management has resulted in their local subsidiaries? Factory management by Japanese firms is influenced by local environmental factors, particularly, by factors of work environment. As such, we shall re-examine this aspect.

Work environment in Europe: presence of functional equivalent

At first, we anticipated that the managerial environment in Europe was naturally different from that in Japan and was closer to that in the United States, because industrialized European countries in the 19th century transferred technologies to the United States and in the 20th century Europe accepted American-style mass production method. Naturally, we were aware of the fact that Europeans are wary of 'Americanization,' while accommodating the US investments, and that they maintain are aware of Fordism or Taylorism and are making efforts to modify them, despite their acceptance of the American mass production method. However, as we visited Japanese subsidiaries and their factories and surveyed their management, we were amazed to discover, contrary to our expectations, the existence of such aspects as compatible with the Japanese system. Europe, being an advanced industrialized region of the world, certainly has a well-established production system. The system, however, is not the same as the American system. The mass production method of the United States was completely different from the Japanese system in nature, whereas the European system was not necessarily in conflict with the Japanese system. Rather, some of their elements, when incorporated into the Japanese system, would in fact functionally facilitate the Japanese system. The Japanese production system consists of such key elements as high-level skill formation of shop-floor workers, streamlined production control to attain both high efficiency and good quality, long-term relationship with assemblers and parts and material suppliers, resultant and reciprocating improvement in parts quality and efficiency, and harmonious labor relations. European manufacturers established their unique production system: tradition of expertise formation of employees, American-style mass production techniques, long-term relationships between assembly manufacturers and parts manufacturers, and works council, and an in-house labor negotiation platform not bound by the framework of industrial trade unions constitute the system. Obviously, each of those components is in nature a coherent system within a European company. What was significant however, was that some of those elements, once incorporated by Japanese firms into their factory management, could function as elements that constitute the Japanese system (Kumon and Abo, 2004). Dividing the components of the system into two categories, namely, form and function, in Europe there are elements whose formal adaptation becomes an application of the Japanese system. Specifically speaking, professional skills of shop-floor employees, performance evaluation in the wage system, works council and others could be functionally equivalent with the elements that constitute the Japanese system. In other words, professional skills of shop-floor workers in line with the historical European tradition of professional training functionally overlap with the in-house-nurtured sophisticated multilateral skills in Japanese industries. European wage system is originally job-centered and is different from the Japanese system, which is complex consisting of diverse measurement criteria including age, length of service and skill levels. However, it is similar to the Japanese system in that it can differentiate each employee from the others by performance evaluation. Works council is a system in which members elected by the votes of employees negotiate with the management about working conditions and it is not a trade union. In Europe, there are trade unions that transcend corporate organizations, having a mandate to negotiate industrial working conditions. Works council, however, could provide a similar function with that of in-house labor negotiation where company union representatives negotiate with the management of the company. As such, the European production system among its vital elements includes functional equivalents, which, though different form-wise, fulfill the same function with the Japanese system. This provides favorable factors for the application and consolidation of the Japanese system in Europe.

Hybrid patterns in Europe

Outline of the surveyed factories

As has been described so far, the strategy Japanese industries adopted in venturing into Europe was to begin local production in a restrained manner and to plan for an expansion through a wait-and-see approach. This was because the market size Japanese industries obtained through trade was relatively small due to the regulation on trade and investment by the individual European governments and the European Commission. What kind of management would be brought about by such a low-key investment strategy? The answer we would expect is a passive attitude in the application of the Japanese system. On the other hand, the existence of compatible elements in the European labor environment is a factor that enables them to actively apply the Japanese system in the factory management. What exactly are the profiles of the hybrid patterns of application and adaptation of the Japanese subsidiaries in Europe? The analysis of this point will follow.

Let us first begin by clarifying the character of the factories surveyed (see Tables 6.1 and Table 6.2). The industries surveyed include automobile assembly, automobile parts, electronics assembly and electronics parts. First, let us review the site locations. The total number of Japanese factories our team visited is 56, 20 of which are located in Britain and the other 36 are in continental Europe. In many cases, Japanese manufacturers chose Britain because the Thatcher Administration welcomed Japanese investments and also because plants in Britain could serve as bases of operations of exporting to Continental Europe. This is reflected in the large number of factories we visited in the UK. Industry-wise, electronics and automobile industries are more or less balanced in terms of number, with 12 factories belonging to the former and slightly less eight to the latter. Japanese multinationals

Table 6.1 Factories surveyed in the UK

Plant	*Industry*	*Location*	*Start of operation*	*Ownership*	*No. of employees*	*No. of Japanese*
UCL	Elec. Assy	Wrexham	1985	100%	175	3
UCM	Elec. Assy	Cardiff	1974	100%	2,424	42
UCO	Elec. Assy	East Lothin	1979	100%	545	10
UCE	Elec. Assy	Lowestoft	1982	100%	383	8
UCF	Elec. Assy	Wrexham	1985	100%	1,080	16
UCG1	Elec. Assy	Bridgend	1982	100%	1,675	22
UCG2	Elec. Assy	Pencord	1992	100%	2,786	39
UCQ1	Elec. Assy	Plymouth	1991	100%	302	3
UCQ2	Elec. Assy	Plymouth	1981	100%	890	8
UDC	Elec. Part	Milton Keynes	1985	100%	530	15
UDK	Elec. Part	Newton Aycliffe	1991	100%	608	29
UDA	Elec. Part	Livingston	1982	100%	1,440	34
UAE	Auto. Assy	Luton	1989	JV	1,800	4
UAO	Auto. Assy	Burnaston	1992	100%	2,459	48
UAR	Auto. Assy	Sunderland	1986	100%	4,100	30
UAS	Auto. Assy	Swindon	1992	100%	2,571	99
UBG1	Auto. Part	Llanelli	1989	100%	1,000	
UBG2	Auto. Part	Washington	1986	100%	147	
UAM1	Auto. Part	Telford	1992	JV (75%)	764	
UAM2	Auto. Part	Shipley	1904	JV	810	

Notes: Elec. Assy = Electronics Assembly; Elect. Part = Electronics Parts. ditto for Auto Industry.
Source: Data is from the plants surveyed.

Table 6.2 Factories surveyed in Continental Europe

Factories	*Industry*	*Location*	*Start of operation*	*Ownership*	*No. of employees*	*No. of Japanese*
GBB	Auto. Part	Germany	1971	100%	174	10
GBC	Auto. Part	Germany	1976	JV	62	1
GBL	Auto. Part	Germany	1996	100%	240	6
GDC	Elec. Part	Germany	1988	100%	225	2
GDH	Elec. Part	Germany	1984	100%	192	7
GDJ	Elec. Part	Germany	1980	100%	650	19
GDO	Elec. Part	Germany	1992	100%	450	11
GDN	Elec. Part	Germany	1984	JV	280	5
GCD	Elec. Assy	Germany	1973	100%	661	13
GCH	Elec. Assy	Germany	1990	100%	430	4
GCP	Elec. Assy	Germany	1991	JV	153	5
FCD	Elec. Assy	France	1984	100%	603	20
FCH	Elec. Assy	France	1986	100%	400	4
FDI	Elec. Assy	France	1985	100%	139	5
FCJ	Elec. Assy	France	1992	100%	140	9
FCO	Elec. Assy	France	1994	100%	517	7
FBH	Auto. Part	France	1984	JV	163	6
FCF	Elec. Assy	France	1989	100%	350	6
FCG	Elec. Assy	France	1987	100%	1,360	23
BDI	Auto. Part	Belgium	1974	100%	328	9
LDB	Elec. Part	Luxembourg	1991	JV	806	25
NAA	Auto. Assy	Netherlands	1991	JV	4,158	35
NEQ	Mach.	Netherlands	1992	JV	438	11
ICG	Elec. Part	Italy	1988	100%	277	3
IBM	Auto. Part	Italy	1991	JV	1,040	0
ICD	Elec. Assy	Italy	1987	JV	662	3
SAR	Auto. Assy	Spain	1980	JV	4,226	26
SBD	Auto. Part	Spain	1990	JV	286	4
SBM	Auto. Part	Spain	1991	100%	267	12
SCF	Elec. Assy	Spain	1986	JV	776	13
SCK	Elec. Assy	Spain	1977	100%	257	6
PAP	Auto. Assy	Portugal	1996	JV	391	14
HAK	Auto. Assy	Hungary	1992	JV	1,450	18
HBF	Auto. Part	Hungary	1993	JV	24	1
HBI	Auto. Part	Hungary	1996	100%	240	2
HDB	Elec. Part	Hungary	1997	100%	699	6

Notes: Auto. Assy = Automobile Assembly; Auto. Part = Automobile Part; ditto for electronics industry.
Source: Data is from the plants surveyed.

naturally invested in continental Europe as well, and we visited 11 factories in Germany, 12 in France and Benelux, 9 in South Europe (Italy, Spain, Portugal) and 4 in Hungary. Since the subject of the study this time is traditional EU countries, of the former socialist countries that are experiencing the economy in transition, only Hungary is included in the survey. In Continental Europe, electronics industry (21 factories) somewhat exceeds automobile industry (15 factories).

Secondly, with regard to the timing of investment in terms of the year when the operation began, many of the factories we visited became operational in 1992 or earlier. This reflects the corporate desire to move into Europe prior to the market integration. In this respect, too, there are some differences between Britain and continental Europe. More specifically, all of the 20 factories in the UK began their operations in 1992 or earlier. In continental Europe, too, most of the factories became operational in 1992 or earlier. Only five began production later than 1992, of which three are in Hungary. It is during this period that Japanese industries made focused investments in the expanded EU member countries and this trend is reflected on the timing when the Hungarian operations began.

Thirdly, the size of the factories in terms of the number of employees should be considered. The average number of employees of all the factories in Table 6.3 and Table 6.4 is 893 per factory. It is not too big and not too small, a medium-sized factory. The size fits in well with the cautious stance taken by Japanese multinationals in penetrating into the European market. By region, however, we see a distinct difference between Britain and continental Europe. Specifically, the average number of employees per factory in Britain is 1,324 *vis-à-vis* 653 in continental Europe. The number is about twice larger in the UK. The average number of employees per factory in Britain by industry is 1,706 in automobile industry compared with 1,070 in electronics industry. The auto industry somewhat exceeds electronics industry, but the latter also maintains a sizable level. The number of employees is also restrained by the nature of the industry the factory belongs to. An auto assembly factory capable of producing 200,000 cars per year requires approximately 3,000 employees, the largest of the industries of auto assembly, auto parts, electronics assembly and electronics parts. The size of the factories in the UK, which accommodates four auto assembly factories, naturally becomes bigger, and besides, the factories of electronics industry in Britain also maintain a sizable scale. In the case of continental Europe, the average number of employees is half of that in the UK, indicating a smaller size. Country-wise, it is 909 in

Table 6.3 International comparison of the application scores for hybrid factories

	Continental Europe	*UK*	*Whole of Europe*	*North America*	*Korea/ Taiwan*	*ASEAN Countries*	*East Asia*
GI. Work Organization	3.0	3.4	3.1	2.9	3.7	3.3	3.5
1. Job Classifications	3.2	4.4	3.6	3.7	4.9	4.5	4.7
2. Multifunctional Skill	2.8	3.3	3.0	2.6	2.9	2.6	2.7
3. Education & Training	3.1	3.5	3.2	2.9	3.4	3.3	3.3
4. Wage System	2.8	2.8	2.8	2.4	3.9	3.1	3.5
5. Promotion	3.1	3.4	3.2	3.1	3.7	3.1	3.4
6. First-line Supervisor	3.1	3.4	3.2	2.9	3.4	2.9	3.2
GII. Production Management	3.1	3.5	3.3	3.3	3.5	3.4	3.4
7. Equipment	3.4	3.9	3.6	4.3	3.5	4.0	3.7
8. Maintenance	2.8	3.0	2.9	2.6	3.3	3.0	3.2
9. Quality Control	3.1	3.6	3.3	3.4	3.6	3.2	3.4
10. Process Management	3.2	3.6	3.3	3.0	3.5	3.2	3.4
III. Procurement	2.8	2.5	2.7	3.0	3.2	3.2	3.2
11. Local Content	2.8	1.9	2.4	2.7	2.9	3.1	3.0
12. Suppliers	2.9	2.7	2.8	3.9	3.5	3.8	3.7
13. Procurement method	2.8	2.9	2.8	2.5	3.2	2.8	3.0
GIV. Group Consciousness	2.7	3.3	2.9	3.2	3.4	3.2	3.3
14. Small group activities	2.5	2.7	2.6	2.5	3.2	2.9	3.0
15. Information sharing	2.8	3.6	3.1	3.6	3.5	3.3	3.4
16. Sense of unity	2.8	3.7	3.1	3.5	3.6	3.3	3.5
GV. Labor Relations	3.2	3.5	3.3	3.6	3.4	3.1	3.2
17. Hiring Policy	3.1	3.3	3.2	3.4	3.0	3.1	3.0
18. Long-term employment	3.2	3.4	3.3	3.4	3.3	3.0	3.2
19. Harmonious labor relations	3.5	4.2	3.8	4.4	4.0	3.3	3.6
20. Grievance procedure	3.1	3.0	3.0	3.3	3.2	3.1	3.1
GVI. Parent-Subsidiary Relations	3.0	2.8	2.9	3.6	2.3	2.9	2.6
21. Ratio of Japanese Expatriates	2.6	2.4	2.6	3.7	1.5	1.6	1.5
22. Delegation of Authority	3.2	3.0	3.1	3.6	2.7	3.2	2.9
23. Position of local Managers	3.1	3.0	3.1	3.6	2.7	3.8	3.3
Overall average	3.0	3.2	3.1	3.3	3.3	3.2	3.3

Source: Based on our author's data.

Table 6.4 Regional comparison of the four perspective evaluation

	Continental Europe	*UK*	*Whole Europe*	*North America*	*Taiwan/ Korea*	*ASEAN countries*	*East Asia*
Human Methods	2.9	3.4	3.1	3.1	3.5	3.2	3.4
Material Methods	2.9	3.2	3.0	2.8	3.4	3.0	3.2
Human Results	2.9	2.7	2.8	3.7	2.1	2.7	2.4
Material Results	3.0	2.8	2.9	3.6	3.3	3.6	3.5

Source: Based our author's data.

southern Europe, 784 in France and Benelux, 603 in Hungary and 320 in Germany.[3]

Analysis of hybrid patterns in Europe

Hybrid patterns of application and adaptation in Europe will be analyzed in comparison with the other regions (see tables 6.3 and 6.4). The characteristic that emerges from the two tables is a medium application degree. In other words, compared with North America and Asia, no clear-cut features can be identified. In our evaluation system, the scores predominantly converged around the 3 points, which indicates medium application degree or demonstrates both aspects of simultaneous application and adaptation.

The overall average application degree of the whole Europe is 3.1 points. The score is slightly lower than 3.3 of North America and East Asia but exceeds the level of 3.0, and this indicates that the Japanese management and production system is introduced to the extent of approximately 50 per cent in the local factories as a whole. It also means that European elements are hybridized with the Japanese elements to the level of approximately 50 per cent. Average application degree of slightly higher than 3.0 is the level universally observed in every region and in every timing ever since we surveyed the United States in 1986, and it is worth noting that the same application level has been found in a broadly classified region of Europe. This implies the functioning of certain logic that despite varied composition of 23-item application in regions and in timings, the average application score converges to the level slightly higher than

50 per cent as a result of those differences offsetting each other among themselves.

Next, let us look at six-group, 23-item hybrid evaluation. By six-group, the scores for the whole Europe are generally around 3 points, and there is neither a conspicuously low-score group nor a group that posted a distinctly high score. The scores of all the groups are between 3.3 and 2.7. Analysis of the six groups by dividing them into three groupings, namely, Group I, Work organization and Group II, Production management, that supposedly constitute the axis of the factory management; Group III, Procurement, that is the secondary axis; and the last grouping of Group IV, Group consciousness, Group V, Labor relations and Group VI, Parent-subsidiary relations, that form the framework of the former, helps to understand in part the characteristics of the factory management in Europe. Specifically, the scores for I, Work organization and II, Production management are 3.1 and 3.3 respectively, both exceeding 3 points, which is not necessarily the case with the other two groupings. The score for III, Procurement, the secondary axis, is 2.7, while the scores for framework-constituting IV, Group consciousness, V, Labor relations, and VI, Parent-subsidiary relations are 2.9, 3.3, and 2.9 respectively, all around 3.0 level. As such, the overall average of the whole Europe is medium, but in a closer look, the scores for Groups of Work organization and Production management, the axis of factory management, exceed 3 points, whereas scores for framework-constituting groups are somewhat lower. This pattern is different from that of North America and relatively close to that of East Asia.

North America, on close examination is clearly different from Europe. Specifically, the score for Group I, Work organization is 2.9, slightly below 3 points, while Group II, Production management shows a high application degree of 3.3. On the other hand, the scores for secondary-axis and framework-constituting groupings all exceed 3.0, and the scores for framework-items are particularly high. The score for Group IV, Group consciousness, is 3.2, and the scores for Group V, Labor relations and Group V, Parent-subsidiary relations are extremely high at 3.6 respectively. In North America, high application degree of the framework-constituting groups thus supports the overall application of the Japanese system.

In the mean time, the pattern in East Asia is an enlarged version of the European pattern. Namely, the scores for axis-forming Group I, Work organization and II, Production management exceed those for framework-forming groups. More specifically, the scores for Group I, Work organization and Group II, Production management are 3.5 and

3.4 respectively, indicating a very high application degree. The scores for other Groups are also mostly higher than 3.0; 3.2 for III, Procurement, 3.3 for IV, Group consciousness, 3.2 for V. Labor relations, 2.6 for VI, Parent-subsidiary relations, but comparatively lower than those for Work organization and Production management. Another characteristic of East Asia is a low score of 2.6 for Parent-subsidiary relationship. We have thus found an interesting result that the hybrid patterns in Europe are different from those in North America and close to those in East Asia.

At this point the items that display the European characteristics should be explained. First, the score of Job classification for the whole Europe is 3.6, almost identical with 3.7 for North America. The score, though in lower than Asia's level of 4, is favorable for the introduction of the Japanese system. In view of the fact that the argument to criticize segmentalized job classification and its adverse effects originated in Europe, we expected to find a minutely segmented job classification system, which was not the case. European wage system is job-centered, in which for each of the wage grades is allocated a job. The wage grades are so diverse that in one case there are only two ranks, production workers and skilled trades, and in another as many as ten classified ranks. Japanese companies have basically accepted the local job classification system. In Britain, there was a case in which job classification was changed to two ranks of skilled trades and production workers, but in Continental Europe, there was no need for the reform as opposed to the case in North America. In North America, there were scores of job classifications, sometimes more than a hundred, and how to simplify them was a challenge to the locally operating Japanese companies. The number of job classifications varied depending on the industry and the size of factories, but job classifications had to be simplified in order to secure work flexibility. Many of the automobile assembly and parts factories simplified them into two, production workers and skilled trades. In contrast, no such reduction took place in Europe, except that a Japanese factory in Britain introduced a new method from a subsidiary in the US, reducing them to two. Rather, the local wage system including the system for skilled trades is accepted as it is. And yet, multifunctional skill can be formed within the company because job rotation is permitted within the same wage rank. As such, in Job classifications, using our terminologies, adaptation without modification can be applied.

A similar situation is found in Wage system. In the Japanese wage system, wages of regular employees including shop-floor employees are determined by manifold elements that include length of service, age and job performance, and naturally individual employees' wages are differentiated by appraisal (performance evaluation). In Europe, the wage of shop-floor employees is basically job-centered and the wage by grade is determined by industry-wide bargaining. The wage rank of the workers in this case finds its own level in the wage grades in the factory depending on the job content. Surprisingly, however, in Europe, performance evaluations have common practice to a considerable degree. Japanese subsidiaries in France, Benelux and the UK did not experience any significant problems in practicing performance evaluations.

The author had a chance to have an interview at a trade union headquarter of the French energy industry. It was a traditional energy industry union, affiliated with the communist party, and they approved the performance evaluation system. I asked why a trade union approves performance evaluations, and they answered, 'It is no longer a Soviet time and it is normal that wage is differentiated. However, performance evaluations require transparency and should not cause unjustifiable discriminations.' I further asked what is the wage difference resulting from the performance evaluations and the answer was 'between the range of five to maximum 25 per cent.' I again asked if there was also an influence of Japanese companies on the practice of performance evaluations, and the answer I was given was rather vague 'there may be.'[4] Performance evaluations thus are being implemented even under industrial trade unions, but not in all the factories. In North America, performance evaluations were hard to implement despite simplified job classifications due to the opposition of labour trade unions. Compared with North America, European trade unions are more flexible.

I will now move on to the skill formation in a factory. In Japanese factories, shop-floor employees learn skills through in-house education and training as well as OJT, while the European system is a combination of a vocational training system and in-house skill formation. The combination varies from one country to another. In Germany, for instance, professional skill training is conducted in the so-called dual education system, a combination of outside vocational training and the in-house training system, the qualification of which is also valid outside the company. Meanwhile, in France, though traditional vocational training is available, it is limited to the jobs of outmoded skills, and skill formation is generally implemented in-house. In France, too, the wage grade earned in a company that corresponds to the skill level is valid in the society, and therefore the employee, changing the company, is eligible for the same wage grade in another company. As such, in Europe, the skill of a shop-floor employee and the wage grade he/she earns through the former has a social nature. Social qualification is somewhat strange to Japanese companies, but the question is how compatible it is with the skill formation required in the Japanese factory management. This is one of our interest areas in conducting our factory survey, and the general impression we had was that Japanese in-house skill formation and the wage system that encourages the process is not inconsistent with the European skill formation. Special technicians (Facharbeiter) nurtured under the German skill training system are equipped with solid skills, though they may lack in flexibility. It is an essential condition required for manufacturing in a factory and the Japanese management, though feeling somewhat uncomfortable with the lack of flexibility, relies upon the skills of special technicians. In other countries, where no such vocational training system is available as in Germany, local employees have generally familiarized themselves with the skill formation through in-house OJT.

The last item under review is Works Council. In the United States, no works council can be organized because labor laws ban in-house organizations other than labour unions. Therefore, Japanese companies, in organizing labor-management consultation system and small group activities, are required to carefully discuss with the labour union, if there is any. In contrast, there exists an employee representative system in Europe, which has been introduced to the entire Europe when the integrated market was formed. The system, in which representatives elected by the votes of employees negotiate with the management in the works council, presents an interesting form to Japanese companies. Usually, those who run as candidates and get elected as representatives for the works council are largely trade union activists, and therefore it is not certain that works council can be an in-house negotiating organization in a true sense. In fact, we heard that in Germany works councils reiterate the views of trade unions. Meanwhile, in the Netherlands, the attitude of employee representatives at works council is allegedly extremely gentlemanly, which makes it possible to discuss corporate matters and works council is actually playing the same role with that of the Japanese labor–management consultation system. I also heard that in the UK, since labor–management issues are mostly discussed and determined at works council, trade unions, though they do exist, are nearly dysfunctional. Works council thus could function (as a functional equivalent) either as a collective bargaining system, or as a labor–management consultation system, apparently depending upon labor–management dynamics in the end. Even so, works council, as it enables labor–management talks concerning in-house issues, is potentially favorable to the Japanese companies in that it could function just like the labor–management consultation system.

Let us refer afresh to Table 6-4 and review the European characteristics in the perspective of technology transfer and on the basis of scores of the four perspective evaluation. It is clear that in Europe the Methods that constitute the Japanese system have been transferred to some extent and that the dependence on Results is low. This pattern is again different from that of North America and closer to that of East Asia. More specifically, for the whole of Europe, the score of Human Methods is 3.1 and Material Methods 3.0, while Human Results is 2.8 and Material Results 2.8. As all the scores are around the level of 3, it is difficult to identify a clear-cut trend from those figures. But we may be able to say that reliance upon methods is high as the score for methods–application exceeds 3 points, whereas results–application is below the level. On the other hand, in North America, the scores of Human Methods and Material Methods are 3.1 and 2.8 respectively, showing a variance in methods-application. In results–application, the scores of Human Results and Material Results are 3.7 and 3.6 respectively, showing a high dependence on results. The application pattern of North America ten years later is different from this, with results-application declining. However, the North American pattern at the time of our survey was clearly different from the one in Europe. In East Asia, methods–application exceeds the 3 points, with Human Method scoring 3.4 and Material Methods 3.2, whereas the score of Human Result is 2.4 and Material Result 3.5, illustrating that Asia realized high level of methods-application not depending upon Human Results. However, as the region consists of developing countries, its dependence on Japan in terms of Material Results is also high. Asia thus achieved a high methods-application level without depending upon Human Results and this is clearly different from North America and closer to Europe.

European hybrid pattern by region

European regional comparison

The scores for whole Europe is in fact a total of the scores for each region within Europe. For the purpose of comparing with North America and Asia, Europe was examined in aggregate. The result shows that the application degree of the Japanese system is medium and its hybrid pattern is closer to Asia than to North America.

Next, we shall undertake European regional comparison (see Tables 6.5 and 6.6). The average application score by European region is 3.2 for the UK and 3.0 for Continental Europe. The score for the UK is 0.2 point higher than Continental Europe. By country, the application scores for Britain and Germany are highest 3.2 respectively, and the scores decline in southern countries. More precisely, the score for France and Benelux is 3.0 and for southern Europe (Italy, Spain, Portugal) is 2.8. For Hungary, the only country we visited in Central Europe, the score was 2.9. As such, the application score for Britain is high, comparable with that of North America and Asia, whereas the score for Continental Europe is somewhat lower than those of North America and Asia. Relatively high application score for the UK coincides with the factory size we have seen in Table 6.1 and Table 6.2. As described earlier, the average number of employees per factory in Britain was 1,324, larger than 653 in Continental Europe. Greater emphasis on the management of the factory by the parent company may as well act as a factor to increase the application level of the Japanese system in the subsidiary management. High application scores for the UK can be interpreted as a reflection of the emphasis parent companies put into the factories in Britain.

Furthermore, 'Method' application we pay attention to shows that the high application score for the UK is accompanied by high 'Method' application. As Table 6.6 shows, 'Human Method' score for the UK is 3.4 and 'Material Method' is 3.2, exceeding the scores of North America and attaining virtually the same level with those of Asia. On the other hand, for Continental Europe, the scores of both 'Human Method' and 'Material Method' are 2.9, slightly below 3 points. Thus, a focus upon 'Method' application would reveal more clearly the relatively high application degree of the UK. 'Method' application is affected also by the local managerial environment, particularly by the factors of working environment deeply related with the factory management. Therefore, let us look at each of the countries. In accordance with four-perspective evaluation, in particular, hybrid patterns of each country shall be examined in the following:

United Kingdom

Hybrid patterns in Britain are 'Methods–application, Results–adaptation,' where Methods–application is high, while Results-application is low. Namely, the scores of 'Human Method' and 'Material Method' are

Table 6.5 Application scores for hybrid factories in European region

	Whole Europe	*Continental Europe*	*UK*	*Germany*	*France/ Benelux*	*South Europe*	*Hungary*
GI. Work Organization	3.1	3.0	3.4	3.1	3.0	2.9	2.9
1. Job Classifications	3.6	3.2	4.4	3.1	3.5	2.9	3.3
2. Multifunctional Skill	3.0	2.8	3.3	2.8	2.8	3.0	2.5
3. Education & Training	3.2	3.1	3.5	3.2	3.0	3.1	3.0
4. Wage System	2.8	2.8	2.8	2.7	2.9	2.6	3.0
5. Promotion	3.2	3.1	3.4	3.2	2.8	3.2	3.0
6. First-line Supervisor	3.2	3.1	3.4	3.4	3.0	2.9	2.8
GII. Production Management	3.3	3.1	3.5	3.4	3.0	3.0	3.2
7. Equipment	3.6	3.4	3.9	3.9	3.2	2.6	4.8
8. Maintenance	2.9	2.8	3.0	2.7	2.7	3.1	2.5
9. Quality Control	3.3	3.1	3.6	3.5	3.0	3.1	2.5
10. Process Management	3.3	3.2	3.6	3.4	3.2	3.2	3.0
GIII. Procurement	2.7	2.8	2.5	3.5	2.7	2.4	2.3
11. Local Content	2.4	2.8	1.9	3.6	2.8	2.0	2.0
12. Suppliers	2.8	2.9	2.7	3.8	2.8	2.1	2.8
13. Procurement method	2.8	2.8	2.9	3.0	2.6	3.0	2.3
GIV. Group consciousness	2.9	2.7	3.3	2.8	2.9	2.5	2.3
14. Small group activities	2.6	2.5	2.7	2.6	2.7	2.3	2.0
15. Information sharing	3.1	2.8	3.6	2.8	3.2	2.7	2.3
16. Sense of unity	3.1	2.8	3.7	3.0	2.8	2.6	2.5
GV. Labor relations	3.3	3.2	3.5	3.0	3.5	3.2	3.1
17. Hiring Policy	3.2	3.1	3.3	3.1	3.1	3.4	2.5
18. Long-term employment	3.3	3.2	3.4	3.0	3.6	3.2	2.5
19. Harmonious labor relations	3.8	3.5	4.2	3.2	3.9	3.1	4.3
20. Grievance procedure	3.0	3.1	3.0	2.8	3.3	3.0	3.3

Table 6.5 *Continued*

	Whole Europe	*Continental Europe*	*UK*	*Germany*	*France/ Benelux*	*South Europe*	*Hungary*
GVI. Parent-subsidiary relations	2.9	3.0	2.8	3.4	2.8	2.6	3.3
21. Ratio of Japanese Expatriates	2.6	2.6	2.4	3.0	2.6	2.4	2.3
22. Delegation of Authority	3.1	3.2	3.0	3.6	2.9	2.7	4.0
23. Position of local Managers	3.1	3.1	3.0	3.5	2.9	2.8	3.5
Overall average	3.1	3.0	3.2	3.2	3.0	2.8	2.9

Source: Based in author's own data.

Table 6.6 Four perspective evaluation for European region

	Whole Europe	*Continental Europe*	*UK*	*Germany*	*France/ Benelux*	*South Europe*	*Hungary*
Human Method	3.1	2.9	3.4	3.0	3.0	2.9	2.7
Material Method	3.0	2.9	3.2	3.1	2.8	3.1	2.4
Human Result	2.8	2.9	2.7	3.3	2.8	2.6	2.9
Material Result	2.9	3.0	2.8	3.8	2.9	2.2	3.2

Source: Based our author's data.

3.4 and 3.2 respectively, both exceeding 3 points, whereas those of 'Human Result' and 'Material Result' are 2.7 and 2.8, both at the 2-point level. From the Japanese perspective, this type of hybrid pattern is almost ideal. The application of the Japanese system would facilitate the efficient manufacture of quality products. On the other hand, high degree of dependence on local procurement and local managers would cut costs for procurement and personnel and guarantee a high level of commitment on the part of local managers. This ideal pattern resulted in part from an active investment strategy of the Japanese companies. At the same time, it cannot be overlooked that the local managerial environment that existed in Britain was highly supportive of the application of the Japanese system. British workers were flexible in their acceptance of the Japanese management and production system. This flexibility was due to various environmental factors including the policies of the Thatcher government in changing Britain's traditional labor practices, a diminished self-confidence in their traditional labor relationships on the parts of both management and labor as a result of a decline in international competitiveness, and the spread of the Human Resource Management style that emphasized motivation, originally from the United States, which formed a ground for the permeation of the Japanese system. Let us have a closer look at the application of Work organization. In the case of electronics assembly industry plants, while the wage system adapted to British industry-specific wage classifications, management applied its practice of performance evaluations. In the case of auto assembly plants, in addition to creating a simplified wage system with only two job classifications of production workers and skilled trades, directly following the experiences in the US, wage increases are determined by performance evaluations. The performance evaluations, the introduction of which was too difficult in the United States, are indeed practices in the UK. In addition, attempts are being made to override the common sense of the British class society. Management abolished the traditional segregation between hourly and salary wages, replacing it with a comprehensive annual salary pay system. All employees are in the same uniform; all employees use canteens in the same manner. Efforts to eliminate classism is regarded in Britain as lacking in common sense, but Japanese managers are comfortable with these measures, which in turn have drawn support from the British workers. Class–society-originated systems thus have been reformed and the Japanese system has been applied. And yet, management failed to bring change to the special treatment of skilled trades. In Japan, production workers and maintenance personnel are hired simultaneously and after the hire, they are assigned to the jobs according to their aptitude. For both of the jobs, workers receive in-house education and training in a similar manner and there is no wage difference between the two. In the UK, however, as long as there is a wage difference between production workers and skilled trades in the external labor market, there is no option for the management but to follow the practice. Such efforts as mentioned above are not only imitated by those Japanese manufacturers in other industries than electronics and automobiles but also became models for local, indigenous companies. Japanese manufacturing factories in Britain thus produced good business results by exporting their products to continental Europe on the basis of high application degree of the Japanese system until they faced with increasingly stronger British pound sterling, which is now becoming an obstacle to their good performance. Britain, though being a member of the EU, has not participated in Euro, and this brought about the appreciation of British sterling, which in turn negatively impacted upon the product export from the UK. Some electronics firms have chosen to exit the country.

Germany

In Germany, hybrid patterns are predominantly 'Results-application.' Specifically, the scores for 'Human Method' is 3.0, 'Material Method' 3.1, 'Human Result' 3.3 and 'Material Result' 3.8, and clearly the Results–application degree is greater than Methods–application. The factories in Germany are largely auto parts and electronics parts manufacturers of medium size (See Table 6-2), where Japanese managers play a big role and they are heavily dependent upon Japan for parts and materials. In Germany, where special technicians are nurtured through a dual education system, skilled trades can be amply hired and the management can rely upon their skills. While '*Tarif*' is accepted as it is, this system permits the mobility of workers among the different jobs within a particular wage classification as well as awarding of extra wage benefits on the basis of performance evaluations. Japanese managers, therefore, are implementing rational production control, while relying upon special technicians and *meisters*. Germany's advantage as a production location lies in this respect that the Japanese system can be applied while adapting to the traditional German-specific systems. The scores of four-perspective evaluation for Germany are higher for results than for methods, but method scores are also relatively high at 3.0 (Human Method) and 3.1 (Material Method), implying half as much of the Japanese system is applied in the local plants. There are, however, impediments to flexible production management. Skilled trades' narrow work range and the demarcation of production departments create impediments to the mobility of workers among different jobs and to the cooperation among departments. Furthermore, as trade union activists are often elected as representatives of shop-floor employees at works council, management have to direct much energy toward the negotiation at works council.

France and Benelux

The scores of application and four-perspective evaluation for France and Benelux are almost identical with those for Continental Europe. The overall average of 23-item evaluation for France and Benelux is

3.0 points, exactly the same with the Continental European average. In four-perspective evaluation, too, the score of 'Human method' is 3.0, 'Material Method' 2.8, 'Human Result' 2.8 and 'Material Result' 2.9, all ranging between 2.8 and 3.0 and indicating no salient characteristics. Meanwhile, the scores for Continental Europe of 'Human Method', 'Material Method' and 'Human Result' are all 2.9, while that of 'Material Result' is 3.0. The only difference is in distribution. In France and Benelux, the score of 'Human Method' is 3.0, while in Continental Europe, the score of 'Material Result' is 3.0 and that, too, is only a minor difference. The scores for France and Benelux and characteristics of their distribution can be interpreted as a reflection of the motivation of rather passive nature on the part of the Japanese industries in investing in these countries. The size of the factories in France and Benelux is medium with 784 employees per factory on average, which also suggests the passive stance of the investors. In addition, geographically, this region is located right in the middle of Continental Europe which and it might be that these countries are between Germany and Iberian Peninsula also in terms of managerial environment. In other words, the passive attitude of the Japanese industries toward investment coupled by the in-between environmental factors might have contributed to creating the almost identical hybrid pattern with that of Continental Europe with all the scores converging around the 3.0 points.

In France, skill training of shop-floor workers is provided basically in house, as is also the case in Japan. The local wage grades system is adapted as the basis of the wages of individual companies, but within that framework, the grade classifications can be changed and management can practice performance evaluations. Japanese companies did introduce performance evaluations. As in Germany, the problem is high labor cost due to short working hours. Automatization has limitations in medium-size plants and high labor cost is automatically passed onto product costs. In this region, too, the works council system is generally formalized, and Japanese companies were solving in-house labor problems through negotiations with employee representatives.

South Europe (Italy, Spain and Portugal)

The overall average score of this region is 2.8, the lowest in Europe and also the lowest even including North America and Asia. The hybrid pattern is a Results-adaptation type. In comparison with the other regions, Results–adaptation is conspicuous in that 'Method' scores are both around 3.0 with 'Human Method' 2.9 and 'Material Method' 3.1, whereas the Results-application is extremely low with 'Human Result' 2.6 and 'Material Result' 2.2. This hybrid pattern of the low average of application and low Result-adaptation is a reflection of the passive nature of the Japanese investment in this region. Let us look at this point in Table 6.2. Factories in this region are mostly medium and small. Only two factories of auto assembly and auto parts have more than a thousand employees and the rest have fewer. Further, the plants are predominantly joint ventures (six out of nine) because Japanese manufacturers placed priority on the cooperation with local manufacturers. Medium-size operations and the prevailing JV operations is the result of passive investment strategy of the Japanese industries, which is reflected on the system application degree, which are not necessarily high. What is interesting in this region is that the Japanese system is more accepted in rural areas rather than in traditional industrial areas. This is the same trend observed within developing nations as in Asia. Another point worth noting is the fact that strong influence of traditional trades unions to some extent constitutes an obstacle to the application of the Japanese system. For instance, due to the strong restraining force of trades unions, performance evaluation for wages is hard to practice and labor negotiations are tough to discuss labor distribution. Also, in-house division of labor is observed, which is typical when unions have strong influence. Specifically speaking, the Japanese system that involves production workers in quality control and maintenance is hard to apply, and they have to be attended exclusively by QC personnel and skilled trades.

Hungary

The overall average of Hungary is 2.9, 0.1 point lower than the European average. Four-Perspective Evaluation of the country is characteristically Results-oriented. Namely, the score of 'Human Method' is 2.7 and 'Material Method' is 2.4, both lower than the level of 3.0, whereas scores of 'Human Result' and 'Material Result' are 2.9 and 3.2 respectively, indicating relatively higher 'Result' scores. Investment in Hungary is to establish bases of operations for exporting products to EU countries and to capitalize on the low wages. As the EU expanded its membership, factories are increasingly relocated from Iberian Peninsula, former European peripheries, to Central and Eastern Europe. This trend is true both for European and Japanese enterprises. The outcome of the survey of Hungary in this perspective is extremely interesting. Unfortunately, however, no definite conclusion can be drawn from our survey, as only four factories were visited and they may not be the typical case in Hungary. Nevertheless, the impression we had from the limited number of case studies is that the acceptability of the Japanese system in the country seems high. In Hungary, there is no regulation by unions concerning wages and labor conditions as observed elsewhere in Continental Europe. Transition economy characteristically lacks nationwide social regulations. Japanese companies are pursuing flexibility inside their subsidiary factories, which is accepted by local environmental factors.

Conclusion

Let us summarize the findings of our survey research concerning the transferability of the Japanese system to Europe. As for transferability, the answer is positive through hybridization. Japanese multinationals employed a cautious investment strategy toward Europe. It was a response to the strict regulations imposed upon trade by the member countries and the European Commission, which continued from the 1970s to the 1990s. In the application-adaptation relationship, Japanese companies encountered an interesting phenomenon that in Europe adaptation to the elements of the local system could be application of the Japanese system. In Europe, Japanese firms could rely upon functional equivalent that the elements of the local system in formality, once incorporated in the Japanese system, could function as application of the Japanese system. This can be seen in wage system, skill formation and labor relations, major elements that form the Japanese system. The hybrid patterns in Europe, to our surprise, are closer to that of Asia. It was because the local labor environment was compatible with the Japanese system despite the cautious or passive attitude toward investment.

Coming into the 21st century, regulation by the European Commission on trade has been removed and the expanded EU is providing Japanese multinationals with new investment opportunities. As this survey of Hungary shows, Central and Eastern Europe as a new European periphery is likely to have flexibility to accept the Japanese system.

Notes

1. Concerning international transferability of the Japanese management and production system, there are more diverse points of contention including universality of the system and difference and similarities between Japan's work organization and Europe's semi-autonomous work group, but here,

only minimum two points, namely, history of the research and functional equivalent in work environment are discussed. This chapter based on the field research in 1997–98.

2. Ministry of Finance, *Ministry of Finance Statistics*, monthly, No.608.
3. By industry, too, the factories in the UK are also relatively large in size. In case of auto-related industries, factories in the UK naturally have a large number of employees, as they are predominantly automobile assembly factories. In electronics industry, too, UK factories are larger. In the latter's case, there are five factories in the UK with more than 1000 employees, whereas in Continental Europe, only one factory in France employs more than 1000 personnel. All the others are relatively smaller in size.
4. Interview at the headquarters of the Fédération Nationale de l'Energie-CGT.

References

Abo, Tetsuo (ed.) (1994) *Hybrid Factory: The Japanese Production System in the United states*, New York: Oxford University Press.

Boyer, Robert, Elsie Charron, Ulrich Jürgens and Steven Tolliday (eds) (1998) *Between Imitation and Innovation: The Transfer and Hybridization of Productive Models in the International Automobile Industry*, New York: Oxford University Press.

Cawson, Alan, Kevin Morgan, Douglas Webber, Peter Holmes and Anne Stevens, (1990) *Hostile Brothers: Competition and Closure in the European Electronics Industry*, Oxford: Clarendon Press.

Dohse, K., U. Jürgens and T. Malsch (1985) 'From Fordism Toyotism? The Social Organization of the Labour Process in the Japanese Automobile Industry', *Politics and Society*, 14(2).

Elger, Tony and Chris Smith (eds) (1994) *Global Japanization? The Transnational Transformation of the Labour Process*, London: Routledge.

—— (2005) *Assembling Work: Remaking Factory Regimes in Japanese Multinationals in Britain*, New York: Oxford University Press.

Freyssenet, Michel, Andrew Mair, Koichi Shimizu and Giuseppe Volpato (eds) (1998) *One Best way? Trajectories and Industrial Models of the World's Automobile Producers*, New York: Oxford University Press.

Freyssenet, Michel, Koichi Shimizu and Giuseppe Volpato (eds) (2003) *Globalization or Regionalization of the American and Asian Car Industry?*, Basingstoke: Palgrave Macmillan.

—— (eds) (2003) *Globalization or Regionalization of the European Car Industry?*, Basingstoke: Palgrave Macmillan.

Kenney, Martin and Richard Florida (1993) *Beyond Mass Production: The Japanese System and its Transfer to the US*, New York: Oxford University Press.

Kujawa, Duane (1986) *Japanese Multinationals in the United States: Case Studies*, New York: Praeger.

Kumon, Hiroshi and Tetsuo Abo (eds) (2004) *The Hybrid Factory in Europe: The Japanese Management and Production System Transferred*, Basingstoke: Palgrave Macmillan.

Liker, Jeffrey K., W. Mark Fruin and Paul Adler (eds) (1999) *Remade in America: Transplanting and Transforming Japanese Management Systems*, New York: Oxford University Press.

Mason, Mark (1997) *Europe and The Japanese Challenge: The Regulation of Multinationals in Comparative Perspective*, New York: Oxford University Press.

Oliver, N. and B. Wilkinson (1992) *The Japanization of British Industry 2nd edn.*, Oxford: Blackwell.

Schonberger, R.J. (1982) *Japanese Manufacturing Technique: Nine Hidden Lessons in Simplicity*, New York: Free Press.

Takamiya, Makoto (1981) 'Yoroppa niokeru Nihon no Takokuseki-Kigyo: Sono Katudo to Kokyo-Seisaku Nitaisuru Ganni' (Japanese Multinationals in Europe: Its Operation and their Public Policy Implications) in Takamiya Shin (ed.), *Takokuseki-Kigyo to Keiei no Kokusai-hikaku (International Comparison of the Multinational Enterprise and its Management)*, Tokyo: Dobunkan, pp. 145–72.

Trevor, Malcolm (1983) *Japan's Reluctant Multinationals: Japanese Management at Home and Abroad*, New York: St Martin's Press.

Tsurumi, Y. (1976) *The Japanese are Coming: A Multinational Interaction of Firms and Politics*, Cambridge, Mass: Ballinger.

Turnbull, Peter (1986) 'The "Japanization" of British Industrial Relations at Lucas', *Industrial Relations Journal*, 17(3).

Womack, James, Daniel Jones and Daniel Roos (eds) (1990) *The Machine that Changed the World*, New York: Rawson Associates and Macmillan.

Yoshino, Michael Y. (1976) *Japan's Multinational Enterprise*, Cambridge, Mass: Harvard University Press.

7

Japanese Hybrid Factories in Transitional Economies in Central and Eastern Europe: with a Focus on Czech, Poland, Hungary and Slovakia

Yuan Zhi Jia

Introduction

In January 1990, immediately after the systemic transformation was enforced upon the former socialist countries in Eastern Europe, a summit meeting of the Conference on Security and Co-operation in Europe (CSCE) was held in Paris. At this meeting, Francois Mitterand, then the President of France, raised an alarm in addressing to the European leaders as follows:

> If the political division is replaced by an economic division, a new crisis shall emerge. A 'curtain of economic disparity' taking over the 'iron curtain' shall divide Europe into 'the rich' and 'the poor', creating a new tension in this part of the world.[1]

Fourteen years later, we witnessed cataclysms in Europe. On 1 May 2004, the European Union received ten countries in Central and Eastern Europe as new members of the organization and EU25 system thus came into being.

The expansion of the EU to the east has made positive contributions to the development of the world economy and is facilitating the mobility of goods, capital and labor. In particular, the capital of developed countries is pouring into Central and Eastern Europe gearing towards the growth potential of the newly affiliated member countries in this region. During the six years until their participation in the EU, five major countries in Central and Eastern Europe (Czech, Slovakia, Poland, Hungary and Slovenia) attracted approximately 80 billion Euro (about 11 trillion yen) of FDI. Direct investment by Japanese firms, whose presence used to be only minor in this region, rapidly increased during this period. According to the statistics of Japan External Trade Organization (JETRO), the number of the Japanese manufacturing companies already operating in Central and Eastern Europe reached 137 as of the end of 2003, doubling from the number three years earlier. Auto-related industries account for nearly half of the direct investment of Japanese firms, reaching a comparable level with that of Germany, a major investor in the region. With sales companies and other non-manufacturing sector included, 300 or more Japanese firms are operating in this region.[2]

This chapter seeks to clarify the current situation, the characteristics and significance of the transfer of the Japanese production system in this region with a focus on the Japanese manufacturing firms rapidly developing local production in Central and Eastern Europe. The following three questions will be the basis of our approach.

First is the question of transferability of the Japanese production system into transitional economies. The Central and East European transitional economies are, as described earlier, in the stage of rapid transition from the socialist planned economy to market economy, and they still retain legacies that are not in line with market economy. Most typically, they labor practices from the socialist time. As stated later, we observed in the testimonies obtained through our field study such legacies in the area of employees' commitment and loyalty to the management. We also observed a few remnants of the practice of the state meddling in labor issues. Can Japanese firms in such an environment possibly transfer in this region their human resource management system and production control practices, which constituent their competitive advantage? And if transferable, how can they live together with those remnants of the former system in the region (using our key terminology, a question of 'application' and 'adaptation')?

Secondly, how viable is the Japanese production system being beleaguered by the European multinationals? It is well known that Central and East European transitional economies, while placed under the powerful influence of the former Soviet Union during the Cold War, were drew strongly influenced, both historically and culturally, by Western Europe, particularly Germany. After the transition began, massive capital came from the EU countries together with the transplanting of their corporate and production systems. As a result, it is likely that the production system of the EU countries gradually became the standard of the Central and East European countries. In this perspective, what kind of production system would the Japanese firms build in the region as they ventured into these transitional economies?

Thirdly, transitional economy is characteristically in the phase of consolidating a pattern for more rational systems amid the process of a new system replacing the old through trial and error. In what way would the Japanese firms, operating in the countries in such a phase, influence the formation of the local systems?

Japanese investments, their characteristics and the local managerial environment

First of all, let us give an overview of the direct investment made by Japanese companies in Central and East European transitional economies. The cumulative amount of direct investment by Japanese firms in the region until 1994 remained at an extremely low level of US$370 million, whereas in the latter half of the 1990s, the investment began increasing at such a pace of over US$100 million per annum from the following reasons:[3]

1. Prompted by the economic growth and the progress of the economic reform in Central and East European transitional economies, by the development of a single currency for the EU, and by the increased production cost of the Japanese subsidiaries in Britain due to stronger British sterling, Japanese companies operating in Europe undertook reviews of their production sites in view of enlarged Europe that includes Central and Eastern European transitional economies. As a matter of fact, when our team surveyed Japanese subsidiaries in Germany in 1998, a top manager involved in a Japanese subsidiary told us that 'the Japanese local production operations in Europe will shift from the west to the east and from the north to the south,' and through our field study this time, we came to realize that this prediction is becoming a reality.
2. Japanese parts manufactures became active in moving into the region as a supplier to Japanese firms in automobile and electronics industries, which were already operating in Western and other parts of Europe. The most typical case is the construction by Toyota Motor Corporation of their factories in Poland (a factory to manufacture transmissions and another for diesel engines) and in Czech (a joint venture with PCA for small cars; producing 300,000 units per annum starting in 2005). Following suit of Toyota, Toyota-affiliated parts and components manufacturers arrived in the region

one after another and built their plants in Central and Eastern Europe. In fact, several Toyota-affiliated parts manufacturers were included in our survey this time.

3. The most important factor was after all the participation of the Central and East European transitional economies in the EU. To auto and consumer electronics manufacturers, those transitional economies not only provide cheap labor but also serve as a foothold for the gigantic market including the EU as well as the neighboring former Soviet Union and its of area influence.

Against this backdrop, at the end of the 1990s, the cumulative amount of the Japanese investment into Central and East European transitional economies increased to US$1 billion. The number of direct investment by Japanese manufacturing companies, which counted only 70 in 2000, nearly doubled in the following three years to 2003 (137 companies as of our survey). In the following paragraphs, we shall look into the characteristics of site locations, triggers of the investment and industrial characteristics of the Japanese investment in the region.

First of all, the site locations of the Japanese direct investment in Central and Eastern Europe is concentrated characteristically in a few countries rather than spreading throughout the region. Specifically, the amount directly invested in three countries, Czech, Poland and Hungary has an overwhelming share in the total amount invested in Central and East European transitional economies. This is shown in Table 7.1, which summarizes the Japanese FDI in 2002. In 2002, Japanese investment in Central and East European transitional economies (EU10) accounted for only 0.5 per cent of the entire Japanese FDI in the amount of 24.4 billion yen, which was heavily concentrated in the aforementioned three countries. Table 7.2 shows the result of the questionnaire survey conducted by *Nihon Keizai Shimbun*, and this also indicates that these three countries are considered the most attractive factory site locations by Japanese manufacturing enterprises.

Secondly, let us consider the triggers of the Japanese investment. Why did the Japanese investment concentrate in a few countries, that is, Czech, Poland and Hungary, as we have seen?

1. The biggest reason we were given was 'wage cost and easy procurement of human resource.'[4] In our field of study, we obtained the same information from a Japanese firm already operating in the region. Table 7.3 portrays the merits of investment for Japanese

Table 7.1 Japanese FDI towards 4 surveyed countries and other regions (2003, 100 million yen)

	All industries	*Manufacturing*	*Pulp*	*Chemical*	*Iron*	*Machinery*	*Electronic*	*Transport*	*Others*
Whole World	44,175	17,757	161	2,336	771	1,570	4,773	5,992	1,651
EU25	18,108	6,007	13	439	35	798	492	3,567	642
Original EU15	17,864	5,771	10	438	27	787	459	3,407	622
New EU10	244	236	3	1	8	11	33	160	20
Czech	166	160	3	0	2	3	4	129	20
Hungary	58	56	–	1	1	–	28	26	–
Poland	20	20	–	–	5	8	2	6	–
Slovakia	–	–	–	–	–	–	–	–	–
USA	9,913	5,991	14	1,361	163	459	2,999	798	85
China	2,152	1,712	26	175	138	191	381	236	383

Source: Institute for International Trade and Investment, 'International Trade and Investment', May 2004.

Table 7.2 The most attractive EU countries for Japanese FDI

Manufacturing (responses of 101 Japanese firms)			*Non-manufacturing (responses of 56 Japanese firms*		
No. 1	Czech	27.70%	No. 1	UK	44.60%
No. 2	Hungary	20.80%	No. 2	Germany	42.90%
No. 3	Poland	16.80%	No. 3	France	33.90%

Source: Nihon Keizai Shimbun, 29 Nov. 2001.

Table 7.3 The competitive advantages in Central & Eastern Europe

1. Emerging manufacturing market.
2. Highly educated human resource.
3. Stable employment (low leave rate)
4. Highly potential of technological ability
5. Advanced logistics
6. Cheap production cost

Source: Based on the data obtained from a Japanese subsidiary in Czech.

firms and it seems that the competitive advantages as a manufacturing market and a production base are found in these three countries.

2. Prospective currency unification (the introduction of Euro) is another driving force of the increasing investment of Japanese enterprises. Namely, when the distribution of Euro cash begins, the consumers within the Euro area are likely to be more price-sensitive. It may well be the case that these three countries were chosen as a supply base in order to capture the Euro-using market.
3. Central and East European transitional economies have an advantage of being located literally in the center of continental Europe. Former Soviet Union and its neighboring countries form a market indispensable for the Japanese firms as a prospective market of tremendous potential. Also attractive is their proximity to the advanced region of Western Europe.
4. Market demand potential of this region is attractive all the same. A manager involved in a Japanese subsidiary told us, 'The population accounts for 15% of the enlarged EU, whereas the market share in sales does not yet correspond to this ratio. Their purchase power, however, is growing, making it a very promising market.' As this statement demonstrates, Japanese enterprises are also going after the market potential of this region.

Table 7.4 The number of Japanese firms that invested in 4 surveyed countries

	Manufacturing *No. of firms*	*Automobile-related*	*Sales company & others*	*Total*
Poland	26	18	48	74
Czech	56	29	62	118
Slovakia	8	5	4	12
Hungary	33	19	54	87
Total	123	71	168	291

Source: Nihon Keizai Shimbun, 19 Aug. 2003.

Thirdly, the industry-wise characteristic of the Japanese investment is simple and clear. They are concentrated on the two industries, 'automobiles' and 'electronics.' Table 7.4 shows the industries in which Japanese firms invested in the four surveyed countries from our field study. According to this data, as of August 2003, there were 123 Japanese local subsidiaries that were already established or the decision had been made to establish, out of which 71 (equivalent to 57 per cent) were auto-related industries. In Czech, for example, in August 2003, when we conducted our field study, 50 Japanese manufacturers were either operational or had decided on local production. Of the 50, there were 32 auto-related firms, 9 electronics and 9 others.[5] Obviously, there are rationales for the focused investment in auto industries. Although the economic size of the newly affiliated EU member countries is only 5 per cent of the enlarged EU, their potential is greater, as compared with that of Western Europe, which has already reached maturity. According to a source of a Japanese auto subsidiary, 'as a stricter environmental standard of the EU is introduced, great replacement demand shall be created. Also promising is the demand for the second cars among the wealthy class.'[6] For instance, 54 per cent of the passenger cars in Poland are 11 years or older after manufacturing. The old cars sold immediately after the collapse of the socialist system, have to be renewed and the car ownership ratio is less than half of that of Western Europe and this makes a great potential demand. The same source also commented, 'Unlike China, Central and Eastern Europe shall not be a world factory due to the limitation in size. However, only Central and Eastern Europe can serve as a production base geared toward the European market, which accounts for a quarter of the world's consumer electronics market.'[7] This rightly reveals the investment trigger on the part of Japanese multinationals.

Table 7.5 The overview of the 4 surveyed countries (by 2002)

	Czech	*Hungary*	*Poland*	*Slovakia*
Population (10 thousand)	1,024.60	992.3	3,862.20	539.82
GDP (million US$)	73,565.70	64,926.50	188,996.90	24,188.40
Per Capita GDP (US$)	7,180.20	6,543.20	4,893.50	4,480.80
Inward FDI (million US$)	39,395.10	28,717.20	47,900.00	8,529.80

Source: Institute for International Trade and Investment, 'International Trade and Investment', May 2004.

And what exactly is the managerial environment of Central and East European transitional economies where Japanese firms are heavily investing?

First of all, the environment in macro-economic perspective is characterized as a 'small economy' plus the 'income level of a less developed country'. As Table 7.5 shows, of the four countries, the size of the GDP of each of the three countries apart from Poland is only equivalent to the annual turnover of a major Japanese firm. In fact, the total economic size of the ten countries newly participated in the EU is less than that of the Netherlands. However, their per-capita GDP is at the level of a less developed country.

Secondly, as shown in Table 7.6, the economic growth rates of the countries where Japanese companies invested are considerably higher than that in Western Europe. Obviously, 2–3 per cent level of growth cannot be comparable with that of East Asia, but in view of the barely growing EU economy, Central and East European transitional economy is a promising region that enhances the potential growth of the EU as a whole and attracts foreign investment.

Thirdly, high unemployment rate is a difficult problem in these countries, but to foreign investors it is an element that makes the hiring of qualified workers easier. The region has so far posted a double-digit unemployment rate. In fact, the Japanese subsidiaries we

Table 7.6 The economic growth rate in the 4 surveyed countries (%)

	2001	*2002*	*2003*	*2004*
Poland	1.0	1.4	2.5	3.0
Czech	3.1	2.0	2.3	2.7
Slovakia	3.3	2.3	4.0	5.0
Hungary	3.8	4.4	3.2	3.5

Source: Nihon Keizai Shimbun, 18 July 2003.

surveyed replied unanimously that 'there is no problem' in hiring quality personnel.

Fourthly, the cheap labor costs in this region, compared with the West European countries, is the most lucrative element to Japanese industries. The current wage level of the Central and East European transitional economies, which varies depending on the type of jobs and from country to country, is generally 10.50 per cent of the West European level. On the other hand, those countries enjoy a high level of education. Allegedly, it would take at least ten years for their living standard and the wage level to reach the West European levels, and the Japanese firms operating in the region can take advantage of the cheap labor cost as it is currently.

Fifthly, the high skill levels of the workers provide Japanese firms with a favorable environment. Taking an example of the same industry in Germany and in Czech, although the wage difference of the two countries is approximately 6 to 1, 'there is no difference between Germany and Czech in the skill level of workers.'[8] Though different from the 'meister system', which has supported the high manufacturing skills in Germany, Czech, too, has a long-established infrastructure for training and educating skilled techniques, enjoying quality labor force that made the country a 'manufacturing plant' of the East in the socialist time. As a matter of fact, in our field survey, we heard a similar testimony from a person involved in a local plant of a Japanese firm.

Overview of the field study in 2003

In the summer of 2003, our research team surveyed 34 Japanese and local companies in Czech, Hungary, Poland and Slovakia. Through the research, valuable and influential information was acquired with regards to the situation of the transfer of the Japanese production system in the Japanese factories engaged in local production in Central and Eastern European transnational economies. As such, through the field study in some of the local companies and the participation of local researchers in the survey, we have been able to obtain a picture of the present situation of the local management and production systems to a certain extent. In Japan, there has been no appropriable large-scale field survey of the corporate management and production systems in Central and East European transitional economies. It is for this very reason that we wish to disseminate the information we have obtained in the research concerning this little-studied subject with a view to making contributions to the various academic areas concerned.

Table 7.7 shows an overview of the Japanese firms the team surveyed in 2003.

As for the location of the surveyed firms, 9 are located in Czech (including one government-affiliated office), 12 in Hungary, 10 in

Table 7.7 Overview of Japanese firms in Central and Eastern Europe (surveyed in 2003)

Firms	*Location*	*Ownership*	*Industry*
C1	Czech	Japanese	Food
C2	Czech	Japanese	Automobile parts
C3	Czech	Japanese	Automobile parts
C4	Czech	Japanese	Fiber
C5	Czech	Japanese	Automobile parts
C6	Czech	Japanese	Electronic parts
C7	Czech	Japanese	Electronic assembly
C8	Czech	Japanese	Electronic parts
C9	Czech	Japanese	NA
H1	Hungary	Japanese	Automobile parts
H2	Hungary	Japanese	Electronic parts
H3	Hungary	Japanese	Automobile parts
H4	Hungary	Japanese	Automobile parts
H5	Hungary	Japanese	Automobile parts
H6	Hungary	Japanese	Automobile parts
H7	Hungary	Japanese	Automobile parts
H8	Hungary	Japanese	Electronic parts
H9	Hungary	Japanese	Electronic parts
H10	Hungary	Japanese	Electronic parts
H11	Hungary	Japanese	Automobile parts
H12	Hungary	Japanese	Electronic parts
P1	Poland	Japanese	Others
P2	Poland	French	Electronic parts
P3	Poland	Local	Others
P4	Poland	Japanese	Automobile parts
P5	Poland	Japanese	Automobile parts
P6	Poland	Japanese	Electronic parts
P7	Poland	Japanese	Automobile parts
P8	Poland	Japanese	Automobile assembly
P9	Poland	Japanese	Automobile parts
P10	Poland	Japanese	Automobile parts
S1	Slovakia	Japanese	Automobile parts
S2	Slovakia	Japanese	Electronic parts
S3	Slovakia	Japanese	Automobile parts
Total	34		

Source: Author's data.

Poland and 3 in Slovakia. All the major recipient countries of the Japanese direct investment are covered by our research.

Secondly, the industries targeted in our survey were predominantly automobile and electronics-related, as is also the case with the target industries of our earlier research teams. Specifically, 18 companies are in auto assembly and auto parts industries, 11 in electronics assembly and electronics parts, and 5 are in others. In fact, Japan's FDI in Central and Eastern Europe is heavily focused on the two areas of automobile and electronics, and our target companies are also in line with this trend.

Thirdly, an overwhelming majority of the surveyed Japanese companies arrived in this region around mid-1990s. Immediately after the regime change in 1989, their economic growth plunged, which was followed by confusion and repeated trials and errors that continued until the first half of the 1990s, and after that the economy began picking up. As shown in Table 7.8, the recovery rates of the four countries we have surveyed rank in the top tier among the new EU member countries. Japanese multinationals thus began their direct investment in this region, which apparently was settling down, and business in Central and Eastern Europe finally picked up.

Fourthly, as for the form of ownership, wholly owned Japanese subsidiaries prevail. This also had a significant impact on the timing of the Japanese investment. At the early stage of the regime change, the governments of Central and East European transitional economies wanted foreign capital to purchase and/or consolidate their state-owned enter-

Table 7.8 Economic recovery rate of Central & Eastern European economies

Country	*Recovery rate*	*Growth rate (%)*	*Year of economic transition*
Czech	95	1.70	1992
Hungary	99	3.10	1993
Poland	122	5.10	1991
Slovakia	100	4.90	1993
Slovenia	109	3.80	1992
Estonia	77	3.20	1994
Latovinia	60	2.60	1993
Lithuania	62	3.00	1993
Bulgaria	67	3.00	1994
Rumania	76	0.00	1992

Note: Recovery rate: 1989's GDP=100.
Source: Institute for International Trade and Investment, 'An Inquirey into the Economic Structure Reform and FDI in Eastern Europe', p. 1, March 2001.

prises. In other words, the initial plan was to promote privatization of state-owned enterprises (SOE) through merger and acquisition (M&A) by foreign capital. However, contrary to their expectations, there was no take-over style direct investment by foreign capital except in certain countries (Poland, for example). In the latter half of the 1990s, taxation on investments was considerably eased and such regulations as limiting the ownership ratio and restricting cash transfer and employment were abolished, which helped foreign capital to shift their focus on green-field investment.[9] Against this backdrop, Japanese multinationals increasingly chose wholly owned subsidiaries for their investment.

Fifthly, in relation with the above, some of the companies we surveyed were not yet in full operation and some plants were test operating. In this respect, there are some gaps in the observation. Nonetheless, we believe the information and data we have gathered are one the whole significant.

Transfer of the Japanese production systems

In this chapter, by way of the 'application–adaptation hybrid model' and the 'five-scale evaluation method' developed by the Japanese Multinational Enterprise Study Group (JMNESG),[10] we shall evaluate how the Japanese production system has been transferred by the Japanese firms in their local plants as they ventured into Central and East European region. Table 7.9 shows the scores for the 29 factories that it is possible to evaluate and that are highly representative of the 34 Japanese companies operating in the four countries of Czech, Hungary, Poland and Slovakia. Let us, by referring to Table 7.9, review and analyse the results of the 'Six-group, 23-Item hybrid evaluation'.

Group 1: 'Work organization and administration'

First, the average score of 'Job classification,' an element, which is typically Japanese, was high at 4.1 points. We had expected that the Japanese job classification system with a high degree of flexibility would meet with much resistance in this region, where the Soviet version of the American mass production system was influential during the socialist era, but the situation was found otherwise. Namely, a simplified job classification system of a Japanese style has been transplanted favorably in the surveyed factories with no opposition coming from their employees. Japanese-style job classification system is applied to most of the Japanese factories we surveyed with virtually no resistance.

Table 7.9 The Japanese production system transferred in 4 surveyed countries

Groups/elements	*Average scores*
Work organization/administration	3.3
1. Job Classification	4.1
2. Job Rotation	2.8
3. Education & Training	3.4
4. Wage	2.9
5. Promotion	3.3
6. Supervisor	3.2
Production control	3.3
7. Equipment	4.0
8. Maintenance	2.8
9. Quality Control	3.0
10. Operation Management	3.4
Parts procurement	2.6
11. Local Content	2.2
12. Suppliers	2.8
13. Procurement Methods	2.7
Team sense	2.8
14. Small Group Activities	2.0
15. Information Sharing	3.2
16. Sense of Unity	3.2
Labor relations	3.3
17. Employment policy	3.2
18. Employment Security	3.0
19. Labor Union	3.8
20. Grievance	3.3
Parent/subsidiary	2.8
21. Japanese Ratio	1.7
22. Power Delegation	3.1
23. Local Manager	3.4
Total Average Score	3.1

Source: Author's data.

The average application degree of 'Job rotation' is the lowest in this group (2.8). Although many surveyed factories said that they are clearly 'practicing multifunctional skill development', yet there is considerable variation in their levels of implementation. One of the auto parts manufacturers affiliated with a major auto maker in Czech and the auto parts manufacturer in Hungary have applied the system and the method of the factories in Japan exactly as it is including the 'skill clearance score sheet', and earnestly promoting multifunctional skill development. On the other hand, we had an impression that the electronics-related factories are somewhat falling behind in introducing multifunctional skill development methods, though at every plant we visited, we were told, 'if feasible, the system shall be introduced.' We consider that the reasons for the delay in the transfer of multifunctional skill development method are as follows: (1) in the former planned economy, division of labor was so strict in the factories of manufacturing industries that multifunctional skill development was not necessarily encouraged. In fact, the author, who made field studies of quite a few factories in China, observed similar phenomenon in local and indigenous as well as Japanese factories in China; (2) in view of the shorter history of operation, the development of multifunctional skills seems to be the managerial challenge for the future, and (3) this is an issue also relevant to local regulation. In Slovakia, for instance, due to the presence of legal regulation that stipulates 'Job is determined by the agreement between the employee and the company and no unilateral direction shall be permitted,' it is difficult to introduce multifunctional skill development to the entire employees.

The score of 'Education & Training' is slightly favorable for Japan (3.4). Many surveyed factories have established OJT-type shop-floor training systems by making efforts to introduce 'skill clearance score sheet' and other relevant methods. The above-mentioned Toyota-affiliated auto parts maker, though yet to be fully operational, is making a strong effort towards education and training at the production floor. They have introduced 'mastering more than two works' as a basic rule for operators of the assembly line, thereby establishing a 'skill clearance score sheet' training system under the control of a team leader. The management introduced a provision that requires the mastering of the skills for all the eight processes in order to be promoted to the first-line supervisor. Some factories introduced training programs and some provide employees with training opportunities in a sister factory in other part of Europe or in a parent factory in Japan.

The 'Wage system,' which is related to job classification, scored 2.9, just at the level of 'hybridization.' In fact, most of factories we surveyed are practicing the wage system that addresses each employee by introducing an appraisal system and placing a greater emphasis on job performance. For example, an auto parts manufacturer in Czech is trying to establish a wage system that involves such an appraisal system, in which 'performance evaluation is implemented twice a year,' 'performance is evaluated by ranks A, B, C and D for wage increase, and annual wage hike is hopefully to be introduced' and 'bonus should be differentiated.' On the contrary, the introduction of Japanese-style wage system still faces some difficulties. For example, one factory in Hungary (H3) practices 'hourly wage system' irrespective of performance. Generally the score of 2.9 is a result that reflects the current practice of wage management slightly favorable for Japanese system. On the other hand, further effort seems to be necessary in the coming days. However, through our field study, we believe that Japanese style wage system is highly possible to be transferred to the region. The reasons are as follows. (1) As described earlier, a drastic change from the old to new systems represents the characteristics of transitional economies. Following the collapse of the systems from the socialist time, new systems to replace them are yet to be established and the wage system is one of them; and (2) the governments of the Central and East European countries, being particularly keen to solicit foreign investments, are not practicing strict labor and wage regulations as in Western Europe. Therefore, the wage system transplanted by foreign companies did not encounter strong legal or political barriers.

The score of 'Promotion' is more favorable (3.3). This is because most of the factories we have surveyed are consistently practicing the policy for promotion inclined toward the Japanese system that emphasizes 'internal promotion' as well as performance result and refrains from promoting and recruiting from the sources outside the company. It is true that there were a few cases in which management executives at a high level were recruited from outside due to the short history of operations, but the factories were predominantly adamant in appointing first-line supervisors by promoting their 'production floor' workers.

The score of 'Supervisor' was 3.2. In relation with the above 'Promotion,' internal promotion was by and by established, but seemingly it will take a considerable time before they reach the level of Japanese counterparts in the parent company in terms of experience and competence.

Group II: Production control

The scores of 'Equipment' reached a high level of 4.0 but the actual situation sharply fluctuated above and below the average (3.3) from one factory to another. Some use 90 per cent or more equipment imported from Japan or exactly the same equipment with those in its parent factory (3 companies) and some use equipment either locally procured or imported from other parts of the EU. And there is no industry-specific tendency. Closer observation, however, finds some kind of rationality. For example, in the case of the auto parts maker in Czech (C5), equipment was purchased mostly from Germany. German-made large equipment is almost comparable with Japanese counterpart in terms of quality and performance. And German makers are willing to serve them whenever needs arise capitalizing on the geographical proximity. On the other hand, they have imported dies, the key part of the equipment, from Japan. In a nutshell, there was a big difference from factory to factory in this item.

The score of 'Maintenance' is 2.8, the lowest among the elements in the Group. This is because maintenance personnel and production floor workers are hired and trained separately. This is how maintenance is served in the overwhelming majority of the factories except in a few factories. Although only a few testimonies were obtained from the survey, we assume that this reflects the strong legacy from the former socialist systems. Namely, in former socialist countries, equipment personnel and production floor workers in manufacturing factories were trained and treated very differently. The status of equipment technicians was higher. Such a practice is indeed frequently observed in factories in China, which is also a transitional economy.

The score of 'Quality Control' is slightly favorable for Japan, reaching 3.0 points. Probably in relation to the equipment we have discussed above, a very clear attitude was observed that careful quality control measures are never to be compromised, no matter if locally procured equipment is used. However, it looks like that the transplant of a practice of 'Building quality in the production process' as we see it in Japan, will take longer than expected. In one case, non-Japanese methods such as sample inspection of half-finished products and checking defects as part of 'Building quality in the production process' are practiced locally, but the reliability test that is hard to implement locally is done in Japan' (H3), and in another case, harsh programs are implemented in such a manner that 'every product has to go through final inspection and the photographs of the employees with many defects are openly displayed in the factory' (S3). Further, as may be related with the unfavorable implementation of small group activities for QC, local Japanese subsidiaries are trying their hardest using a variety of tools for the sake of quality control.

The score of 'Operation management' remains at a high level of 3.4 unaffected by the above. However, in our field survey, we very often heard it stated that the industrial sense of the workers and technicians in Central and Eastern Europe is superior to that of the Asian counterparts. Despite shorter period of operation, many of their work standards of the production floor have been developed locally. In many factories, Japanese managers and engineers highly commended the ability for improvement and problem-solving skills on the part of local technicians. This is a phenomenon not often observed in the Japanese subsidiaries in Asia.

Group III: Parts procurement

The average score of this group was the lowest in all 6 groups (2.6). On the other hand, the low application score reflects the special situation about Europe's solid foundation of manufacturing industries.

The low application degree of 'Local content' (2.2) and 'Suppliers' (2.8) is partly a reflection of the unique condition in Europe. Many of the surveyed companies, asked for the reason for purchasing materials and parts from local markets or from the EU, answered that they deliberately increased the local procurement rate to benefit from 'Euro 1' (an EU regulation that stipulates that a company with less than 60 per cent local procurement rate cannot receive the full benefit of the favorable tax duty). What is significant is the point that many of the surveyed companies are parts manufacturers and that they are contributing to increasing the local procurement ratio of their clients by raising their own. However, a closer look into the local procurement reveals that many factories purchase either general-purpose and/or low-value added goods from the local market, while importing special materials and core parts from Japan. Many factories also use Japanese factories operating in Europe as local suppliers when they purchase from the EU or local markets.

Group IV: Team sense

The average score of 'team sense' is fairly low (2.8). Of the Group, 'Small group activities' posts the second lowest of the 23 items (2.0). Many factories said that they are not doing small group activities at all. Even those who said that they did, are in the initial stage of trial and error and very few have attained any substantial result. Due to the shorter period of operation, the management is probably still fully occupied by the work to start up the production, and apparently small group activities are left on the back burner. In contrast, the scores of 'Information sharing' and 'Sense of unity' are somewhere in the middle at the same score of 3.2, slightly leaning toward Japan. This result can be interpreted that there are aspects that offset the weakness of being reluctant in practicing small group activities. The majority of the surveyed factories are trying to organize various measures and activities to enhance information sharing and the sense of unity among employees (meetings, employee house organs and social get-togethers). However, the elements of this group apparently require ingenious plans to be worked out as an important challenge for the future.

Group V: Labor relations

'Employment policy' scored 3.2. 'The hiring and securing of homogeneous employees by multi-step selection process' is guaranteed by the local environment. Hundreds or even a thousand times more applications of the actual number of hires that reflect the high unemployment rate in the region, provides the Japanese subsidiaries with ample leeway to select qualified personnel – in the case of C6, located in Czech, from a large number of applicants selected candidates who are likely to fit into the company. This is followed by a thorough interview (to check the language ability, former jobs, education level, resident-place, etc.). This means that the employee hired after all this are 'nice young people with good quality.'

In contrast, the score of 'Employment security' is relatively low (3.0). Most of the Japanese factories our team has surveyed, rather than adopting the policy of 'guaranteeing long-term employment,' often conclude contracts of short-term employment. According to a testimony of a manager in a Japanese factory, 'individual contracts are the local customary practice' (Czech, C6). One of the factories said that 'the contract is for two years and there are cases that the contract is not renewed' (P3). Such a situation seems to display the 'extravagance' the Japanese multinationals are enjoying in Central and Eastern Europe, which is suffering from two-digit unemployment rates.

As for 'Labor union' (3.8), too, there seem to be aspects commonly observed in China. That is the notion that 'good labor relation is taken for granted.' Of the most factories we have surveyed, many have no labor union at all. In the case of the factories that have labor unions, one said, 'labor relations are extremely favorable' (H3) and another said, 'the union does not negotiate wages' (P6). The overall impression we received about the labor unions in Central and Eastern European region is that they are 'peaceful unions' rather than militant organizations like UAW in the United States or Germany's IG Farben. And as part of the system reform required prior to the participation in the EU, in most of the Japanese subsidiaries, 'Works Council' is organized and the issues involving labor relations are discussed between the management and the Works Council to find agreeable solutions. Works Council is likely to play a bigger role in the future.

'Grievance procedure' also leans toward Japan (3.3). The result has much to do with the high score of 'Labor union.' Grievance is handled and solved predominantly through corporate ladders and via Works Councils.

Group VI: Parent–subsidiary relations

The average score of this group is 2.8, the second lowest of all the groups. In a nutshell, the score signifies 'strong adaptation to local systems' in parent–subsidiary relations. For example, the score of 'Japanese ratio' is 1.7, indicating that a small number of Japanese expatriates are controlling the local management through a large number of local managers. Presidents of several companies testified that they would 'continue to manage the factory with a small number of Japanese expatriates.' As for the relationship with the parent company, many supported the practice that 'the home office approves what has been proposed by the local subsidiary' and we had an impression that the operation is based on the local initiative from the very beginning. In reality, the managers of many of the surveyed factories apparently included Japanese expatriates competent and qualified for international management with much experience of working abroad in North America and the EU.

Conclusion: world comparison of hybrid factories and the characteristics of Central and Eastern Europe

So far, we have analysed the situation of the transfer of the Japanese production system in the Japanese factories operating in Central and Eastern Europe by '6-group, 23-item hybrid evaluation.' In conclusion, based on the result of the analysis, I shall point out the regional characteristics in broader perspective in comparison with the other Japanese operations throughout the world. Table 7.10 summarizes the level of hybridization of the Japanese firms operating throughout the world including Central and East European transitional economies. By referring to this, I shall explain the characteristics of the Japanese factories in Central and East European transitional economies.

First, as shown by the 'Average score' on Table 7.10, the hybridization level of the Japanese factories in Central and East European transitional economies is 3.1 points, a score between those placed in the middle of the UK and continental Europe. Table 7.10 demonstrates that our conclusion of the evaluation, that is, 'the management in Japanese factories in any region of the world is a hybrid of slightly

Table 7.10 The comparison of the hybrid factories all over the world

	N.A (1989)	*N.A (2001)*	*UK*	*C & E Europe*	*Cont. Europe*	*KRA/ TWN*	*ASEAN*	*China*
Work organization/ administration	2.9	3.2	3.4	3.3	3.0	3.7	3.3	3.5
Production control	3.3	3.4	3.5	3.3	3.1	3.5	3.4	3.3
Parts procurement	3.0	2.6	2.5	2.6	2.8	3.2	3.2	3.0
Team sense	3.2	3.3	3.3	2.8	2.7	3.4	3.2	3.0
Labor relations	3.6	3.7	3.6	3.3	3.2	3.4	3.2	3.1
Parent/subsidiary	3.6	2.8	2.8	2.8	3.0	2.3	2.6	2.7
Total Average	3.3	3.2	3.2	3.1	3.0	3.3	3.2	3.2

Source: Central & Eastern Europe's score was assessed by JMNESG. Other scores came from Abo (2004).

more than 50 per cent of Japanese elements and slightly less than 50 per cent of local elements,'[11] is also true in Central and East European transitional economies.

Secondly, as illustrated by the comparison of the scores of 'Work organization and administration,' Japanese factories in Central and East European transitional economies posted the third highest score next to Korea/Taiwan and the UK. As everyone knows, Korea and Taiwan, being extremely close to Japan both historically and culturally, may well score high points while the UK has a relatively flexible environment of labor and social regulation. But what exactly are the reasons for such a high score for Central and Eastern Europe, which is considerably remote from Japan in historical, cultural and geographical terms? Following rationales could be cited: (1) Japanese firms, being a minority in Central and East European transitional economies unlike multinational enterprises in the EU countries, need to secure footing from the very beginning of the operation. To this end, the elements in this Group that constitute the core of the Japanese production system presumably are prioritized in transferring the system; and (2) the regional environment in which labor and social regulations are looser apparently contributes to the higher score. In the case of the wage system, for example, unlike Western Europe, the region lacks a well-established wage system bound by regulations and customary practices, and this may make it easier to introduce a Japanese system.

Thirdly, the score of 'Team sense' is the second lowest of all the regions. The interpretation that emphasizes only the short history of the operation is not fully convincing. The author wishes to point out that this probably comes from the 'systemic inertia' from the former socialist era. The issues of human consciousness and the sense of incentives nurtured under the government and bureaucrat-led planned economy over half a century cannot be transformed only through the participation in the EU and the change of the system.

Fourthly, the score of 'Parent–subsidiary relations' is also as low as East Asian level. In other words, local subsidiaries take a fairly independent position. First of all, the result of 'a few Japanese expatriates controlling the local management' is largely due to the geographical position of the region. Namely, the region presents a pattern in which a few Japanese managers who are knowledgeable about the conditions of Central and East European transitional economies and have rich experience in working for European operations, control the local management in cooperation with local managers who are capable enough for the task. (This is a significant difference from South East Asia, where the role of local mangers is minor.) And this is something that proves the competitiveness of the Japanese multinationals that have gradually gained confidence in the international management. We were quite impressed by the high level of the international mind Japanese management demonstrated in responding to our survey.

Finally, I shall compare the hybrid pattern of the Japanese factories in the region. As shown in Table 7.10, the hybrid factory in Central and East European transitional economies has a pattern placed in the middle between the continental European type and the British type. The proximity level to the Japanese system is: the UK – Central and Eastern Europe Continental Europe, in that order. However, in comparison with the 'continental European type,' the application degree of Japanese core elements (Group I) is higher than that of continental Europe, while that of 'Parent–subsidiary relations' is lower. Explaining this phenomenon is not necessarily easy. We may as well say that the local managerial personnel in Central and Eastern Europe are fairly compatible with Japanese firms or their management system. At the same time, it may be the case that the Japanese management and production system that has reached as far as Central and Eastern Europe via North America, Asia and Western Europe, has now entered the phase in which they can be transferred effectively without any rigid control by the parent companies in Japan thanks to the accumulated experience of Japanese expatriate managers in international management. In view of this, the Japanese production system may as well be entering the phase of maturity after experiencing the expansion phase in the 1980s and the period of ordeal in the 1990s.

Notes

1. Tanaka (2004), 'Phase II of the historical transformation in European international relations: Road to one Europe', *International Trade and Investment*, Vol. 12, May 2004, Institute for International Trade and Investment (ITI), p.3.
2. *Nihon Keizai Shimbun*, 19 August 2003.
3. Institute for International Trade and Investment (ITI) (2001), Research study concerning direct investment in Eastern Europe and the economic structure, March 2001, ch. 3.
4. *Nihon Keizai Shimbun*, 29 November 2001.
5. Materials prepared by a local Office of JETRO at the time of our field survey.
6. *Nikkei Sangyo Shimbun*, 29 April 2004.
7. *Nikkei Sangyo Shimbun*, 20 May 2004.
8. *Nikkei Sangyo Shimbun*, 28 May 2004.
9. Iguchi (2000) 'Changing needs for corporate strategy and technology transfer and human resource movement in Central and Eastern Europe: An analysis based on the field survey of the Japanese enterprises, Kansai Gakuin University, *Kansai Gakuin Economic Review*, vol.54, No.1.
10. For 'Application–Adaptation' model, see Chapter 1 and Abo, (1994).
11. Testsuo (2004), p.47.

References

Abo, Tetsuo (ed.) (1994) *Hybrid Factory: The Japanese Production System in the United States*, N.Y: Oxford University Press.

Abo, Tetsuo, (2004) 'Kokusai Iten Kara Mita Nihonteki Keiei Kanri Hoshiki no Ippansei to Tokushusei – Nihon Gata Haiburiddo Keiei Moderu no Kentoh' ('Universality and particularity of the Japanese management and production method in view of international transfer: Analysis of Japanese hybrid management model') *Sekai Keizai Hyoron*, July 2004. (The main parts of this article are included in the chapter 1 of the present book.)

Heinz-Jurgen Stuting, Wolfgang Dorow, Frank Claassen and Susanne Blazejewskim (ed.) (2003) Chang Management in Transition Economies: Integrating Corporate Strategy, Structure and Culture. Palgrave Macmillan.

Iguchi, Yasushi (2000) 'Chutouou Shokoku niokeru Kigyou Senryaku Gijutsu Iten Niizu no Henka to Jinzai Ido' ('Changing needs for corporate strategy and technology transfer in Central and Eastern Europe and human resources movement: An analysis based on the field survey of the Japanese subsidiaries') Kansai Gakuin University, *Kansai Gakuin Economic Review*, vol. 54, no. 1.

ITI (2001) *Touou he no Chokusetsu Toushi to Keizai Kouzou ni Kansuru Chousa Kenkyu (Research study concerning direct investment in Eastern Europe and the economic structure)*.

Sadowski, B.M. (2001) 'Towards Market Repositioning in Central and Eastern Europe: International Coorperative Ventures in Hungary, Poland and the Czech Republic', *Research Policy*.

Strzelczak S. (ed.) (2003) *Economic and Managerial Development in Asia and Europe, Comparative Studies*, Karamist Ltd.

Tanaka, Tomoyoshi (20040 'Oushuu Kokusai Kankei no Rekishiteki Tenkanki Fe-zu2-EU25 25Kakoku Taisei to Hitotsu no Oushuu he no Doutei' ('Phase II of the Historical transformation in European international relations: Road to one Europe') *International Trade and Investment,* special issue vol. 12, May, 2004, ITI.

8 Discussions

Tetsuo Abo

In this chapter the main parts of discussions on the reports at the Teikyo symposium, included in Chapters 1 to 7, are recorded with small editorial adjustments. We chose this way to reproduce as far as possible the real processes of questions and answers at the symposium as we believed that would be an interesting and stimulating way of conveying to readers of this book very vividly the significant points of merits and demerits concerning the overall research results of the JMNESG. This is so important, not only for receiving outside evaluations on the existing research results but also for having a very important opportunity to improve and develop them further by finding out the positive and weak points involved. The discussions, as readers will see, were not always well organized, but we did not try, in the editing process, to reorganize questions and answers so they would be more consistent. It would not be fair to change the contents after the discussions ended.

Basically, almost all the questions by commentators and the replies by presenters of the reports are re-recorded with the exceptions of greeting words, and so on. On the other hand, it is a regret that the questions and answers between participants and reporters could not be included in this book due to a rigid limitation of space. At the end of this chapter only the names and some points of questions and comments raised are mentioned.

All the parts of discussions in this chapter were produced by transcribing the cassette tapes that recorded the simultaneous translations in Japanese and English in the process of comments and replies at the symposium. Therefore, the English itself cannot be expected to be completely correct even though the standard is very high. I hope generous readers will understand the usefulness and significance of these discussions.

Fujimoto to Abo

Fujimoto to Abo

I would like to congratulate the stability of the membership of the Professor Abo's team. I think this is rather characteristic of Japanese professionals, their workers. The turnover rate is very low, this is very outstanding and also I'd used the word 'integrated type of production system,' but it's very close to the Japanese-style production system in Professor Abo's team. And this has been compared with the American and the European types of 'division of labor,' and they are two extremes at the ends of the spectrum, and this approach can be criticized, but I think this approach is still very interesting and has been applied to many Japanese companies going out to every part of the world. And I believe that Japanese and American companies can also be subject to this approach – not only the Japanese subsidiaries operating in the world, but also, the, for example, MIT and other members have been applying this similar method, and for the last 5 years, I think the Japanese consumer electronic companies have changed greatly, so these changes could be incorporated into the method.

And also 'application and adaptation,' this is very interesting, and has useful terminology. Application and adaptation, it's easy to pronounce for all of us in both English and Japanese. And hybridization has become one of the terminologies used by the other renowned researchers, and I think, it is under the heavy influence of Professor Abo and his team's results. Professor Boyer, here we have today, is one of the good examples for that. And for the last several years, many other researchers have changed their positions, but Professor Abo and his team maintain the consistent positions and have had big influence on the changing situation of the Japanese economy itself. So I think this is another strength that the Professor Abo and his team have had in their research activities.

It might sound self-serving, but I said I use the word 'integral' in the management product system. I believe it's equivalent to the Japanese Production System. I think this is the result of the last half century at least but I think some reflect that for the last 500 years by Musasi Miyamoto's book, *Gorin no sho* (a text written by a Japanese great swardsman), for example, is the kind of involvement in which the activity in the field is what matters. But we still pay attention to the social background of a given country or location. But anyway, culture is exactly what matters, and particularly for the last 50 years, Japan experienced rapid economic growth and, of course, the experience at that time is reflected in what we are going through. But, of course, these are very exciting applications by the Toyota's integration method and other companies. But, Toyota's integration and other sectors' integration methods, I think, are basically the same and Professor Abo, extracted the essential factors for his analysis.

And then, specializing in production and the engineering management, and their positioning in the entire system, I like, therefore, his method of analysing and the part of information analysing – to read it as 'information of design.' So, designing information is invisible, but without that, we cannot look at the entirety. For example, it is rather complicated, and this is what I'd like to convey here in my message. But anyway, all the routines are orchestrated, so that everything will be operated smoothly until the information production is flowed into the customer. I think this is the most sound characteristic of the Toyota style, and Japanese style, the production method and all of these factors, almost the same as the factors that are identified and picked out by Professor Abo's team.

And this is the routine of the system, so the production processes are compared. First, the products are compared among various companies, which were carried out by Abo's team, for example (see Table 8.1), at the top is the auto industry, and at the bottom is the consumer electronics industry. So this is about the organization capability, and I think this is very interesting to see comparison between electronics and auto industry, because they have a different 'architecture' and also their products are different. This reflects what we have experienced for the last 10 years. And on the left-hand side, you see the functional designing, and also the right-hand side, the structural designing. So

Table 8.1 Basic types of architecture

	Integral	*Modular*
Closed	Closed/Integral type automobile, motor cycle, 'light/thin/short/small'-type consumer electronics, game software, etc.	Closed/Modular type main frame computer, machine tool, lego, etc.
Open		Open/Modular type personal computer & its systems, inter-net products, bicycle, some financial products, etc.

how to match these two is what is required. This is an example of PC, that I call 'modular type.' All functions are already developed and designed, just by simply connecting them in the best way. But the upper right, you see in the case of passenger car, that I call 'integral type,' there are functionalities, and the parts and components have to be more connected in a more complicated manner, otherwise they can not end up with good products.

I think consumer electronics should be positioned somewhere between these two, I mean between the PCs and the passenger cars. And smaller electronic products can be close to the passenger car, but the rather larger consumer products can be produced in a more modular production method, and automotive is here. Therefore, Professor Abo, as a result, is comparing the difference in architecture by taking up automobile and electronics industries. The passenger car comes into the integral, and motorcycles also in the integral, and Chinese motorcycles in the modular. Chinese passenger cars and Chinese PCs are all open-modular section. So in this central section there are many very commonly used parts and components, for example, the mainframe computer consists of many multipurpose parts and this is the lego. So you see this is the closed modular, because this doesn't connect with the similar toy with another brand. And so, if there is some affinity between organizational capability and architecture the competitiveness can be improved, product performance can be improved. If the affinity is poor, then I think the adaptation becomes more important. The hypothesis can be applied to home consumer electronics.

According to Professor Abo's theory, I think, we can make this kind of prediction on right bottom, right is the American type, and of course, this is the rather very subjective. This is not at all scientific, but Japan has scarce national resources, so long-term employment and long-term contractor relations is very important. And in Europe, this is my defined European, but they need strong brand appeals to other countries, otherwise they cannot compete with their neighbors who are relatively similar in thier size and type. So I think they have very high level of the skills in specifying themselves, and I think this is not similar to the American, because America is an immigrant nation where society itself is modular type, and in South Korea, chaebol is very strong, and their leadership in strength has been exerted in the capital intensive modular-type products, like in the other world cup of the football. As China has the strength in the mobilization they can mobilize perhaps in manufacturing labor intensive modular-type products. And I think in Southeast Asian countries, they are inexpensive in mobilizing more skilled workers for manufacturing labor incentive integral-type products. So each country, each nation has its own strength and characteristics.

And in the 20th century, Japanese and American production systems were representative, so I think these two are enough for the time being in our analysis, because all others are in a way of hybrid or mixture of the components of these two production methods – American or Japanese. So I think the dichotomy between Japan and America adopted by Professor Abo's team is very useful. But of course, China has its own model, judging from its history that it introduced the Russian production methods. However, I have a question for the competitivness of that model, so it is not directly compared with Japanese model, but I think there is some value in analysing Chinese model. But if you add that Chinese model the model itself becomes more complicated, so perhaps we can use Chinese model in identifying whether there are some similarities between the American and Chinese models and so on. And after that, the bottom at the diagram can be converged into the top of that diagram, so, but of course, should this hypothesis of mine be very fine? I'd like to do that perhaps in my research in the future.

Abo's reply to Fujimoto

As I introduced Professor Fujimoto's theory in passing, he has introduced the concept of the architecture, not just for myself, but for all of you as well. This is very useful for my replies and our discussions.

One of the questions raised by Professor Fujimoto is as to whether the parent plants in Japan have been the same, have not changed throughout these years. You are right. Within our group, we have been concerned with this point at all times as we had our discussions. But it's not that we have come up with a definite conclusion as of yet. Especially in regard to the electronics industry, and for its assembling sections in particular, there could be substantial changes, and also for the automotive more or less, as we looked at the model that was made at the 1980s as a benchmark. That was the time when Japanese automotive industry was most glorious. Subsequent to that, there must be changes, and we need to consider that. However, we are most interested in knowing how the transplants are judged from the benchmark established in the mid-1980s in Japan. That's the basis. Subsequent to that, if you look at the parent plants even in

Japan, they are the same or different from the plants in the 1980s. And we might be able to learn something from it. That is an idea that I think is quite interesting.

Next, as to whether the culture should be incorporated or not, of course, it's not that we speak in one voice, and as said, culture is not that static, nor is it absolute. But relatively, it changes, and you said that the culture was generated in 50 years in a country. And if you were in the United States, it was the other extreme vs. Japan. I would agree that there could be possibilities to change, for this is a matter too big to debate, but if I made touch on it just for one point, you need to consider that there are people come together to form society, and they pursue their lifestyle. And when they do it, it's from their perspective of organization theory. It's something that can't be changed that easily. Having said that, it doesn't mean that something has happened over here is never going to be transplanted to the other side, no. If you look at the United States, in order to get closer to the other side, it's going to be quite costly, and if you pay the cost, it's going to pay off. That would probably be the strategic judgment to be exercised by management.

Another point, which is important as Professor Fujimoto concluded, is that Japan and US are situated at two extremes. But others may be in between the two countries. Professor Boyer, you are right. And in our group, we had a heated debate on this issue, next to the US, maybe, we should look at Asia, and if US and Japan are the two poles, that's the application and adaptation model of 5 scales, and so it would be applicable, for example, in Korea, Taiwan, and other countries. But each time, if you are going to have Korean type of management, Malaysia type and German, French type of management style, and if you change your counter party, that's going to be very useful. But at the same time, if you want to make comparisons worldwide, and after, let's say, 10 years, it will be quite difficult to do so. For the good example about that, in 1989 and 2001, we should be able to make the comparison. And that if you include China, France, UK, and Germany, we should be able to compare the two time series and different zones. That's the strength of the model. But in France, what it is, and how is it in China, of course, we've gone through many plants in different countries, and we look at unique needs of locality, and unique needs of management style. And at the very end, we have included a descriptive explanation as a result of the analysis, so that we come to the integrated overall judgment, and we believe that we are making such efforts.

Okamoto to Kawamura

Okamoto to Kawamura

Professor Kawamura's report has carried out extensive analysis of the current situation and evaluation of the Japanese-style management and production system in North America, including a very meticulous research of the underlying social and environmental elements.

I think that Professor Kawamura's report was a kind of summarization of the research project of the JMNESG that Professor Abo has been leading. I was involved in similar projects before but currently are not really involved in them, so this was quite informative.

He remarks that the general application score of the Japanese factories surveyed in North America is 3.2 with no major change in this since the last survey in 1989. He explains that this would be the result of mutual-offsetting effects of two factors on the score: on the one hand, there is advancement in the localization in humans and materials that means lower application; on the other hand, the higher application in the management system. That is why there is no major change in the score.

The report emphasizes that there will be no changes in the long-term creation of the American system's competitive edge. It is also pointed out that great competitive pressures in North America under globalization, including ones from china, may affect the hybrid pattern of Japanese transplants in the area.

One point that I feel is problematic about the basic perspective of the 'Hybrid Model' is that its specific message is not clear. For instance, the research outcomes show that the ratio of Japanese expatriates is much lower now and also the condition or title of the local managers is being enhanced and decision-making has been led by local people more and more in factories, which have made the lower application scores. I would like to know the co-relation between these situations and the enhancement of the application in the Japanese-style management method aspects. Many of researchers of international business often discuss these facts to emphasize the localization issues. Such local adaptation has been treated as the major restraints to promotion of the competitiveness of local plants. So how to overcome the restraints constitutes one of the most important managerial tasks for the local plants, I think. Is that task of these two mutual-contradicting aspects resolvable well by head quarters or by the overseas local plants? In this context, the emotional cooperation aspects of localization are not very important for the management, because the survival of the company by increasing competitiveness is by far the first priority for them. Of course, it is definite that there are many applications of Japanese-style institutions in work organization and its administration. However, the deterioration of them has been found in their real functions. Job rotation, whose purpose is to create multi-skilledness, actually tends to be nominal, or only conducted nominally or superficially.

Well here arises one question. In the Abo model, does this type of substitution constitute application or adaptation? It is apparently an application, but virtually adaptation that shifts to the local practice. Many understand that it causes a retardation of production capability in the Japanese local plants. As for the 'functional equivalents,' to adopt them by Japanese firms in the US might mean that the appearance is Japanese-style but the virtual function is reversed in the American context.

All of these things are problematic and the localization of Japanese firms is quite a multi-tiered one. Accordingly, the application–adaptation relations in localization have multi-tiered aspects. It seems to me problematic by what degree the model incorporates such complexity.

Professor Kawamura also points out that Japanese factories in the US are placed under the strong pressures shifting toward a 'revised American-type.' This aspect needs to be reconsidered deliberately. It should be made clear whether the American version of revised Japanese management system of the Japanese local plants are actually deviating from the Japanese-type, or should be understood as in the process of transition though they basically maintain the Japanese-type.

Lastly, I have one more point. How we can think about the relationship between the slippage of the realization of Japanese system in local plants and the inevitability of the introduction of the lean system under the strong competitive pressures in a global level?

It is true that, in electronics industries, rapidly advanced modularization has induced Japanese firms to become inadaptable to the situation. Consequently Japanese electronics factories have deteriorated their performance. On the other hand, automobile companies have steadily increased their output. The question whether it is mere the result of the past investment constitutes a very important controversial issue, I think.

Kawamura to Okamoto

Professor Okamoto's comments cover a wide range of the issues and include some fundamental problematic points of our methodology and our understandings. My time is limited. I would like to answer the questions just focusing on main points.

One of the most important questions for me is the one about the conversing tendency of Japanese factories in the US toward a 'revised American-type' in the 1990s based on our research outcomes. The terminology of a 'revised American-type' that I use is that a management and production system of which is organized on the basic logic of the American-type or the Ford–Taylor type mass production but 'Japanized' in a way that it incorporates many Japanese-type elements. Of course, much more should be done further in its conceptualization. Professor Okamoto pointed out that I might think of it as an end of convergence in the long run in the US. I think that there has been such tendency that will be quite probable even in the future in the US.

We have found that there have been some factors that have been brought about that tendency even in the Japanese factories in the US in the 1990s. The one factor is that the restraints to the local application of Japanese-style methods from the local conditions have still persisted, especially from traditional work rules and practices closely linked with the traditional American labor relations, even though it is said that they have considerably changed in these two decades. It seems that they are deep-rooted in the American industrial society in the 100 years or more of historical developments. Of course, Japanization has exerted the transformative pressures on them but, it is not probable the Japanese-style methods are able to replace them completely in the US (or even in Western Europe as well in similar sense). I think the basic logic of the American-style system stubbornly persists in the US.

I would like to emphasize that these restraints would especially constrain the local transfer of the Japanese-style capability-building system – it is the very core of the system. In the US in the 1990s, under the strong localization pressures, Japanese firms have also increased dependency on the local staff and managers as well as the revised application or the utilization of functional equivalents which emerged in the changing work practices and labor relations in the US. It is probable that the insufficient realization of the Japanese-style capability-building system in the local transplants in the US might constitute the major cause of a shift of their management and production system toward a revised American-type. The 'functional equivalents' easily changes their functions to the American ones in that context.

In addition to these underlying factors, the expanding macroeconomic environment might bring about the deterioration of the Japanese system. It is notable especially in the auto industry. Japanese companies have experienced successive expansion of their production to cope with vastly increased demands, partly because of their relative competitive advantage of the increased application of the Japanese-style methods. Ironically, it induced them to incline toward the mass-production logic.

The conjunction of these factors has constrained the local full-application of the basic logic of the Japanese-style management and production system. It might have brought about an inclination toward a 'revised American-type.'

Kenney to Kawamura

In 2000–01 the Group resurveyed some of the same plants they visited in 1986–89. This is significant because they now have two points in time from which to examine the transfer of the Japanese production system to North America.

Their new study finds that Japanese automakers became more localized while the consumer electronics industry has become less local as Japanese makers have been withdrawing from the US and the Maquilas. They find that the importation of production equipment is still high, but this may not be unique to Japanese firms because most MNCs try to standardize their factories globally. Intel, for example, operates on a 'copy exact' formula for all of its plants operating around the world. As Kogut (2004) observes, MNCs may not know any other way to be efficient except to operate around the world in as similar ways as possible.

Professor Kawamura finds that the substantive functions of the Japanese system have been rather diluted. The wage system has not evolved since 1989, i.e. what was in place then is largely the same in 2001. Moreover, in the auto assembly plants job rotation has even weakened more and is now being administered on a seniority basis. Not surprisingly, this is most true in plants organized by the UAW – in other words, a US labor relations regime reproduces the US pattern most closely. Where there seems to be more of a movement toward the Japanese system is in 'education and training' and 'quality control.'

Echoing Adler *et al.*'s (1999) findings, Kawamura finds is the creation of 'functional equivalents' in many cases and thus argues that there is a 'revised application' being created in the transplants. These does leave somewhat unresolved whether the basic logic of the Japanese system has been transferred.

What is most interesting in this chapter is a rethinking of the entire problem of measuring application along two lines.

First, the case where functional equivalents have been created within the logic of the foreign system. Judging whether a functional equivalent is present is problematic, but necessary, because one needs to evaluate the equivalent in the context. Thus context must be judged.

Secondly, there is what might be seen as the converse of the first problem, i.e. the case of lax implementation. Here, the problem is that the form exists, but it has little meaning. Seen differently, it is quite possible that the plants or even sub-sections of the plants have evolved in a variety of directions thus making them more heterogeneous than they were at the time of the first survey. He attributes this heterogeneity and movement toward the US environment as being due to a lack of capacity building. An alternative is that, in the anthropologist's term, the plants 'went native,' something that would be expected in the brown field plants and at the firms that did not have a strong management system in the first place.

He found that one of the greatest problems was the transfer of the human capability-building system to the US. This conclusion is one with which I agree most wholeheartedly, and was roughly our conclusion when Richard Florida and I (1993) I worked on these topics in the 1980s. I commend Tetsuji for this rethinking and urge him to continue to deepen his theoretical work along these lines.

Finally, it is interesting to analyse why the Japanese auto firms, Toyota and Honda, and the partially Japanese firm Nissan have become increasingly dominant in the global auto industry and are able to use their foreign plants so effectively, while in consumer electronics Japanese firms have had a much more difficult time. I have no explanation for this, but it could be due to the complexity of the auto production process versus the rather simpler electronics assembly.

References

Adler, Paul, Fruin, W. Mark and Liker, Jeffrey (eds) (1999) *Remade in America* (New York: Oxford University Press).

Kenney, M. and Florida, R. (1993) *Beyond Mass Production: The Japanese System and Its Transfer to the US* (Oxford University Press 1993).

Kogut, B. (2004) 'From Regions and Firms to Multinational Highways: Knowledge and Its Diffusion as a Factor in the Globalization of Industries,' In M. Kenney with R. Florida (eds) *Locating Global Advantage: Industry Dynamics in a Globalizing Economy.* (Stanford: Stanford University Press), 261–84.

Kawamura to Kenney

I think basically his comments endorsed my approach. It encourages me to continue my methodology and research direction. Of course, situations have become more complicated and the Japanese operations have expanded to many regions including China. Japanese companies should upgrade their operation management and their business strategy. We have to be enhancing our research activities and upgrading our methodology accordingly.

Kenney to Carrillo

Kenney to Carrillo

Professor Carrillo reports on a survey he and colleagues undertook examining the production systems US and Japanese firms have adopted in Mexico.

In the first part of the chapter, he analyses the role of Mexico in two powerful macro-geographical tendencies. The first is the development of the North American manufacturing region and the second is the entrance of China on the global manufacturing scene. The tension between the macroregion and the global manufacturing hub is quite possibly the most important dynamic in the world today with the possible exception of the rise of India as a critical service hub for the world's MNCs.

Carrillo has found that in Mexico US firms have more Japanese production systems than do the Japanese firms operating in Mexico. He finds that US firms have adapted more of the 'Human–Methods,' while the Japanese have applied a Materials–Results system. This result may be confounded by the fact that the industries in which the Japanese operate, i.e. consumer electronics and the US operate, i.e. automobiles and auto parts are very different. This conflict could bias his results. For example, he finds that Japanese firms are more likely to import equipment from Japan than are US firms likely to import equipment from the US. This is interesting, but what does it mean? For example, it could be that the US factories, such firms Ford Hermosillo, are importing equipment from Japan. This would show a trilateral organization of the automotive industry, but, this might only signify that both industries are importing equipment. I would submit it might also suggest that the US-owned factories in the US are also importing equipment from Japan!

This leads me to two methodological points that increasingly bothered me when I was undertaking this research in the early 1990s. First, I had to go to the mother plant to be sure as to whether there were differences. This was one of the towering strengths of the Abo group's work, i.e. they visited the parent plant and compared it with the overseas plants.

Secondly, it is absolutely important to control the industry and the activity (and this must be at the micro-level). So a television tube production operation cannot be compared to television assembly operation. This is so important that it might outweigh everything else. Auto plants labor and work organization simply cannot be compared with consumer electronics assembly.

In the case of the consumer electronics transplants, elsewhere I have argued that the overseas factories are 'reproduction' factories (Kenney *et al.* 1998). The overseas factories are not meant to improve the process simply to reproduce it. Thus they can not be compared with the parent plant because their purposes were different.

One important result Carrillo finds is that in electronics the Mexican factories are upgrading. The evidence for this is that they are assembling flat panel televisions, however what is the evidence that this is a more sophisticated function, when the high technology is in the FPD (Flat Panel Display) production and that is in Asia. At the macro-level, one could argue that it is evidence of the skills in Mexico declining, because it is replacing CRT (Cathode-Ray Tube) production which is relatively capital intensive and was where Mexico had an opportunity to move to a more capital and technician-intensive production process (Kenney 2003).

Carrillo is to be congratulated for doing the painstaking work necessary to evaluate the evolution of US and Japanese auto and electronics facilities in Mexico. This paper provides an excellent insight into their evolution, and finds a optimistic scenario for Mexico. I think their finding that the US firms provide more discretion to their Mexican managers is right, but may have always been the case. In contrast to Japanese firms, US firms tend to manage by the numbers, i.e. I don't care what you do as long as you make the numbers. By its very nature such an attitude gives greater discretion.

I wonder if some of the advances he attributes to the Maquilas, such as e-business, supply chain management etc., are anything other than normal business and are implemented from headquarters and signify little in terms of upgrading.

Unfortunately, at the political–economic level, I am not as sanguine. My feeling is that Latin America and, to a lesser but significant degree, Mexico are becoming increasingly peripheral nations for the global economy. This is, in large measure, is due to a rather cavalier response by the Mexican government, business, and polity to the manifold opportunities presented by the growth of the Maquilas during the 1980s and 1990s. Upgrading in terms of universities, R&D capability building, and entrepreneurship were barely discussed – in fact, it was only Jorge Carrillo, Oscar Contreras and few others that were raising the alarm. They were ignored and now it is very late. I am struck at how aggressively China and now India are working consciously to upgrade their economies, because they believe that this historical moment of opening will be brief and they must break through now.

Without a doubt, Professor Carrillo has made an important contribution that extends the work of the Abo group to Mexico.

References

M. Kenney (2003) 'The Shifting Value Chain: The Television Industry in North America,' in Martin Kenney with Richard Florida (eds) *Locating Global Advantage* (Stanford: Stanford University Press).

Kenney, M., Goe, W. R. Contreras, O., Romero, J. and Bustos, M. (1998) 'Learning Factories or Reproduction Factories?: Labor–Management Relations in the Japanese Consumer Electronics Maquiladoras in Mexico,' *Work and Occupations* 25, (3): 269–304.

Carrillo to Kenney

I want to mention four points. First, is that comparison with the same activities, of course, is always important. And that for all different activities, I mean that apply in all the cases, we compare CKD, SUV cars, Toyota Tijuana, so we cannot compare in that sense the auto industry in Mexico and in other countries as well. So, in the sense of the Japanese production system's transferability, I think we can compare different types of activities, but don't always take it into account, in the same industry, but they are participating in the same value chain.

Second, 'reproduction' factories, yes, globalization brings a more homo- geneous pattern to all of the world, for the same multinational and the same affiliates, but I think the building in capabilities are different in each case. So, when we are talking about, for instance, the case of Sony, Samsung, or Delphi in the case of Mexico, we are talking about more than a reproduced factory. That is beyond this type of reproduced factories because they are incorporated in new functions, such as a kind of headquarter function like in the Dephi case. The third comment is related to CRT and flat television production. Yes, I have the same feeling, because, of course, the design of the panel display is in Korea and Japan, but not in the other countries, but not for Korea and for Japan, the issue is their capability to quick learning and quick change for the new niches. Because if you want to still produce CRT, because more skills are needed, then you are out of the market, because more CRTs are now produced in China. So to move to other value-added segments and to different niche segments are so important, and in this case, not only university but also company people are trying to be very aggressive, trying to implement the local design. And we did care about headquarters' policies with some capabilities to bring local capabilities. I am optimistic, in the near future, about that there could be some R&D facilities in the Mexico as well.

And the final comment related with China, India, Mexico and also opportunity for Mexico I totally agree. Mexico as well as North America, but especially Mexico has followed the pattern of being very peripheral to the integration of United States. That's the very decision-making taken by the local government and also by the affiliate. So in that sense, that explains the pattern, and so if we can still be competitive in terms of large size production, short inventory production, and quicker response production, then probably will still play a good role in the American economy.

Tamura to Itagaki

Tamura to Itagaki

Being an editor of *Nihon Keizai Shimbun*, I do have quite a bit of knowledge about the Asian situation. And I have seen and heard what happens at the very forefront in writing the articles for the *Nihon Keizai Shimbun*, thus I decided to accept the invitation to comment on Professor Itagaki's presentation. On the paper written by Professor Itagaki I must say it's very challenging and provocative – and as a journalist, especially for those journalists covering economic arena, often at times we have the tendency of emphasizing ROI and financial aspects in evaluating the Japanese companies. In that sense, it was an eye opener listening to Professor Itagaki. Any time you talk about the Japanese type of production system, and as 'hybrid type' as advocated by Professor Abo, these words do sound very refreshing to me.

But the Japanese type of production system is often viewed from a political perspective. Why? Because I have lived in the United States for an extended time, and in the days of President Clinton. Right around 1993, in the West Coast of the US, UCB would have professors who were very much interested in the Japanese type of production system, in which they were experts (at UCB). And these professors at Berkeley were the so-called 'revisionists,' saying that Japan was different from others. And, from that perspective, they were critical of the

Japanese type of production system, saying that it is evident from this that Japan is different and unique from the US. The nature of how they criticized is that they said it was closed, and that they were not open to the outsiders. They were asking whether the Japanese production system had universality or not and could be ransferred to others.

That was a question posed, and since then this question has never left my mind, and listening to Professor Abo and Professor Itagaki, I get the feeling that it is quite universal. And you could say that the Japanese type of production system needs to be looked at from the viewpoint that it does have quite a high degree of universality. Another point: Korea, Taiwan – to what extent has the Japanese production system rooted in these countries? And, as cited earlier, in the example of Southeast Asia for Toyota, it was stated that it is long-term and there is continuity that exists to the present day. I have listened to that presentation with great interest.

Having said that, what is the contribution that the Japanese type of production system would have on the development of economy? From the perspective of macroeconomy, what is its contribution? Can we say that it is an epoch-making event in the stage of the economic development, or is it that it has triggered another phase? Here again, I would say that it needs to be viewed from a high level.

The third point: as the Japanese type of production system, multiple numbers of products can be produced in small lots. If you go to, for example, the Guangdong province in China, some of the companies are using a belt conveyor, and some woman starts to produce parts and components for the cell phone, it does show what the Japanese companies have done. This is an effort on the part of the Japanese SMEs – having located themselves in Hainan province, they were very quick in adapting to the system so that it could be introduced locally without hesitation. I must say I was quite perplexed, and surprised in the good sense, as to how they were able to do it! Listening to Professor Abo, may be we need to consider the Japanese tradition and practices as well. Probably, I would say that flexibility on the part of the Japanese needs to be the focal of attention.

Itagaki to Mr Tamura

There are many comments, given by Mr Tamura, I don't have time to respond to all of them, and I appreciate that he gave supplementary comments to my chapter. Therefore, I would like to choose three points to respond.

First point is whether Japanese production system has provided epoch-making effects from a macroscopic point of view. I also emphasize this point. I would like to paraphrase it. Japanese technology, I think, has had a continuous impact on the industrialization of East Asian countries. There are three aspect of technology transfer. One is the technology related to products themselves – 'lighter, thinner, shorter, and smaller' type products – which Japanese companies modified American-type products into. The other is Japanese production technologies, which have transformed Taylorism and quality control methods originated from United States into Japanese ways and have brought them to East Asian countries. I mentioned about the Japanese companies' attitude of continuing with operations under Asian economic crisis. However, I didn't talk about how such behavior produced results in the economic performance of East Asian countries. Immediately after the crisis I went to Toyota's new factory in Indonesia, and each process was in operation only for five days a month. Then, 50 per cent of the employees were ordered to stay at home, and 50 per cent of them were ordered to come to the factory to receive training and education, which seemed to enhance the capability of quality control. They showed me the painting process. They explained that keeping painting liquid clean at the line stopping was very difficult and that the cleanness was a good proof of the high, improved skills of the local staff members. Third is the technology embodied in the equipment and parts brought from Japan – we called it transfer of 'Results–Material'. This technology transfer has played important roles in not only enhancing the capability of the Japanese affiliated plants but also promoting the industrialization of the local economy.

The second point is the importance of the flexibility of the Japanese production system: yes, I agree with what Mr Tamura said. I also usually emphasize that, but I didn't do so in my presentation today. The cell production system is a representative example of small-lot production on a diverse product line. The actual processes of the system must be changed depending on the characteristics and number of product models and also depending on the skill of the workers. The cell production system requires flexibility. This system has been already brought into China. But it cannot work well without continuous improvement originated by parent factories in Japan. And this continuous improvement is sustained by the flexibility of the mother factories.

The third point is the argument that Japanese companies should utilize M&A more. I believe that Japanese companies are not very good at the M&A. Of course, M&A should be utilized more than previously, but not to the level that the European and the American companies have utilized. Even the European and the American companies, which are better at M&A than Japanese counterparts, have experienced many failures in M&A.

Zhang to Kamiyama

Zhang to Kamiyama

First, the JMNESG raised a very important issue, and the results of the research are quite impressive. This group made a study and the research about the so-called 'DNA of Companies,' and this type of study is quite difficult – especially in China. The Chinese companies' managements are not really willing to share information to those who came from outside the country. So in order to get the quality research, I imagine that the liaison and other related work were quite difficult and painstaking. And, as far as I know, Professor Kamiyama is one of a few Japanese who went into China for this study and visited many of the plants, including the auto assembly plant in mainland China. So I was, first of all, greatly impressed with the results and the fruits of the study.

His chapter as a whole shows us at micro level the stories. However, prior to entering into the main content of the paper, he gave us a macroscopic other perspective of Chinese economy. In terms of the research methodology, I think he combines the macroscopic and microscopic views in a very delicate and well-balanced manner, and such research was quite detailed. As you know, the basic infrastructure and institutions in social and economic matters are quite different between Japan and China, and these two countries share a lot of difficulties in terms of history and territory. And there might be some other flaws in the mutual trust from time to time.

Some people say that China is about to break down, or other people say China is a great threat, and hybrid transplants of Japanese companies developed in China show that those companies or plans have a strong vital force. So in very complex issues and social problems, why could Japanese companies increase their presence in China and enhance the operations in China? I think there are two reasons for that. First, there is demand from the Chinese side for Japanese hybrid plants. That means Japanese hybrid factories bring benefits to Chinese economic development. One of the benefits is to alleviate the lack of capital in Chinese companies. Another benefit is promotion of employment in local markets. The last benefit is the transfer of the Japanese management system into China. An additional benefit is the increase in trade with other countries – more than half of the exports 'that was' China has been brought about by Japanese companies operating in China.

And the other thing is there is a demand from the Japanese side for the Chinese market. Up until 2000, for a long time, the Japanese foreign director investment has been primarily directed towards Western countries. However, these have all matured, and the developed countries have a similar level of industrial maturity and equality, and economic issues/challenges are similar in nature. However, China is completely different from the United States and European countries. First of all, China is less developed, and this is a newly-emerged market with big potential for the future. And, we have cheap labor, and labor is rich in its quantity. We have a 1.3 billion population, so the potential demand for the market was enormous. So, I think the Chinese market is quite important for the Japanese economy.

I think there are four main functions of Japanese transplants in the Chinese market. First, one actually is a prolonged life cycle of already-established and produced products and production facilities. Even if the life cycle of those equipment and machines, finished in Japan, they can still be brought into China, which can extend the life cycle of those tools and equipment. The other thing is the reduction in cost. Japanese companies have perpetual problems of high-cost structure, and by transferring operations into China and other countries, those cost problems can be solved.

And at the same time, Japanese imports can increase. For example, last year, 68 per cent of total exports from Japan are supported by the increase in the exports to China. And the majority of the exports to China have been created from the demand of Japanese transplants in China. As Professor Kamiyama pointed out, in the case of the electric industry, the equipment and the parts were brought from Japan as they are into China. According to some statistics, out of the exports from Japan into China, the ratio of the electricity reaches 54.1 per cent, so the Japanese transplants in China are a driving force to increased imports from Japan. And also, the Japanese transplants in China can alleviate the trade friction between Japan and Western countries. The products which were made in bases in China were actually based on the imported materials and intermediary products from Japan. However these were products made in China, as indicated, so this is indirect export from Japan via China to the Western countries. So, the transplants in China have the effect of alleviation of trade friction between Japan and Western countries.

With these four main functions, I believe Japanese hybrid factories are contributing to the improvement of Japanese economy. So, as a total, hybrid factories in China play a very important and fundamental role for the realization of a win–win situation between China and Japan. And there are some very interesting themes covered by the paper of Professor Kamiyama. There was analysis of application of Japanese production and management systems in China, and the average score was 3.2 – so overall, this is a similar level to America and European countries.

Between China and Western countries, you might think that the basic institutions and economic situation might be completely different. However, in the case of the application level of Japanese management system, those two areas are similar. So, what are the main reasons for that particular other point?

Kamiyama to Zhang

The most important point of your question is why the application score for China is almost at the same level as the other countries and regions investigated. I would say that the main reason for that is the high level of application in the electrical industries, especially in the 'Results intake' aspects. That is, the Japanese electrical and electronics firms in China have brought in a considerable amount of the facilities, the raw materials and parts and components from Japan into their Chinese plants. Whereas, in the case of the automotive industry, such 'Result application' activities by Japanese automobile firms were rather low because there is a strong impetus on the part of the Chinese government and Chinese joint venture partners in China toward domestic production of automobiles.

These circumstances explain why Japanese electrical and electronics firms lessened their market share in China; that is, it is too costly for them to import parts and components from Japan, assemble them into final products, and sell them in Chinese markets. Whereas, in the case of the automotive industry, the situation is just the reverse. The Chinese government has strongly encouraged domestic production of automobiles and this policy has caused the market prices of foreign automobiles to rise higher in Chinese market than in other countries, even though recent prices lower due to the intense competition. On the other hand, the biggest goal of the Chinese government is to acquire the latest foreign (Japanese) technology. In a knock-down assembly, the parts and components are brought in, all this does not facilitate the acquision of technology and necessary skills. Thus, the Chinese government sought to increase the localization ratio and carry out R&D activities in China as well. That's the reason why the automotive industry had to bring a Japanese-style production system into Chinese factories.

One more point I want to add is that the Chinese government did not recognize the importance of parts and components for the automotive industry until around ten years ago. At that time, they thought that producing one or two foreign automobile models was the same as being able to produce all types of automobiles. So as long as foreign car manufacturers were brought in, the Chinese government thought that China could produce automobiles that have the same performance and quality as those in foreign countries. But nowadays, the Chinese government has come to understand the importance of parts and components. So, rather than having a mere knock-down assembly system, it is necessary for China to localize the automotive industry to the highest possible extent through joint ventures with foreign car manufactures and parts makers. However, it is difficult to raise the localization ratio while assuring a level of quality as in foreign countries if there are no capable parts makers.

Boyer to Kumon and Abo

Boyer to Kumon

I'd like to thank Professor Abo and his team for inviting me, and also for that I owe very much to them when I co-edited the book *Between imitation and innovation*, I borrowed from them the concept of hybridization, so for me it is a pleasure to comment now on the paper by Professor Kumon that is a follow up of this long series of research. I appreciate the paper because it suggests, I think, very general interesting questions.

First, the new information about the process of hybridization in Europe is quite interesting. On one side, Europe is now being unified into the EU and its extensions, but on the other side, the chapter provides a disaggregated analysis between Germany, France, South Europe and Hungary. So Europe seen from Japan might seem very homogenous, but it is very diverse. Last but not least, Professor Kumon concludes that after all, the transfer of Japanese methods is very similar in Europe and in Asia.

And to be frank, I will discuss a little bit this hypothesis. Let me summarize the main finding according to my understanding. First, firms won't have major difficulties, but they have to hybridize their organization since the model is transformed by going to Europe with totally distinct institutional configuration of markets or styles of governments and firms. Second element – and it was, I think, the star concept of this conference – the model diffuses itself via functional equivalents, using the specificity and idiosyncrasy of the local environment, just to develop the same objective as the Japanese model, but with different means. The third element: Europe would be very close to Asia. And you see, just visiting Asia and Europe, I've not got the feeling that they are in the same macro mood, nor the same managerial style.

Professor Kumon mentions that there are three waves of transplanting in Europe. First, firms react to protectionism. Second, they react to merger and concentration (both in the car industry and in the electronics industry). And third, now they adapt to the entry of new members – as you know, now we are 25 members in the EU, and maybe 10 more during the next decade. Therefore, what is quite interesting, Professor Kumon contemplates a very bright future of transplant in Central and Eastern Europe.

Nevertheless, this analysis raises many problems and questions.

- First question: all over the presentation, I was surprised – the global score is very near 3, with minimalist variance (at most 2.8 to 3.4). So for me it was a question: don't you think that is a problem of methodology? This might be explained by the history of your research: you started comparing on the horizontal axis the Japanese system and the American system. Consequently, the scale runs from 1 to 5, and the scoring is clear. But when you introduce Europe, you might have a totally different system that runs from A to E. When comparing Europe to America, you need another ranking from I (in Roman capital) to V. Therefore, the average score of Europe, 3, might be the consequence of the projection of the European model along the axis that describes the opposition between the Japanese and the American models, whereas it might define an autonomous model. So the question is the following: could you extend the concept of adaptation/hybridization to more than two models? This could be a quite interesting complement.
- Second question. Professor Kumon did not distinguish so much the car industry from the electronics sector. By contrast, Professor Fujimoto this morning pointed out that in the case of electronics,

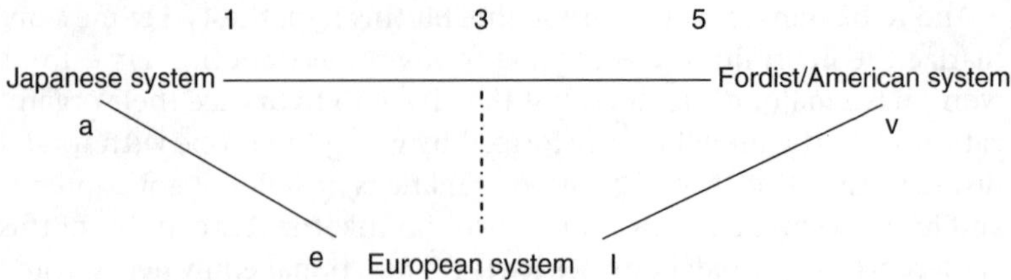

Figure 8.1 How to rank three different productive systems

you get modular systems, whereas the car industry displays integrated systems. Therefore, the managerial style of subcontracting labor force management and innovation policy might be different and the analysis should distinguish between the two sectors. Therefore, would it be possible to disentangle the scoring among the two sectors, and how do they comply with the Fujimoto model?

- Third question: the literature (at least in the US) opposes greenfield plants to different forms of restructuring when the transplant operates in an old industrial site. Could the data be used in order to test whether the localization in a new site (or an old one) matters for the performance. Is this conventional wisdom, according which the transposition of the Japanese principles is easier in greenfield plants, supported by the data?
- Fourth question: my reading of hybridization is that it is the final outcome of a series of trials and errors. Therefore the transposition takes time, because the managers and the employees have to learn how to adapt. Consequently, the period since the opening of the transplant could be an important variable in determining the proximity to the typical Japanese model. Table 8.2 computes the score according to the date of opening in order to test if there exists a clear correlation: the older the transplant, the better the adaptation. Surprisingly, that it is not the case, in the sense that you don't have

Table 8.2 Does the date of opening matter for Japanese transplants?

	UK	*Germany*	*France/Benelux*	*South Europe*	*Hungary*
Average date of opening	1986	1982	1987	1987	1994
Application Scores					
General	3.5	3.2	3.0	3.0	3.0
Equipments	3.9	3.9	3.2	2.6	4.8
Production management	3.5	3.4	3.0	3.0	3.2

Source: From Tables 6.1 and 6.5 in Professor Kumon's chapter.

any clear relation, and other presentations during this morning have already exhibited similar results. For example, Professor Kawamura found that, in the electronics sector or car industry, sometimes the score moved up, and sometimes it declined. This is a challenging issue, since hybridization is supposed to be a dynamic process.

A possible explanation stresses that the learning process might be different according to the components of the Japanese Model. The more recent the equipment, the more efficient is the productive organization. The older production management, the better is the economic performance (compare lines 4 and 5 in Table 8.2). This might be a reason why no correlation is observed at the level of the general application score.

Therefore, I could propose to make a variance analysis in order to decompose the score into a country effect (a_i) a sector-specific effect (b_j) – electronics or car industry – c_t (a temporal effect), and last but not least, the firm-specific ability d^l. I would bet that the Toyota transplant and the Nissan transplant are not the same, because by definition you observe firm specificities. Why not to use this wonderful data set in order to estimate this global model, which would teach us a lot about the problem of hybridization?

$$S^l_{ijt} \quad = \quad a_i \quad \div \quad b_j \quad \div \quad c_t \quad \div \quad d^l$$

Score in country i in sector j at time t for firm l	Country effect	Sector specific effect		Temporal effect	Firm specific ability

- Fifth question: seen from Japan, Europe looks like the tiny territory at the end of the continent, but seen within Europe, the management styles are quite diverse. The reading of the paper by Professor Kumon gives the impression that the typical productive model is the German system. For instance, the description of UK labor industrial relations is quite surprising: the very adversarial and balkanized industrial relations are perceived as a minor variant of co-managed labor market institutions. A quite intuitive hypothesis suggests that different institutional configurations should trigger definite diverse adaptation/hybridization of the Japanese model. Therefore, it should be quite interesting to try to use the analytical framework proposed

Table 8.3 Hybridization between diffusion and innovation

The firm adopts / *Foreign institutions*	*Same principles and routines*	*Same principles but different routines*	*New principles with previous routines*	*New principles and new routines*
Similar to the domestic ones	East Asia		(Eisenach)	
Dissimilar but permissive	North America	UK		(Resende)
Dissimilar and rather constraining		Germany France	(Fasa–Renault)	
	Diffusion	*Adaptation*	*Hybridization*	*Innovation*

by '*Between imitation and innovation*' (1998: 53). Basically, the issue of hybridization is related to the conjunction of two factors (Table 8.3). The first one (horizontal axis) captures the degree of standardization of the principles and routines that are brought by the transplant according to the business model of the mother company. The second factor (vertical axis) represents the degree of similarity of the institutions between the domestic economy and the economy from where the mother company originates. One can update a previous analysis with the data collected by Professor Kumon.

According to the findings of this previous comparative study, some factories in Eastern Germany (Eisenach) or in Brazil (Resende) have clearly been innovating, reproducing neither the domestic nor the international productive models. According to Professor Kumon's intensive knowledge, is such an innovation operating for example in Eastern Europe?

- Sixth question: Professor Kumon delivers a quite optimistic prognosis about the diffusion of Japanese model in Eastern Europe. A decade ago, the multinationals have been eager to open factories in Eastern and Central Europe countries, since they expected a fast catching-up and the benefits of rather low wages for rather skilled-workers. Nowadays, a large fraction of foreign direct investment goes to China, especially for electronics, and more recently for the car industry. The same pattern is observed in Mexico, where Maquiladoras are currently shut down and the production delocalized to China. Furthermore, Asia is a fast growing region, whereas the core of Europe experience quasi-stagnation. Can Professor Kumon's optimism be still sustained?

- Seventh question: the survey is rather old since historical time matters, and if the macroeconomic trends change, probably the results might be quite different nowadays. Does Professor Kumon contemplate the possibility to visit again the same plants and update the related scoring? A more mundane question: why did Toyota choose France for producing Yaris and not UK or Germany? Incidentally what is the ranking of the Toyota transplant in France and does it confirm that the adaptation has been quite successful in spite of quite distinctive labor market institutions with respect to Japan?
- May I ask a last question to Professor Abo: when you started your pioneer study, the Japanese model was well defined configuration, but it has been continuously evolving both at home and abroad by the very process of hybridization. Actually, some innovations invented abroad have been imported back to the Japanese mother plants. For instance, I was told by some Toyota managers that the just in time was significantly transformed by the factories operating in the US and this new configuration has been used as an innovation back to Toyota city. Could Professor Abo extend his method and take into account that the Japanese model itself has been significantly transformed during the last two decades?

Kumon to Boyer

My answer to the first question on the methodology is as follows. Europe has a firmly established production system. However, unlike a production system in the United States, it was not completely opposite to Japanese system. At first, we supposed that the European system would be similar to the American system, because of historical relationship between two regions. Different from this supposition, we found functional equivalents in the European managerial environments with the Japanese system. When Japanese firms attempted to blend the local system with the Japanese system, formal adaptation to those elements (e.g. wage system, employment security, works council, etc.) supported functional application of the Japanese system. It is in this sense that Japanese firms relied upon functional equivalent within the European environment. However, we keep five points grading system in Europe, because we need to conduct the evaluation from the perspective of its application.

I reply to the second question, regarding to no difference in the scores between electronics sector and automotive sector in Europe. There was a big gap of the scores in the United States, 2.7 for the electronics sector and 3.6 for automotive sector. This is very interesting point unique to Europe. One of the main reasons is difference in managerial environments between two regions. Japanese firms should make great effort to apply the unique system in the United States where the indigenous production system is completely opposite to the Japanese system. The automotive firms spent a lot of energy in the Unites States. So they recorded high point of application scores. In Europe where the original system has similarity with the Japanese system, they can rely upon the functional equivalent. Therefore two sectors exhibited almost same scores in application.

Third point, it is true that the Japanese system, peculiar to the local environment, is more applicable for greenfield plants. Japanese firms have a tendency to choose greenfield plants in rural districts.

Regarding the fourth point, I think these four effects are quite interesting. We put great importance in firm effect and region effect. When we look at application scores overseas, firm effect is the biggest factor and then followed by regional effect.

I go to the fourth question, on the variety of functional equivalents stemming from differences in labour market, industrial organization and management style among European nations. Yes, there are some differences among countries. France is not much different from Japan in wage system and training system within firms. Japanese firms rely upon the German *Facharbeiter*, who are trained under the dual system and hold professional skills, even though they show lack of flexibility in cooperation with others.

Professor Boyer mentioned innovation at overseas plants. There are two aspects on innovation according to his explanation, principle and routines. Japanese firms in Europe don't do anything new in principle. In term of routines, they have to have some modifications of techniques adapting to local situations. In this sense, you can evaluate it as an innovation.

On the sixth point, transferability in central Europe. According to our field research, Japanese firms are more confident in application their system there. Later other speakers will discuss this it.

Finally I'd like to answer the last question. Yes, our data on Europe is rather old. So I'd like to update the data as much as possible.

Abo to Boyer

To the question from Professor Boyer whether reverse hybridization of the Japanese model exists or not. Reverse can mean two things. Reverse on one hand means that the Japanese hybrid systems overseas can come back to the parent companies in Japan, probably you mean that is the reverse. And the parent companies in Japan are now going through the some transformation and transition in terms of 'structural reform' reflecting on American-style 'market fundamentalism,' so that could mean the reverse as well. But, I think that you are talking about the first one. This reverse means that something hybridized which happened in a local area can come back to Japan and may be partly adopted to the parent systems. I think this is quite interesting argument and this is an internal globalization within Japanese companies.This is probably due to the change in Japanese environment.

But, we don't have any systematic methodology to evaluate such phenomena. I just want to share some of the interesting samples with you. In my report, I have already shown you an example. That is the division line – 'self fulfillment line.' This is the example of the Kentucky plant of Company T and that system was used by Company T in Kentucky and that it spread into other areas in the United States and has been brought back to Japan as well. Traditionally, there is one continuous line at a final assembly process of the plant of Company T and when a problem occured at one point of the line the operations would be suspended. This creates stress for the operators alongside the line. In the United States, they actually divided the line into ten or so portions and they put the buffer for 3 or 5 units of car between the divided lines. So after that, even though there are some defects they can actually stop only one divided part of that line using those buffer. They can continue or maintain the smooth operation for the line itself. Of course, efficiency may be affected; however, on the other hand, there is better quality control.

Anyway, this divided line is a quite interesting example and especially useful overseas and after that I saw plants of Company T in Australia, India and UK. And also that system was introduced to the parent plants of Company T in Japan, such as the plant in Kyushu and Motomachi. But, this is a quite convenient interpretation for me because, according to people of Company T, the first one was developed in Tahara and so on in Japan, then they were brought to the Kentucky plan. Of course, I think the original idea was conceived within Japan, but the real implementation of the idea was probably in Kentucky and that was quite useful there. Then that was brought back to Japan.

Strzelczak to Yuan

Strzelczak to Yuan

I would like to present some of my views on Professor Yuan's comments on Japanese hybrid factories in Central and Eastern Europe. Before, I would like to stress that to a great extent they are supported by my professional experience, rather than by research results.

Professor Yuan refers to Francois Mitterand's (the former French President) opinion from 1990, who was worrying then about the risk of new division of Europe. He meant particularly 'the iron curtain' between poor and rich, caused by economic disparity. In recent years we had many comments on a new division in Europe, mostly among the political establishment, supported rather by political references, e.g. approach to the war in Iraq. Many of them suggest, that a new political and business and environment is shaping now in Europe. I personally believe, that if we look carefully what is really the new and old Europe, different distinctions of countries can be identified, depending on the criteria applied. An important example may be the clustering of a new and old Europe on the basis of business culture, i.e. depending on the work habits, expectations of social security and the role of state in economy and society, attitudes to globalization issues etc. E.g. in Germany and France, the protection of employees' security is very high, just opposite to Central and Eastern Europe or the UK. The societies in countries of 'old Europe' strongly oppose proposal of economic and social reforms, which could enhance productivity and competitiveness of economies, for the price of social security. I would like to refer these comments to Professor Yuan's analysis of Japanese style management adoption in Central and Eastern European countries. The new Europe, according to the recent understanding of this term, and especially Central and Eastern Europe, is much more open for Japanese style management. Personally I strongly support Professor Kumon's comments, who noticed high level of acceptability of Japanese style management in Hungary, and I will come to this point later.

Professor Yuan indicated, that some countries in Central and Eastern Europe tend to be the manufacturing center of all Europe. I strongly support this belief, as it is supported by many statistics. Perhaps the danger, that manufacturing totally might disappear in Europe is not as high, as Professor Boyer says, because there are economic factors, that should protect the manufacturing sector in Europe, e.g. the logistical costs. We should not expect, that all manufacturing will be concentrated in China. But, it is visible that many industries from Western Europe migrated to China or Central and Eastern Europe. It is worth noting, that it also means migration of some other activities, not just only operations, from Western Europe. For example, there were several examples of back office activities, recently shifted by MNEs from Ireland (where they were moved just few years ago due to the cost advantage) to Central and Eastern Europe. Now research and development activities are also shifted to the Central and Eastern Europe, e.g. by ABB, Philips, TRW, Delphi etc. This is a rather surprising phenomenon, as one could expect, that knowledge related activities should be protected in the home basis by MNEs.

Considering Central and Eastern Europe as the environment for a Japanese production system adoption, Professor Yuan believe, that typically transitional economies retain human behaviors and labor practices from the socialist past. According to my personal observations in many Japanese and multinational companies in Central and Eastern Europe, as well as to recent surveys published by Ernst and Young and other renowned sources, something opposite might be valid. I rather believe that the behavior and thinking of workers in France and Germany is much socialistic than the one in Czech Republic or Poland. There are several factors behind that phenomena, for example, tough labor market causes a big valuation of job. People have more respect for an employer, who offers them safety, competitive salary, good treatment and so on. In Western Europe many employees dream of early retirement, enjoying life and free time huge is the main focus. The major interests of people are not linked to the job. It is not possible to meet such attitudes in Central and Eastern Europe, because the welfare and social security is much lower and people have totally different valuation of job.

Secondly, Professor Yuan believes that Western European production systems are like standards and benchmarks for the Central and Eastern Europe. I personally visited plenty of multinational companies operating in the Central and Eastern Europe and from their management I have learned about a specific pattern: after 2 years of operations, the branch of multinational company operating in Central and Eastern Europe is for sure within the top 3 branches of the multinational worldwide, and very often it is the best one. This is a very common pattern and it is very well justified by statistical data. It neglects the belief, that Western Europe can serve as a positive pattern. It seems to be just the opposite. It would be interesting to run this kind of analysis of this phenomenon. There are good reasons to speculate, that many Western European branches of multinationals show low performance, low flexibility, low adaptativeness and low innovativeness. This is a recent and new phenomena.

Referring to the second section of the discussed paper, I would like to stress the importance and relevance of comments by Professor Yuan on the concentration of Japanese foreign direct investment in Poland, Hungary and Czech. Using an example of company we have visited in Poland, i.e. the French Thomson Multimedia, we can learn that Chinese entrepreneurs follow this way of thinking. The Chinese giant TCL took over the Thomson business, including the factory we have visited in Poland. Recently Haier started to use Poland as the entrance gate to the EU. This is very valuable section of comments, but they do not apply only to Japanese investors, but also to Chinese who realized the potential to expand worldwide, including Europe. The only comment, about which I disagree with Professor Yuan, is about labor force. He said, that there is no difference between German and Czech in this skill level of workers. Considering the quality factors of the labor force, like flexibile attitude toward the time of work, for example, which is very demanded by the employers the comparison gives another result. Labor force flexibility is very limited in many Western European countries, e.g. in Germany, France or U.K. To contrast, the readiness to work longer, when needed is high in Central and Eastern Europe. Such comments are very common among Western European managers running the companies in Central and Eastern Europe. Of course, these comments do not apply to the behavior of the governments.

Professor Yuan has noted, that Japanese managers and engineers highly commended the ability for improvement and problem solving skills on the part of local technicians in Central and Eastern Europe. However, it is interesting to note, that this is not followed by application of group consciousness. I am personally not sure about the actual reasons of these phenomena. Maybe the Japanese managers focus the business development, as many Japanese businesses are quickly growing now in Central and Eastern Europe. Perhaps the top management puts most of their efforts on the steady business growth, rather than workshop level activities. Or maybe they treat the local labor forces in an utilitarian way.

I cannot agree with Professor Yuan, that labor unions in Central and Eastern Europe are peaceful and peacemakers, it is not so at all. There is also another reason, why they quickly disappeared from foreign investments. It is because they could not get support from the employees, to confront the owners of the company. If the employees experience better treatment and a better salary, there is no reason for employees to complain. This explains, why in most cases there are no labor unions in multinational companies, including the Japanese one. The reason is not the fight from the top management against the labor unions, but just lack of support from the labor force. This interdependence is very clear, but you have to be inside the company to understand this phenomenon.

Considering the conclusions on transferability of Japanese production system, Professor Yuan commented on the high level of hybridization of Japanese companies, in some aspects like work organization and so on. He cited some rationales, which from my experience might not be so crucial. I would like to propose a very different explanation which refers to some historical roots. First of all I would like to contrast Central and Eastern Europe to Western Europe in a specific way. Central and Eastern Europe has always had a mix of nations and cultures, looking back in history, e.g. the in the Austrian Empire, or in Poland, which included Asians. There are no so rigid divisions between nations and cultures in Central and Eastern Europe, like in the West. It means, that facing globalization issues is now easier. Eastern Europeans are far more open to cultures. Just the opposite, in Western Europe, the sense of nationality is very strong. There is also a strong sense of national identity and people are very proud of their nations, e.g. in France or in Germany. This kind of thinking does not exist in Central and Eastern Europe. That is why people in Central and Eastern Europe are far more open to Asian cultures especially to Japanese culture. Perception of Japan in Central and Eastern Europe is usually very positive, in many ways. Furthermore, the impact of the communist system in Central and Eastern Europe developed special attitudes of labor force. People expect fairness a fair wage system, good treatment, and they can get it from Japanese employers. An interesting conclusion can be drawn from an example of a Toyota plant operating in neighborhood of French Faurecia plant in South-West Poland. The employment turnover ratio in Faurecia is very high and in Toyota very low. Employees from Faurecia are ready to move to Toyota, despite the salaries there are lower by ca.1/6. The probable reason is a better treatment of employees inside Toyota. What makes the difference – not the salary, but the work conditions, job security, perspective for growth, etc. People are ready to accept less money, considering the low level of their salaries, only because of the differences of the behavior of Japanese managers and the way, how people are protected by the employer. There is a kind of readiness for this type of culture, such as that provided by the Toyotism, in the Central and Eastern Europe. Another factor is the Christian background of Central and Eastern Europe – people are demanding fair treatment, for some human values at the workplace, such as respect for the people, fairness, etc. and this is not the case in Western Europe. The Western managers are totally ignoring traditional Christian values, just focusing on profits and treating employees in a utilitarian way. That is why many people in Central and Eastern Europe, especially in Poland, welcome this kind of approach, and they can get this from Japanese companies.

Another explanation should be given about the low level of Japanese expatriates in Central and Eastern European companies. My explanation is very simple: there are few Japanese operating in a typical company in Central and Eastern Europe, because they can just easily survive without them, as the Central and Eastern Europe is very open to Japanese management culture. Furthermore, the knowledge of Toyotism in Central and Eastern Europe, is very deep. That's why, sometimes just one Japanese manager, like in the big Bridgestone factory in Poznan (Poland), can easily manage the whole business working only with the local managers.

There are further factors, which explain why the Japanese production system, fits very well to the industrial culture of Central and Eastern Europe. One of them refers the core concepts of human resources management. The American hire and fire way is perceived as being much worse than the Toyota's approach to employees. The business values is another area of difference. The Toyota's long term approach can be compared with the short term results-orientation, so common in USA, driven by the stock market expectations and huge incentives for top management, which not surprisingly recently resulted in many frauds. The business and organizational culture and management styles, for example, the Japanese Hoshin kanri approach to corporate planning that integrates everybody around strategic goals, contrasts sharply with the traditional French style, in which the top manager is the God, who knows better, who enforces his decisions on the company

Looking forward, at the research of adoption of the Japanese style of management, it would be worth to put attention to these aspects of what is really the Japanese production system. Perhaps there are good reasons to reconsider the existing matrix for adoption of the Japanese production system and to extend its scope to the cultural aspects of the Japanese production system. This proposal results from the Central and Eastern Europe experience.

Considering the experience of Japanese companies in Central and Eastern Europe two more interesting comments can be added. One refers to the type of ownership. Japanese companies have very specific ownership, compared to the Western ones, which is probably significantly influencing the behavior of top management. This might influence the way of adoption of the Japanese production system, like the organizational behavior and the business culture. It should be considered in the future research. This impact was clearly visible in the Fujitsu service business history in Poland. Fujitsu took over the British ICL company after its collapse, but never decided to replace the top management. There was no involvement of Japanese management in Fujitsu in Poland at all. The business survived after the Japanese took over only two more years. An even better example is visible from Sumitomo Electric and Yazak plants comparison in Slovakia. We have visited these two plants and although both are Japanese, the management is totally different. In the Yazaki it is Japanese. The Sumitomo Electric in the past belonged to the British Lucas, and still the British and Slovak managers operate the company. It is visible gap between a culture and organization of these companies. For example, Sumitomo Electric is using ERP, while Yazaki is using Kanban. And the ratio of absenteeism is totally different in these 2 companies. The only factor that can be linked to this difference is just management. The managers in Sumitomo Electric are British and Slovak, some of them openly denying the senses of Japanese management, particularly Kanban. Not surprisingly, it was visible inefficiency of this factory layout, as the smooth materials flow was not valued by the managers. Furthermore, the foremen in the Sumitomo Company, were operating like clerks. They were surrounded by big stacks of the paper print from the computer system, mostly involved in data processing, instead of the typical jobs of foreman in Japanese companies, which lie in supporting and developing the low level staff.

Yuan to Strzelczak

First, I would like to discuss briefly the transitional economies that still might have a legacy of the socialist ages. We talk about France, Sweden and Germany and compare them with the Central Europe. You might say that they are more socialistic and Central Europe may be more capitalistic. Amusingly, this is the kind of argument that we sometimes have, regarding the interesting phenomenon between Japan and China at the moment. Chinese people are probably more capitalistic than Japanese. Anyhow, this is not the area of my expertise, but related to what we have been looking by our group, I can say the following. In Czech, I heard about the sick leave which is a serious problem for the Japanese managers there. We were told this was a typical habit in socialism ages and this system seems to be existent even today. I think it related to our 23 items. What about the management commitment? Here again, looking from the Japanese system, I would say that there are still some remaining problems. Loyalty to the company here again, lots of problems do remain.

Next, I would like to talk about the currently restructuring institutions in Eastern Europe that might be deeply influenced by the western systems. They are probably reacting to the standards in Eastern Europe gradually. Well, we need to take time in observing that, for example, Czech is still the best example. The Works Council, for example, that is coming back. In other words, they are introducing the system that was in existence in Western Germany gradually. So that gradually it's changing in a peaceful way.

Now the third point, Germany and Czech, what about the difference in quality of labor? I have said not much about of the difference between them. Based upon our research, I've observed at least more that 200 factories. And the Japanese management rarely encourages and compliments the local labor. It has happened only in Germany and Czech. I don't know much about other countries, but especially in regard to the quality of engineer and labor, Czech has high quality. And the Japanese management has complimented them, which is quite rare. We need to collect further information and I'd like to reserve my position.

The fourth vital point is that the quality of engineer in Eastern Europe is high. The highly qualified engineer in Eastern Europe, the score is high. There is regardless of the fact that they have a strong willingness to be part of the team. The engineers were carrying out the production control and they are of the highest caliber. The application score of production management is 3.2 and 2.6 is for the score of team loyalty. And I believe these scores still represent the prevailing situation.

Moving along to the fifth point, on the unions, you say they are peaceful unions are ducking issues more than superficially because of the high rate of pay. Most likely, this is the point that we discuss most internally, especially any point related to labor and human relations. They are also related to the situation. How are we going to deal with that? It is still under debate at the moment and I will say that we need a little bit more time before we can come to any conclusion. We are going to look into the literature of Eastern Europe and maybe next autumn we'd like to publish a book as the result of our observation made in 2003. It is a major problem for us and I'd like to take enough time to consider it.

The sixth point, Central Europe has a mixed culture not like France and Germany. They do not hesitate to introduce different cultures from France and Germany. Maybe this is the same as China which is another economy in transition. This is probably a common trend.

Moving along to the seventh point, the Japanese production system, it seems that they represent socialism and Christianity in Central and Eastern Europe. Many years ago, Max Weber pointed out, that the Christian culture and the Buddhist culture have quite substantial differences.

The main points of questions and comments raised from the audience

(a) Q: Difference between the Asian standard and the American standard in the application and adaptation model (Professor Tsutomu Idemizu, Osaka Sangyo University).
    A: In Asian local production systems for Japanese firms to adapt to are not clear so that we have chosen, for a while, to evaluate only application aspect of Japanese system (Professor Kamiyama).

(b) The JMNESG's evaluation results that the overall average scores of application for the most overseas Japanese plants are around 3.2 would show, on one hand, that the basic policy of Japanese parent companies is to bringing-in the Japanese sytems to their overseas plants. And also, on the other hand, that there are still significant differences between Japanese systems and European systems, such as the length of lead time in production (short v. long), quality control methods (supplier involvement–system v. supplier–assembler relationship via market transaction) (Mr Shiomi Araki, Sumitomo Corp., former Komatsu, Ltd).

(c) In Thailand the Japanese production control systems have been largely brought in but not yet for the Japanese management systems including human resource system. The point is how

Japanese firms can build up HRM system adaptable to a local society. Then the key is human development practices (Ichiro Sato, former president at Toyota Thailand).

(d) Mazda is planning to set up a JV auto plant with Ford in China. This must be a very complicated task, judging from our experiences of the JV plant with Ford in the US. The case of VW may be able to reach us some lessons as it has various successful experiences in China as well as in the former East–West Germany (Masato Karasawa, Mazda Motor Corp.).

I have some doubt about the success story of VW in China (Professor Kamiyama).

(e) Q: About the relationship between application–adaptation scores and managerial performance.

A: There is no doubt that this question should be a key to evaluating our research results, however, I have no clear-cut answer to this very difficult question. Since the 1989 research in the US we have tried and spent so much energy in calculating performances at local subsidiary plants such as productivities, quality levels, earnings ratios. Yet there are so many obstacles to attain those tasks: principle problem of company secrecy, then theoretical and technical problems such as differences in scale of production, modern mix, machines and equipment, quality of human resources,and so on, between parent and subsidiary plants. Still we have been somehow trying to collect various relevant data from managers at local plants such as profit or loss, simple comparisons between parent and subsidiary plants regarding their levels of quality and productivity (Professor Abo).

Yes, companies did not want to show us their data when I was doing research on productivity of R&D lead time for twenty years at Harvard University. As for factory level data MIT has been carrying out plant surveys for a long time. If it is a matter of plant level performance, i.e. I call it 'bottom competitiveness,' it could be gained somehow. However, it would be very difficult to reach profitability at local plant level because that kind of performance can be affected by various factors such as managerial policies of parent companies in particular (Professor Fujimoto).

(f) Q: Relating to Professor Kawamura's remark that the current situation of the production system in many cases of Japanese transplants in the US is not necessarily a Japanese-system-based 'Japanese hybrid model', but rather the American-system-based one, or a 'revised American-type'. This includes the important issue of how we can distinguish the two levels of transfer of the Japanese-style management and production system. One aspect is the transfer of the forms or elements of the Japanese system, another one is the transfer of logic or principle of the system.

A: This issue is complicated. I pointed out that as long as we measure the degrees of application of individual elements of Japanese system, our evaluation scores do not necessarily reflect the reality of the actual functions of Japanese system as a whole. We found that Japanese local transplants have borrowed many of the similar local practices or 'functional equivalents,' facing the difficulty of direct application of Japanese methods due to the restraints from the local conditions. It brings about the higher application scores because the similarity of them to Japanese-style ones. However, when the local transplants do not succeed in realizing the basic logic of Japanese production system of which the essential character is the 'large variety and small lot production' system. In these cases, especially in the US in the 1990s, their production system is just a 'revised American-type,' which is based on the basic logic of the American-type mass production system, but incorporates many of Japanese-style elements at the same time (Professor Kawamura).

There were many other questions and answers but here we have to mention only the names of other people who actively participated in the questions and answers. Professors and Messrs.: Shigeo Asano (JFE Steel Corp.), Yukou Beppu (Teikyo U.), Akira Kurita (Shukutoku U.), Kuniko Mochimura (Josai U.), Masatake Wada (Teikyo U.), Mantaka Kanayama (Meiji U.)

Overall summary by Okubayashi

I will try to summarize. We tend to have the third party evaluation for our research at this symposium. Professor Abo's team's result is of great significance academically and globally.

I say so because this symposium has been funded by the Academic Frontier Promotion Program of the Ministry of Education of Japan and the funding is given to the state of art academic research projects in Japan.

Our project is comparable to the high level achieved by the Harvard and MIT research projects. The Institute of Social Science at the University of Tokyo has developed a distinct approach and Professor Abo's team adopted and further developed that approach. So in that sense we pay high regard and have a keen interest in this research. So what should they do for the next step? I think this is what we would like to discuss and suggest in this symposium. I think there can be three things that can be considered by his team.

First, as was said, the transfer of systems and also the transfer of philosophy or the code of conduct. So how should these two take balance? And second, in the 1980s the international competitive advantage of the Japanese style management was often discussed. So what was exactly the advantage that the Japanese style management had at that time? In the 1920s Fordism was praised and then is it the case that the Japanese management style made a breakthrough after Fordism? Then that should be clarified. And that should be demonstrated not by simply looking at Japanese companies but by the success or failure of the Japanese companies' operations in other countries. So in terms of the history of development of the production and management systems, we should analyse the successful advantages of the Japanese production and management system through this research. So what should they do next is what we would like to discuss and suggest in this symposium.

And thirdly, in this study, this is an international study. That is, we are conscious of national borders separating Japan and other countries. At the same time in the era of globalization the companies try to constantly overcome the cultural and social barriers in obtaining competitive advantages. So from that perspective the team should revisit the Japanese operations overseas. And in that way perhaps we can have some direction that the Japanese companies should go towards, in the future. I sincerely hope that this study will be sustainable and continue in to the future.

9
Concluding Remarks: Japanese Hybrid Factories in Global Perspective – Diverging or Converging?

Tetsuo Abo

In the previous chapters and discussions, we have analysed, described and discussed the dynamic situation and overall picture of Japanese hybrid factories that are spreading worldwide. Now, I will try to summarize, including the latest data, and predict the directions of Japanese management and production systems, focusing on the terms of 'diverging or converging,' from the strategic point of view of the world production activities not only for Japanese manufacturers but also for non-Japanese world firms.

Our findings are that these 'hybrid factories' show two distinctive directions, either toward divergence or convergence. The direction of the movement is found to depend on two major factors – local management environment and corporate strategy – which in turn are primarily affected by market conditions such as production costs and scale of sales.

Divergence and convergence of Japanese hybrid factories worldwide

The degree toward divergence is principally determined by differences in the managerial environment, a factor that influences 'adaptation.' The differences are twofold: the degree of difference from the original Japanese system, and the number of variation patterns. The first type of difference depends on the socio-cultural distance from Japan. For example, Japanese plants in the United States and, to a certain extent, Continental Western European countries, may require far greater adjustments than their counterparts in the East Asian region. The second type of differences relates to the scope of Japanese subsidiaries' expansion overseas, since the managerial environment differs to some extent in each country or region. The broader the geographical scope, the greater the number of variation patterns.

Convergence can be observed as a process in which a system becomes closer to what we call the 'East Asian pattern.' This pattern, compared to the conventional 'American' or 'Fordist' system, and the traditional craftsman system of Continental Europe, places heavy emphasis on human-related elements by maintaining flexible and group-oriented organizational structures and administration systems, process-oriented engineering techniques in production control, and long term-oriented relations between end-product producers and associated parts and components suppliers. This system, which is similar to but not identical with the original Japanese-style system seen in Japan, may be a possible global model that retains some of the essential core elements of the competitive advantages of the JMPS.

What we are going to see in this final chapter are two possible and interesting trends: increasing divergence on the one hand and deepening convergence on the other. An ever greater variety of 'hybrid factories' is emerging as Japanese manufacturers expand their geographical scope of operations with economic globalization, and move into emerging markets such as China, India, Central and Eastern Europe. At the same time, however, it is likely that there will be a notable trend toward convergence or a reduction in differences in the application–adaptation patterns of 'hybrid factories.' Hereafter, we will try to elucidate these trends and their strategic implications for the Japanese and world manufacturing companies, using the data, analysis and discussions in the preceding chapters.

Table 9.1 summarizes again the overall pictures of Japanese hybrid factories worldwide, including those in China (2002) and Central and Eastern Europe(2003) which were added to Table 1.1 in Chapter 1.

Meaning of the average scores of 23 items: convergence?

In Table 9.1 it should be first mentioned, as was in Chapter 1, that the total average score of the 23 items for each region falls again in a range between 3.0 and 3.3. This is very interesting and even unexpected in the sense that such a situation is seen also in the targetted regions, such as China and Central and East Europe, which were recently extended and so the new data were added to those in Chapter 1. Here, however, it would not be necessary to add any explanation to the above. It is, however, more important, from the standpoint of the prime theme of this chapter, to examine the semantic content of

Table 9.1 Application ratios of the Japanese production system at overseas Japanese plants

	NA (01)	*NA (89)*	*UK (97)*	*CWE (98)*	*WE*	*K/T (92)*	*SA (93)*	*China (02)*	*EA*	*CEE (03)*
I Work organization and administration	3.2	2.9	3.4	3.0	3.1	3.7	3.3	3.5	3.5	3.3
1. Job classification	4.1	3.7	4.4	3.2	3.6	4.9	4.5	4.4	4.7	4.1
2. Multi-functional skills	3.0	2.6	3.3	2.8	3.0	2.9	2.6	3.0	2.7	2.8
3. Education and training	3.7	2.9	3.5	3.1	3.2	3.4	3.3	3.5	3.3	3.4
4. Wage system	2.3	2.4	2.8	2.8	2.8	3.9	3.1	3.4	3.5	2.9
5. Promotion	2.9	3.1	3.4	3.1	3.2	3.7	3.1	3.4	3.4	3.3
6. Supervisor	3.2	2.9	3.4	3.1	3.2	3.4	2.9	3.3	3.2	3.1
II Production control	3.4	3.3	3.5	3.1	3.3	3.5	3.4	3.3	3.4	3.3
7. Equipment	3.9	4.3	3.9	3.4	3.6	3.5	4.0	3.8	3.7	3.9
8. Maintenance	3.1	2.6	3.0	2.8	2.9	3.3	3.0	3.1	3.2	2.8
9. Quality control	3.4	3.4	3.6	3.1	3.3	3.6	3.2	3.2	3.4	3.1
10. Process management	3.5	3.0	3.6	3.2	3.3	3.5	3.2	3.3	3.4	3.3
III Procurement	2.6	3.0	2.5	2.8	2.7	3.2	3.2	3.0	3.2	2.7
11. Local content	1.8	2.7	1.9	2.8	2.4	2.9	3.1	3.0	3.0	2.6
12. Suppliers	2.9	3.9	2.7	2.9	2.8	3.5	3.8	3.3	3.7	2.8
13. Methods	3.1	2.5	2.9	2.8	2.8	3.2	2.8	2.8	3.0	2.7
IV Team sense	3.3	3.2	3.3	2.7	2.9	3.4	3.2	3.0	3.3	2.9
14. Small group	2.6	2.5	2.7	2.5	2.6	3.2	2.9	2.6	3.0	2.2
15. Information sharing	3.6	3.6	3.6	2.8	3.1	3.5	3.3	3.1	3.4	3.2
16. Sense of unity	3.7	3.5	3.7	2.8	3.1	3.6	3.3	3.4	3.5	3.2
V Labor relations	3.7	3.6	3.6	3.2	3.3	3.4	3.1	3.1	3.2	3.4
17. Hiring policy	3.6	3.4	3.3	3.1	3.2	3.0	3.1	2.9	3.0	3.2
18. Long-term employment	3.5	3.4	3.4	3.2	3.3	3.3	3.0	3.0	3.2	3.0
19. Harmonious labor relations	4.2	4.4	4.2	3.5	3.8	4.0	3.3	3.7	3.6	3.8
20. Grievance	3.7	3.3	3.0	3.1	3.0	3.2	3.1	3.0	3.1	3.4
VI Parent–subsidiary relations	2.8	3.6	2.8	3.0	2.9	2.3	2.9	2.7	2.6	2.9
21. Ratio of Japanese	2.1	3.7	2.4	2.6	2.6	1.5	1.6	1.8	1.5	1.9
22. Delegation of power	3.1	3.6	3.0	3.2	3.1	2.7	3.2	3.0	2.9	3.1
23. Position of local managers	3.1	3.6	3.0	3.1	3.1	2.7	3.8	3.2	3.3	3.6
Average of 23 Items	3.2	3.3	3.3	3.0	3.1	3.3	3.2	3.2	3.3	3.1

Notes: NA: North America, UK: the United Kingdom, CWE: Continental West Europe, WE: Western Europe, K/T: Korea/Taiwan, SEA: South East Asia, EA: East Asia, CEE: Central and Eastern Europe

Source: From the database of JMNESG (research year).

the dynamic combinations between the similarities and differences at the various Japanese hybrid factories worldwide.

Diverging patterns

We can see various diverging patterns for the surveyed hybrid factories by region and by industry.

By region

While the total average scores are unbelievably close from region to region, as shown above, in Figure 9.1, a great variety of differences in 23 element items of Japanese production system is shown by region

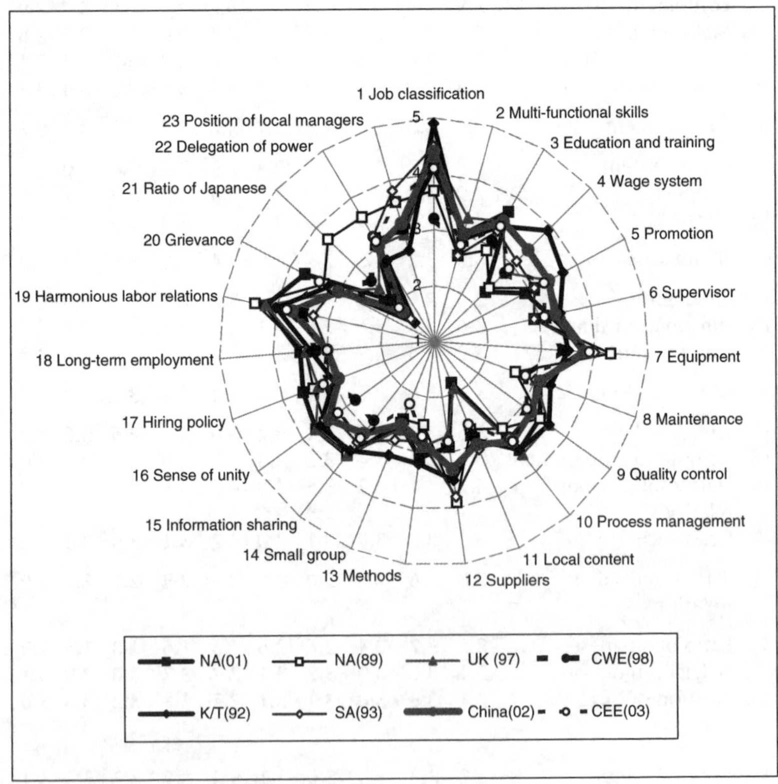

Source: Table 9.1.

Figure 9.1 Hybrid factories in seven major regions: 23 items

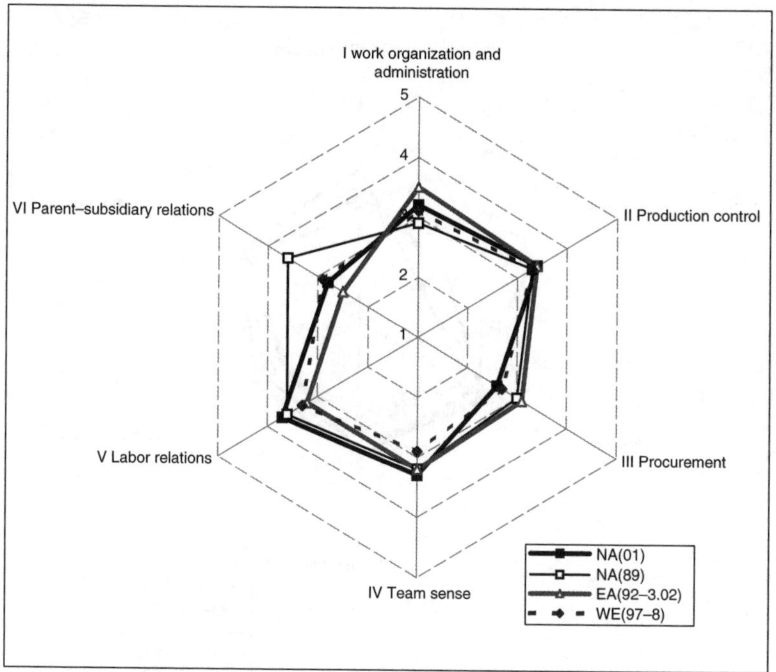

Source: Table 9.1.

Figure 9.2 Hybrid factories in three major regions: six groups

and by items. However, hereafter, I will not enter such details but will describe the more principal diversity in the Japanese hybrid factories worldwide using six groups and, to some extent, four perspective evaluation method.

In Table 9.1, principal regional differences can be seen in scores for the six groups, between the three major regions, North America (89 and 01), Western Europe and East Asia(92–93, 02, China included), and in Figure 9.2, so different shapes of the hexagons are observed.

In Figure 9.3, sharp differences in the six-group hexagons can be seen between the four typical regions of North America (89 and 01), the UK, Continental Western Europe and Korea/Taiwan, a typical East Asia.

In Figure 9.4, looking at three European regions (the UK, Continental West Europe and Central and Eastern Europe), some differences in the shapes of the hexagons are seen in the new European community.

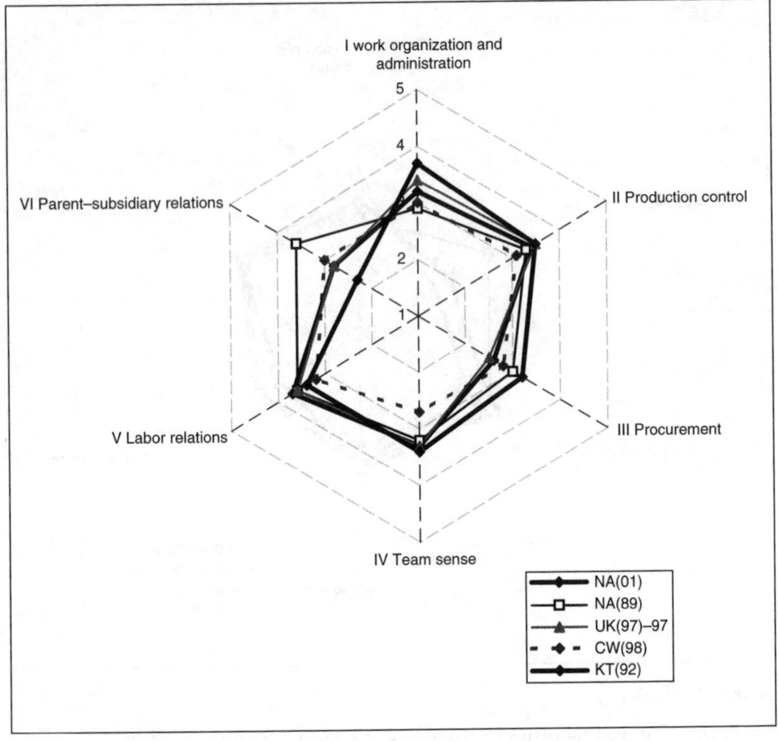

Figure 9.3 Hybrid factories in four typical regions: six groups

By industry

In Figures 1.4.1 and 1.4.2 in Chapter 1, between the automobile assembly and electric and electronics machinery assembly, somewhat symmetrical relational patterns can be seen in North America (89, 01) and Southeast Asia (93). While in North America, overall application scores for the automobile assembly far exceed those for electric and electronics assembly, in Southeast Asia the application scores for electric and electronics assembly are higher than those for automobile assembly. Meanwhile, no significant gaps between the two industries are observed in Britain, Continental Europe, South Korea or Taiwan.

Converging patterns

By time

The most noteworthy change in terms of the convergence of hybrid patterns at Japanese overseas plants is observed between North America (89)

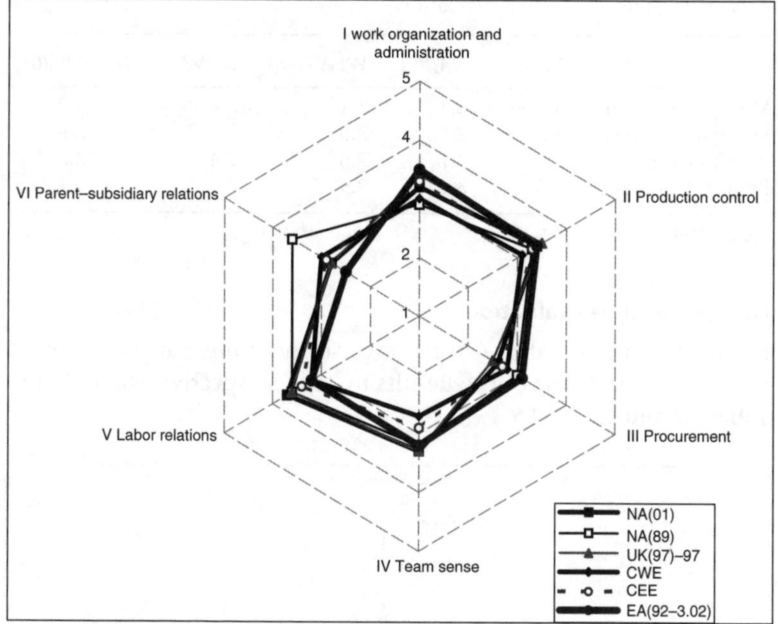

Figure 9.4 Hybrid factories in NA (89,01), UK, CWE, CEE and EA: six groups

and North America (01) (see Figure 9.1 and Chapter 2). This is a large scale convergence of the six-group hexagon for North America (01) from an extreme North American type (89) to a similar pattern to Western Europe, or an intermediate between North America (89) and East Asia, or in other words, toward an 'East Asian pattern,' as described a little later.

The 'East Asian pattern' in the shape of the hexagon for the UK is very significant. There is yet no research evidence showing a historical change from a more typical European type to the present one in the long run, as was observed in a short period of just ten years or so in North America.

By region

So far, as clarified above, while there are many divergent shapes in the six-group hexagons by region and industry for Japanese hybrid factories worldwide, some especially important cases of convergence, such as North America (01), can be observed. As a whole, early in the 21st century the shapes of almost all the hexagons observed, except for that of Continental Western Europe (also North America (89)), seem to be converging toward the 'East Asian pattern' (see Figure 9.3).

Table 9.2 Four perspective evaluation

	NA(01)	*NA(89)*	*WE(97,98)*	*EA(92,93,02)*	*CEE(03)*
Methods–Human	3.3	3.1	3.1	3.4	3.2
Methods–Material	3.2	2.8	3.0	3.2	2.9
Results–Human	2.6	3.7	2.8	2.4	2.8
Results–Material	2.8	3.6	2.9	3.5	3.1

Sources: Tables 1.1 and Table 9.1.

Four perspective evaluation

In addition to the above, the converse situations can be observed more clearly in terms of the Results by four perspective evaluation in Table 9.2 and Figure 9.5.

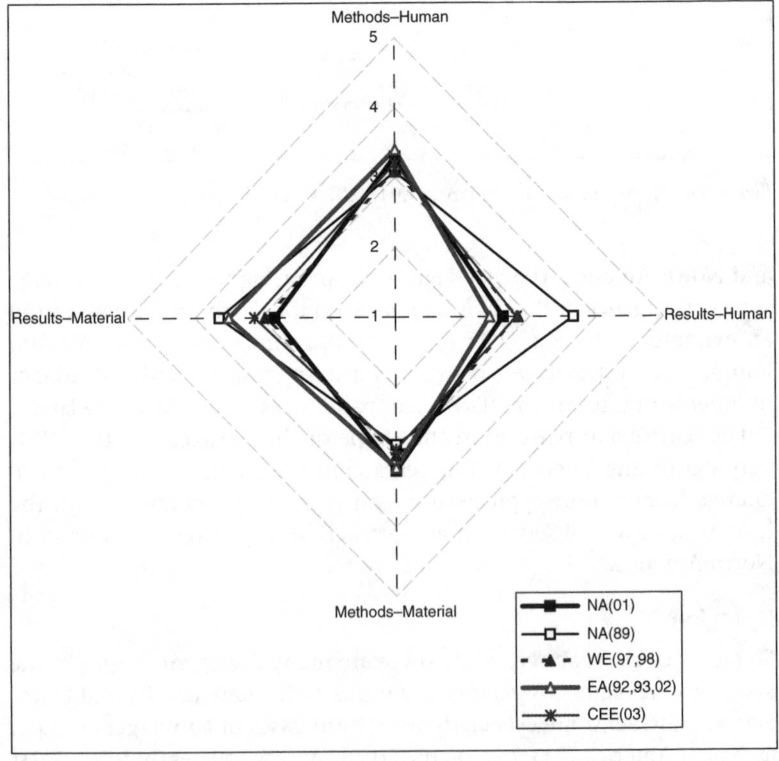

Source: Table 9.2.

Figure 9.5 Four perspective evaluation

The most remarkable is the change of the tetragons of 'four perspective evaluation' between NA(89) and NA(01). The change includes desirable combination of two opposite directions. Along the Results axis both Human and Material lines decreased sharply to become among the shortest, showing significant localization of stuffs and procurements of machines, materials and parts. On the other hand, on the Methods axis Human and Material lines increased a little, meaning substantial rooted-in, to some extent, of essential logics of Japanese production systems.

Apart from the above change in North America, there are not many differences among the shapes of tetragons in other regions, i.e. in the 'four perspective evaluation' almost all of the tetragons are very close to each other in their shapes and sizes. And importantly, the salient feature of the shapes are that the scores on the line of Methods are longer than those of Results, with exception of the distinctly high score of Results–Material for East Asia (high import ratio of machines and parts from Japan) as well as the case of North America (89). The higher ratios of Methods to Results generally mean that at most of the Japanese hybrid factories the methods or logic of the Japanese systems introduced have held a slight edge over the ready made material or human directly brought-in from Japanese parent companies. In other words, local people there have to a considerable degree understood and known how to manage the essential aspects of the systems and to handle the Japanese type machines and materials parts by themselves. This must be substantial technology transfer beyond national boarder.

Why the trends towards the 'East Asian pattern'?

As mentioned above, the 'East Asian pattern' of Japanese hybrid factories can be seen as the most desirable one among many, so this direction of the convergence should be welcomed by Japanese companies. However, why is the converse situation observed among many regions?

There are likely two main reasons for the trend toward the 'East Asian pattern.' First, needless to say, the 'affinity' for Japanese systems may be critical in East Asian countries, where the socio-cultural background is familiar to Japan's. Yet, this is not the case in the UK, where historical and political changes in the social structure may have created a kind of 'affinity' or compatibility with Japanese systems.

Secondly, the strategic responses by Japanese companies to local market and business conditions are also thought to be decisive in other regions. This is typically the case for North America (01), or more precisely, of Japanese automobile makers in the US and Canada, though they had to make great additional investments to compensate for the application gap originated from socio-institutional differences.

Why the 'East Asian pattern'?

Why, then, is the 'East Asian pattern' seen as recommendable? It cannot be called an ideal model for Japanese hybrid factories, but rather as a relatively desirable model. The average application level (3.3) of this pattern is not very high (Table 9.1). In the case of Korea/Taiwan, whose shape for the six-group hexagon is closest to the ideal Japanese model, the average score is just 3.3 and the real application level for each element in GI at shop floors in Japanese hybrid factories in Korea/Taiwan is even lower than the application scores shown in Table 9.1, judging from our observations in terms of the actual Japanese parent plants. However, in this case a higher application score is not necessarily better for the Japanese hybrid model. Given a different socio-institutional environment, it may be impossible or extremely costly to have a full Japanese-style production model in foreign countries.

Anyway, the 'East Asian pattern' can be seen as a desirable one for Japanese hybrid factories in the sense that, above all, the higher human-core portion of Japanese production systems, as shown by the higher application score for GI, is realized with much lower involvement by the Japanese parent company (higher involvement of local management people with profound understanding of the Japanese management systems), represented by the low score of GVI, although the level of local procurement of materials is also low, represented by a high score in GIII (mentioned above).

In conclusion, the 'East Asian pattern' is recommendable since it can function practically in a foreign environment as an international or global model for Japanese hybrid factories. It can smooth the global spread of the Japanese model, including the case of its introduction by foreign manufacturers. Of course, at the same time, it is necessary to point out that the present 'East Asian pattern' has some limitations, such as a slightly too high level for GIII (3.1, lower local procurement), insufficient level in GIV (3.2, relatively low team sense), and not a very high overall application level (3.3).

Needless to say, in addition to that, as described in the discussions above related to technological breakthrough, the Japanese-style management and production system itself is not the only one global competitive production model but one of the epoch-making production models, as the 'integral-type' technology, in the present world.

Another limitation of the system as a global model is the inherent weakness of the Japanese management systems in terms of social scope, i.e. within a relatively homogeneous environment such as within Japanese large companies: women, part-timers, and small companies are often excluded. It is not an easy task to take away from the Japanese society the problems concerning social fairness such as the unequal wage distribution for women and workers at small and medium firms (See Abo, 2005). In this sense, a type of international hybrid factory should be recommended in order to relieve the above-mentioned weak aspects of the Japanese management systems at the cost of reduction in competitive efficiency to some extent.

Reference

Abo. T. (forthcoming) 'Socio-Economics of Wage Differentials: A suggestion from Japanese-style gradual differentiation system of wage', PEKEA international conference, University of Rennes, 4–6 November, 2005.

Appendix: Criteria for the Application Scores in the Hybridization Evaluation of 23 Items, 6 Groups*

I Work organization and administration

(1) Job classification

Evaluation of this item is based upon the number of wage grades that are applied, and the number of job classifications within each wage grade.

5: 1 or 2 wage grades and job classifications
4: 3–5
3: 6–10
2: 11–50
1: 51 or more

(2) Multifunctional skills

5: Job rotation (JR) is common within work teams and also planned and conducted beyond the work teams to train multi-skilled workers. Ordinary production workers utilize score sheets (or tables) and actively engage in quality control, preventive maintenance, and problem solving.

4: JR is common within work teams but limited beyond. Ordinary production workers do participate in quality control and preventive maintenance, although to a somewhat limited extent.

3: JR is almost exclusively carried out within work teams. There is supposed to be a certain amount of participation by ordinary production workers in quality control and problem solving, however, in practice this is rather limited.

2: JR is not commonly carried out, however, in response to fluctuations in demand, model change, or extraordinary situations, job assignments may be switched or job duties expanded. In principle, ordinary production workers do not participate in activities such as quality control or preventive maintenance.

1: There is no JR and job assignments are fixed. There is strict separation between those jobs done by ordinary production workers and those that require specially skilled workers, such as quality control or maintenance.

(3) Education and training

5: Based upon a long-term, systematic education and training program that relies upon OJT and makes use of an in-house training center, the plant is actively engaged in skill formation at every level from ordinary production workers, to maintenance personnel, first-line supervisors, technicians and managers. Personnel are frequently sent to Japan for training, and instructors are often dispatched from Japan. Maintenance personnel and first-line supervisors are chiefly trained from within.

4: Although its program is less planned or systematic, the plant enthusiastically pursues in-house training, primarily on the basis of OJT. Personnel are sent to Japan for training, although this is generally restricted to core personnel such as maintenance personnel or first-line supervisors.
3: Although it is not very systematic, in-house training and education is carried out chiefly through OJT. To the extent that the in-house training of core personnel is inadequate, these personnel are either sent to Japan, trainers are dispatched from Japan, or there is some reliance upon external sources for training and education. There may also be an apprenticeship system.
2: OJT is not very highly regarded. Personnel are expected to pick up whatever skills they need, naturally. At best, there may be some utilization of external sources for training and some personnel may be sent to Japan. Many of the personnel requirements are met from outside.
1: There is no emphasis at all upon in-house training. Necessary skilled personnel are hired from outside.

(4) Wage system

5: Wages are fundamentally the same as in Japan. Basic wages are person-centered and determined by age, seniority, job qualifications, and individual merit. Bonuses are paid and there are periodic raises. There is little discrepancy between the wage system or the amount of wages paid to blue-collar or and white-collar personnel.
4: The extent of supplementary wages paid by the company is broader than in the case of 3 points and there is much scope for merit. Wages also reflect age and seniority.
3: Wages are basically determined by the national wage agreement with some supplementary wages. Merit is the major determinant of supplementary pay.
2: Wages are determined by the national wage agreement and the company's supplementary wages. Merit is not a determinant.
1: Wages are determined by the national wage agreement, and in accordance with numerous job classifications and in-house wage grades. There is no pay for merit.

(5) Promotion

5: The plants adopts an internal promotion system where production workers, including technicians, can be promoted to first-line supervisors and sometimes to middle management positions according to ability. Receiving a promotion is also partly determined by length of service. This means that long-term employees can rise to upper ranks of in-house qualifications, whereas even skilled employees must remain at specified ranks for a specified number of years. Recommendation by the supervisor is a necessary condition for promotion. The speed of promotion is, however, affected by the individual performance evaluation.
4: The plant adopts almost the same type of internal promotion system as described above, however, production workers are unable to be promoted any higher than the position of first-line supervisor.
3: Managers, including first-line supervisors, are partly promoted from within the company, and partly recruited from outside. Ordinary production

workers and technicians can rise to higher wage grades based on their length of service and performance evaluation.

2: Internal promotion is only partially implemented, and there is a basic separation between the promotion of shop-floor workers and that of managers, including first-line supervisors. Promotion is influenced by academic background and state or community qualifications. Where labor union regulations exist, seniority has priority over the performance evaluation in determining production workers' promotion to higher wage grades.

1: There is a clear separation between the promotion of shop-floor workers and the promotion of managers. Promotion to different jobs or to higher wage grades is determined by academic background and community or state qualifications. Where labor union regulations exist, the promotion to higher wage grades is determined by seniority.

(6) First-line supervisor

5: First-line supervisors are internally promoted and they actively participate not only in labor management (maintaining workplace discipline and carrying out individual performance evaluations) but also in the management of work teams (examination of daily production plans, workers' job assignments, analyzing operational situations, securing parts and materials, and education and training), and in the technical control of production processes (setting up work standards, equipment maintenance, quality control, *kaizen* activities). They also play important roles in coordinating different workplaces.

4: First-line supervisors have slightly inferior management skills compared with their Japanese counterparts.

3: First-line supervisors are partly internally promoted and partly externally recruited. They participate in the management of work teams and in the technical control of production processes, but there are weaknesses in their management skills and they require technicians for support.

2: First-line supervisors lack considerable skills for the management of work teams or the technical control of production processes.

1: First-line supervisors are only concerned with labor management. The plant does not adhere to internal promotion of first-line supervisors.

II Production control

(7) Equipment

5: 100% of the equipment is the same as in Japan.

4: 75% of the equipment is the same as in Japan. Or, 100% but older, perhaps less automated machines are utilized.

3: 50% of the equipment is the same as in Japan.

2: 25% of the equipment is the same as in Japan.

1: Equipment is different from that used in Japan.

(8) Maintenance

5: Shop-floor maintenance personnel are chosen from among production workers and trained internally, or enter as new, inexperienced employees, hired separately from ordinary workers. Ordinary production workers actively participate in preventive or other easy maintenance operations. Without the support of Japanese expatriates, the skills of maintenance personnel are so advanced that the stoppage ratios (downtime-to-operating ratios), even for new types of machines, are almost the same as in Japan.

4: Ordinary production workers participate in maintenance to a lesser extent, and stoppage ratios are slightly higher than for plants assigned 5 points.

3: Some maintenance personnel are trained internally, and some have external experience. Ordinary production workers do not participate so actively in maintenance. Skills of maintenance personnel are not very high and the support of Japanese expatriates is required.

2: Maintenance personnel are mainly recruited externally as experienced workers. Ordinary workers do not participate in maintenance, and maintenance is led by engineers including Japanese expatriates.

1: Maintenance personnel are solely recruited externally as experienced workers. Maintenance is carried out under the leadership of engineers.

(9) Quality control

5: The plant emphasizes 'building quality into the production process'. Production workers actively participate in quality control in various ways: (attending to quality, referring to standard work procedures that specify items to check for quality, applying their ability to recognize defective products, and exercising authority to stop production lines, as well as participating in quality improvement activities, active QC and ZD movements). In-process defect ratios and product quality at the shipment stage are both almost equivalent to what is achieved at Japanese plants.

4: The plant emphasizes building quality into the production process, but there are fewer concrete measures. In-process defect ratios are slightly higher than in Japan.

3: The plant tries to build quality into the production process but finds it difficult. Therefore, it assigns more QC personnel or inspectors, or it sets up more check points than in Japan, so as to secure product quality at the shipment stage.

2: Ordinary production workers seldom participate in quality control and quality control or inspection specialists reject defective products after meticulous inspection at many stages in the production process.

1: The plant emphasizes procedures to reject defective products during final product inspection.

(10) Process management

5: Small-lot production on a diverse product line is carried out as smoothly as in Japan, and through the following practices and measures: a diverse model mix on the same production line, frequent product changes, die and jig changes on-the-fly, strict in-process inventory management, applying and achieving the same standard times as in Japan, coordination of line balances led by first-line supervisors, preventive maintenance, quick trouble response through close inter-divisional coordination, and *kaizen* activities.

4: Small-lot production on a diverse product line is carried out, but to a lesser extent than above.

3: Ordinary operations go smoothly, but the support of Japanese expatriates is required to respond to trouble or to major operational changes such as the introduction of new models. A smaller number of models is produced.
2: Mainly engineers and Japanese expatriates should respond to trouble and to carry out operational changes. The number of models is not large. *Kaizen* activities at the shop floor are not expected. There are some problems with production efficiency.
1: Process management is mainly carried out by engineers, including Japanese expatriates, and not by shop-floor workers. The number of models produced is extremely small. There are major problems with production efficiency.

III Procurement

(11) Local content

5: Less than 20% of parts are locally produced and procured.
4: From 20% to less than 40%.
3: From 40% to less than 60%.
2: From 60% to less than 80%.
1: From 80% to 100%.

(12) Suppliers

5: Parts and materials and are mainly procured from Japan, with remaining parts procured from Japanese affiliated suppliers.
4: Key parts and materials are procured from Japan. A high proportion of components procured in host or third countries are from Japanese affiliated suppliers, including sister plants.
3: Only some of the key parts and materials are procured from Japan. Among parts procured in host or third countries, half is from Japanese affiliated suppliers and the other half is from non-Japanese affiliated companies.
2: Parts and materials are procured mainly from non-Japanese affiliated suppliers in host or third countries with the only exception being some of the key parts.
1: Almost all the parts and materials, including key ones, are procured from non-Japanese affiliates suppliers in host or third countries.

(13) Procurement method

5: Practices such as just-in-time, maintaining quality without inspecting at time of procurement, or technological assistance and cooperation (sometimes joint product development or design-in) are implemented through long-term transaction relationships with suppliers.
4: The practices mentioned above are only implemented with some suppliers.
3: Though it is impossible to implement practices such as just-in-time, or maintaining quality without inspecting at time of procurement, some arrangements are made to reduce parts inventory or to facilitate smooth plant operations. Technological assistance is attempted with local suppliers in order to improve quality, cost, and punctual delivery.

2: Local suppliers are relied upon to maintain quality standards and observe delivery times.
1: Transactions with local suppliers are mainly characterized by spot trading. Parts inventories are quite high in order to cope with defective parts and delayed delivery.

IV Group consciousness

(14) Small group activities

5: Most of the workers participate voluntarily and actively in small group activities. They suggest subjects for the activities and achieve a substantial effect with regard to quality, productivity and safety.
4: More than 50% of workers participate voluntarily and actively in small group activities, which enhance workplace morale, but have limited substantial effects. Or, most workers participate actively, although their participation is mandatory.
3: 20% to 50% of workers participate voluntarily, or, most workers participate where such participation is mandatory. The activities are carried out but without much enthusiasm.
2: Less than 20% of workers participate, or activities exist only in special model cases. Or, arrangements such as a system for suggestions is made to improve the atmosphere at the workplace.
1: Neither small group activities nor suggestion systems exists.

(15) Information sharing

5: The plant tries to communicate the intentions of management to employees, to perceive employees opinions, and to facilitate communication within the company, through meetings and gatherings at all levels, through the disclosure of information from management, and through small group activities. There are no significant linguistic communication gaps.
4: Various provisions for information sharing exist, but to a lesser degree than in the case of five points.
3: Attempts are made at information sharing through meetings and other means at each level of the company.
2: The only information sharing is at meetings before work begins.
1: There are no special provisions for information sharing.

(16) Sense of unity

5: The following devices and practices are fully implemented to facilitate a sense of unity among employees: cafeterias open to all employees, uniforms, open-style offices, company-wide social events, morning ceremonies, open parking, company-owned recreational facilities, and so on.
4: Many of the devices and practices mentioned above are implemented but to a lesser extent.
3: Only some of the above are practiced.
2: Only some social events are held.
1: There are no special practices.

V Labor relations

(17) Hiring method

5: All applicants, including those for ordinary production jobs, are carefully screened (through paper examinations, interviews, and multi-tiered selection). The plant can select employees from among many applicants. The plant emphasizes new graduates in the case of recruitment at a higher level of academic background. The company selected the site for the plant by taking characteristics of labor into consideration.
4: Applicants are carefully screened but to a lesser extent than above.
3: Applicants are screened, but there are restrictions stemming from less competition among applicants and a high mobility of labor.
2: Employees are hired only by a very simple test because there are not so many applicants or because the plant must hire frequently.
1: There is no special selection.

(18) Long term employment

5: The plant is explicit about its intention to avoid layoffs on managerial grounds as much as possible and, in fact, the plant has never laid off employees. Provisions for long-term employment are implemented and employees actually do stay with the company for a long time.
4: The situation is basically the same as above, but to a lesser extent with regard to vigorously expressing its intentions. Or, the stability of the workforce is slightly less.
3: The plant does not adhere firmly to a policy of avoiding layoffs (employees have been laid off in the past) although it is not desirable to lay off employees on managerial grounds. The plant hopes key personnel will stay with the company for a long time, but at best, the only measures to secure long-term employment are slightly higher wages. Employee mobility is equal to the local average.
2: Managers think that it is unavoidable to lay off employees on managerial grounds, and in fact the plant has laid off several times. There are no special provisions for long-term employment. As employee mobility is high, the plant can adjust the number of employees without resorting to layoffs.
1: Managers believe it is natural to lay off employees on managerial grounds and the plant has frequently laid off employees. Employee mobility is very high.

Note: Employee mobility was considered both as an absolute ratio and with respect to the local average.

(19) Labor relations

5: Management maintains harmonious relations with the labor union, the works council plays a similar role as the labor–management consultation system in Japan, and there is a determined effort to achieve good communication with personnel. Or, if there is no labor union, then management builds friendly relations with personnel via the works council and takes great care to treat the employees well.

4: There is a labor union and management maintains harmonious labor relations. Efforts to establish a good communicative relationship with personnel are slightly less vigorous than in the case of 5 points.
3: There is a labor union and while negotiations with the union have been arduous at times, there has been no labor dispute. On account of the works council, there have been no particular personnel-related problems.
2: There is a labor union and although there are no major disputes, confrontations about wages or working conditions have, in the past, led to strike action.
1: Labor relations are adversarial. There have been frequent strikes.

(20) Grievance procedure

5: The plant actively attempts to satisfy employee demands such as improved labor and workplace environments, and grievances are resolved mainly at the shop floor or through managerial channels.
4: The plant attempts to satisfy employee demands. In addition to the managerial channel, the personnel department intervenes in the process of resolving grievances (the 'open door' approach).
3: The plant appears to pay some attention to employee demands. Grievances are resolved both on the shop floor and by official grievance procedures through a union.
2: The plant does not put much effort into responding to employee demands or complaints. Grievances tend to be resolved through the labor union channel.
1: The plant pays almost no attention to employee demands. There are many grievances and they are resolved only through the labor union channel. There were cases where grievance procedures reached the stage of external arbitration.

VI Parent–subsidiary relation

(21) Ratio of Japanese expatriates

5: Ratio of Japanese expatriates is 4% or more.
4: 3% to less than 4%.
3: 2% to less than 3%.
2: 1% to less than 2%.
1: less than 1%.
Note: For plants with less than 500 employee, one percentage point was added to each of the above ratios.

(22) Delegation of authority

Regarding products, investment, market, local personnel, R&D, etc.
5: Parent company in Japan makes basically all plans and decisions.
4: Parent in Japan makes decisions to a substantial degree, while subsidiary submits suggested plans.
3: The subsidiary submits plans and the parent evaluates them, and gives or withholds approval.

2: The subsidiary makes substantial plans and decisions while sounding out the intention of parent.
1: The subsidiary basically makes all plans and decisions.
Note: The share of equity held by the Japanese company in a joint venture, as well as the characteristics of the local partner should be taken into consideration.

(23) Position of local managers

5: The most important senior management positions, including president (top management), are all held by Japanese.
4: The president is Japanese and the majority of important positions are held by Japanese.
3: Japanese and local people share management and other important positions fairly equally.
2: The president is a local person and the majority of important positions are held by local people.
1: The most important senior management positions, including president, are held by local people.
Note: Even if the number of Japanese expatriates holding senior management positions is small, if they hold strong authority, the application is higher. The working language used at meetings serves as a reference.

Note

*For more detailed explanations see Abo (1994a), pp. 29–35, Itagaki (1997b), pp. 36–44, and Kumon and Abo (2004), pp. 19–29.

Bibliography

Books and journals

Abegglen, J.C. (1957) *The Japanese Factory*, MIT Press.

Abegglen, James C. and George Stalk Jr (1985) *Kaisha* (Basic Books).

Abo, Tetsuo (ed.) (1990) *Local Production of Japanese Automobile and Electronics Firms in the United States: the 'Application' and 'Adaptation' of Japanese Style Management*, Research Report no. 23 (Tokyo: The Institute of Social Science, University of Tokyo).

Abo, Tetsuo (ed.) (1994a) *Hybrid Factory: The Japanese Production System in the United States* (New York: Oxford University Press).

Abo, Tetsuo (ed.) (1994b) *Nihonteki Keiei Seisan Shisutemu to Amerika: Shisutemu no Kokusai Iten to Haiburiddoka (Japanese Management and Production System in America: the International Transfer of the System and Its Hybridization Process)* (Kyoto: Minerva Shobo).

Abo, Tetsuo (1997) 'The Electronics Assembly Industry', in H. Itagaki (1997b).

Abo, Tetsuo (1998a) 'Hybridization of the Japanese Production System in North America, Newly Industrializing Economics, South-East Asia, and Europe: Contrasted Configurations', in Robert Boyer, U. Jurgens, and S. Tolliday (eds) *Between Imitation and Innovation: The Transfer and Hybridization of Productive Models in the International Automobile Industry* (New York: Oxford University Press).

Abo, Tetsuo (1998b) 'Changes in Japanese Automobile and Electronic Transplants in the USA, 1989–1993', in Hasegawa Harukiyo and G.D. Hook (eds) (1998).

Abo, Tetsuo (1998c) 'Toshiba's Overseas Production Activities: Seven Large Plants in the USA, Mexico, the UK, Germany and France', in H. Mirza (ed.), *Global Competitive Strategies in the New World Economy* (Cheltenham: Edward Elgar).

Abo, Tetsuo (2000) 'Spontaneous Integration in Japan and East Asia: Development, Crisis, and Beyond', in G.L. Clark, M.P. Feldman and M.S. Gartler (eds), *The Oxford Handbook of Economic Geography* (New York: Oxford University Press).

Abo, Tetsuo (200l) 'Competition and Cooperation Between the Japanese and British Management Models in the UK: International Transfer Problems of Intangible Management Systems', in P. Banerjee and F-J. Richter (eds), *Intangibles in Competition and Cooperation: Euro-Asian Perspectives* (New York: Palgrave Macmillan).

Abo, Tetsuo (2002) 'Toshiba', in Allan Bird (ed.) (2002).

Abo, Tetsuo (2003) 'Japanese Hybrid Factories in Germany: Survival in a Different Environment', in Park, S-J. and Horn, S. (eds) (2003).

Abo, Tetsuo (2004a) 'An Integrated Theory of Mangement Geography: Japanese Hybrid Factories in the Three Mager Regions', in Gupta, V. (ed.), *Transformative Organizations* (New Delhi: Response Books).

Abo, Tetsuo (2004b) 'A Shortened Path to Transplant the Japanese Management System', in Strzelczak (2003).

Abo. Tetsuo (2005) 'Socio-Economics of Wage Differentials: A suggestion from Japanese-style gradual differentiation system of wage', PEKEA international conference, University of Rennes, 4–6 November, 2005 (forthcoming from Cambridge Scholars Press).

Adler, Paul S. (1993a) 'Time-and-Motion Regained', *Harvard Business Review*, Jan.–Feb.

Adler, Paul S. (1993b) 'The "Learning Bureaucracy": New United Motors Manufacturing, Inc.' in Barry Staw and Larry Cummings (eds), *Research in Organizational Behavior* (Greenwich, Conn: JAI Press).

Adler, Paul S. and Robert E. Cole (1993) 'Designed for Learning: A Tale of Two Auto Plants', *Sloan Management Review*, Spring.

Alonso, J., Carrillo, J. (1996) 'Gobernación Económica y Cambio Industrial en la Frontera Norte de México: Un Análisis de Trayectorias Locales de Aprendizaje', in *Revista Eure*, no. 67, Santiago, Chile, December.

Alonso, J., Carrillo, J. and Contreras, O. (1994) 'Mercados laborales y condiciones de trabajo en la transición de la industria maquiladora', paper International Seminar 'Las Maquiladoras en México: Presente y Futuro del Desarrollo Industrial', El Colegio de la Frontera Norte and International Institute for Labour Studies ILO, Tijuana, 23–25 May.

Alonso, J., Carrillo, J. and Contreras, O. (2000) 'Trayectorias tecnológicas en empresas maquiladoras asiáticas y americanas en México', *Serie Desarrollo Productivo*, no. 72, División de Desarrollo Productivo y Empresarial, Santiago de Chile: Naciones Unidas (CEPAL-ECLAC). Agosto.

Aoki, M. (1989) *Information, Incentives, and Bargaining in the Japanese Economy* (Cambridge: Cambridge University Press).

Aoki, M. (2000) *Information, Corporate Governance, and Institutional Diversity: Competitiveness in Japan, the USA, and the Transitional Economies* (Oxford: Oxford University Press).

Arias, A. and Dutrenit, G. (2003) 'Acumulación de Capacidades Tecnológicas Locales de Empresas Globales en México: El Caso del Centro Técnico de Delphi Corp', Ponencia Congreso Anual ALTEC 'Conocimiento, Innovación y Competitividad: Los Desafios de la Globalización'. México, 22–24 October.

Asanuma, Banri (1997) *Nihon no Kigyo-soshiki Kakushinteki Tekio no Mekanizumu: Choki-Torihiki Kankei no Kozo to Kino (Japanese Corporate Organization. Mechanism of Innovative Adaptation: Structure and Function of the Long Term Transaction)* (Tokyo: Toyo keizai shinposha).

Baba, Yasuo, and Norio Okazaki, (eds) (1999) *Itaria no Keizai – 'Meido in Itari' wo Umi dasu Mono (The Italian Economy – Creating 'Made in Italy'* (Tokyo: Waseda University Press).

Babson, Steve (ed.) (1995) *Lean Work: Empowerment and Exploitation in the Global Auto Industry* (Detroit: Wayne State University Press).

Beechler, S.L. and Bird, A. (1999) *Japanese Multinationals Abroad* (Oxford: Oxford University Press).

Berger, Suzanne and Ronald Dore (1996) *National Diversity and Global Capitalism* (Ithaca: Cornell University Press).

Berggren, Christian (1993) *The Volvo E. Kperience: Alternatives to Lean Production in the Swedish Auto Industry* (London: Palgrave Macmillan).

Berggren, Christian (1994) 'NUMMI vs. Uddevalla', *Sloan Management Review*, Winter.

Besser, Terry L. (1996) *Team Toyota: Transplanting the Toyota Culture to the Camly Plant in Kentucky* (New York: State University of New York Press).

Bird, Allan (ed.) (2002) *The Encyclopedia of Japanese Business & Management* (London: Routledge).

Boeki no Nihonsha (1997) *Kigyo Katsusha Sirizu – Soritsu 60-shunen Canon – Kyosei wo Rinen-ni. Yuryo Kigyo Gurupu wo Mezasu (Lively Pictures of Corporation Series: 60th Anniversary of Canon, Aspiring to Become an Excellent Corporate Group under the Philosophy of Living and Working Together for the Common Good)* (Tokyo: Boeki no Nihonsha).

Boyer, Robert, Elsie Charron, Ulrich Jurgens and Steven Tolliday (eds) (1998) *Between Imitation and Innovation: The Transfer and Hybridization of Productive Models in the International Automobile Industry* (New York: Oxford University Press).

Bratton, John (1992) *Japanization at Work: Managerial Studies for the 1990s* (London: Macmillan).

Brewster, Chris (1995) 'Towards a "European" Model of Human Resource Management', *Journal of International Business Studies*, 26(1).

Buitelaar, R., Ramón, P. and Urrutia, R. (1999) *Centroamérica, México y República Dominicana: Maquila y Transformación Productiva, Cuadernos de la CEPAL 85*, Santiago de Chile, Naciones Unidas.

Bureau of National Affairs (1996) *Employer Bargaining Objectives*.

Carrillo, J. (ed.) (1993) *Condiciones de empleo y capacitación en las maquiladoras de exportación en México*, Secretaria del Trabajo y Previsión Social y El Colegio de la Frontera Norte, Tijuana.

Carrillo, J. (1995) 'Flexible Production in the Auto Sector: Industral Reorganization at Ford-Mexico', in *World Development*, vol. 23, no. 1 (Oxford: Pergamon).

Carrillo, J. and Gomis, R. (2004) 'Medición de las generaciones de maquiladoras', in Frontera Norte, *El Colegio de la Frontera Norte*, Tijuana.

Carrillo, J. and Hinojosa, R. (2001) 'Cableando el Norte de México: La evolución de la industria maquiladora de arneses', in *Región y Sociedad*, vol. XIII, no. 21, Hermosillo, January–June.

Carrillo, J. and Hualde, A. (1998) 'Third Generation Maquiladoras?. The Delphi-General Motors Case', in *Journal of Borderlands Studies*, vol. XIII, no. 1, Spring, San Diego, pp. 79–97.

Carrillo, J. and Hualde, A. (2004) 'De la TV de cinescopio a la TV digital: trayectoria evolutiva o imposición del mercado', in Carrillo J. and Barajas (eds), *Escalamiento industrial y aprendizaje en las maquiladoras fronterizas. Resultados de investigación*, COLEF, Tijuana.

Carrillo, J. and Lara, A. (2003) 'Maquiladoras de cuarta generación y coordinación centralizada', in *Cuadernos del CENDES*, no. 54, September–December.

Carrillo, J. and Montiel, Y. (2004) 'American versión of Japanese Production System: The Plants of Ford-Hermosillo and Delphi Automotive System-Ciudad Juárez', in Kawamura (2005).

Carrillo, J., Mortimore, M. and Alonso, J. (1999) *Competitividad y Mercados de Trabajo Empresas de Autopartes y de Televisores en México* (Plaza y Valdéz: UACJ y UAM).

Cawson, Alan, Kevin Morgan, Douglas Webber, Peter Holmes and Anne Stevens (1990) *Hostile Brothers: Competition and Closure in the European Electronics Industry* (Oxford: Clarendon Press).
Chishima, A. (2003) *Chinese Labor Organizations and Labor Relations, Organization and Function of Labor Unions*, Productivity & Labor Information Center.
Christman, J. (2004) 'Maquiladora Industry Outlook', *Global Insight*, January.
Christman, J. (2003) 'Maquiladora Industry Outlook', *Global Insight*, March.
Choi, D. and Kenney, M. (1997) 'The Globalization of Korean Industry: Korean Maquiladoras in México', in *Frontera Norte*, vol. 9, no. 17 January–June.
Church, Roy (1995) *The Rise and Decline of the British Motor Industry* (Cambridge: Cambridge University Press).
Clark, Kim B. and Takahiro Fujimoto (1991) *Product Development Performance* (Harvard Business School).
Coase, R.H. (1937) 'The Nature of Firm', *Economica*, N.S.1937, 4.
Cole, R.E. (ed.) (1981) 'The Japanese Automobile Industry', *Michigan Papers in Japanese Studies*, No. 3.
Cook, M.L. (1998) *Trade Union Strategies Under NAFTA: The Unit States Automotive Sector* (Cornell University).
Cutcher-Gershenfeld *et al*. (1995) 'Japanese Team-based Work Systems in North America: Explaining Diversity', *Califomia Management Review*, 37(1), pp. 42–64.
Dallas Federal Reserve Bank (2003) 'Conference Maquiladora Down Turn: Cyclical or Structural Factors?', Isla del Padre, 21 November http://www.dallasfed.org/news/research/2003/03maquiladora.html
De la Garza, E. (2004) 'La Polémica de la Maquila en México: nuevas evidencias', Ponencia, LASA, Las Vegas, 8 October.
Delbridge, Rick (1998) *Life on the Line in Contemporary Manufacturing: the Workplace Experience of Lean Production and the 'Japanese' Model* (New York: Oxford University Press).
Doeringer, Peter, B., Lorenz, Edward and Terkla, David G. (2001) 'The Transferability of Efficient Organizational Regimes: Evidence From Japanese Multinationals' (www.bu.edu/econ/ied/neudc/papers/).
Dohse, K., Jurgens, U. and Malsch, T. (1985) 'From Fordism to Toyotism? The Social Organization of the Labour Process in the Japanese Automobile Industry', *Politics and Society*, 14(2).
Dore, Ronald P. (1973) *British Factory – Japanese Factory* (Berkeley, Ca: University of California Press).
Dunlop, John T. (1989) 'Have the 1980's changed U.S. industrial relations?', *Monthly Labor Review*, May 1988.
Durand, Jean-Pierre, Paul Stewart and Juan Jos6 Castillo (eds) (1999) *Teamwork in the Automobile Industry: Radical Change or Passing Fashion?* (London: Palgrave Macmillan).
Dussel, E. (2003) 'Ser maquila o no ser maquila, ¿es ésa la pregunta?', in *Comercio Exterior*, Mexico, vol. 53, no. 4, April.
Dussel, E. and Xue Dong, Liu (2004) 'Oportunidades y retos economicos de China para Mexico y centroamérica', CEPAL, LC/MEX/L.633, Mexico, 27 September.
Dutrenit, G. and Veracruz, A. (2004) 'La IED y las caapacidades de innovación desarrollo locales: Leccines del estudio de los casos de la maquila automotriz y eletrónica en Ciudad Juárez', CEPAL, LC/MEX/L.604, México.

Elger, Tony and Smith, Chris (ed.) (1994) *Global Japanization? The Transnational Transformation of the Labour Process* (London: Routledge).

Elger, T. and Smith, C. (2005) *Assemling Work* (Oxford: Oxford University Press).

Freedman, Audrey (1988) 'How the 1980s have changed industrial relations', U.S. Department of Labor, BLS, *Monthly Labor Review*, May 1988.

Freyssenet, Michel, Mair, Andrew, Shimizu, Koichi and Volpato, Giuseppe (eds) (1998) *One Best Way? Trajectories and Industrial Models of the World's Automobile Producers* (New York: Oxford University Press).

Freyssenet, Michel, Shimizu, Koichi and Volpato, Giuseppe (eds) (2003) *Globalization or Regionalization of the American and Asian Car Industry?* (Basingstoke: Palgrave Macmillan).

Fruin, W. (1997) *Knowledge Works: Managing Intellectual Capital at Toshiba* (Oxford: Oxford University Press).

Fuchs, M. (2003) 'Learning in Automobile Components Supply Companies: The Maquiladora of Ciudad Juárez, Mexico', in Lo, Schamp *Knowledge, Learning, and Regional Development* (Berlin).

Fucini, Joseph and Fucini, Suzy (1990) *Working for the Japanese* (New York: Free Press).

Fujimoto, Takahiro (1999) *The Evolution of a Manufacturing System at Toyota* (New York: Oxford University Press).

Fujimoto, T., Takeishi, A. and Aoshima Y. (2001) 'Bijinesu Ahkitekucha (Business Architecture)', Yuhikaku Garrahan, Philip, and Paul Stewart (eds) (1992) *The Nissan Enigma: Flexibility at Work in a Local Economy* (London: Mansell).

General Accounting Office (GAO) (2003) 'International Trade. Mexico's Maquiladora Decline Afeects U.S. México Border Communities and Trade; Recovery Depends in Part on Mexico's Actions', Report to Congressional Requesters, United States, July.

Gerber, J. and Carrillo, J. (2003) 'Competitiveness Characteristics of the Electronics Maquiladora on Mexico's Northern Border', Annual Conference Association of Borderlands Scholars (ABS). Las Vegas, 9–11 April.

Ghosn, Carlos (2001) *Runessansu: Saisei heno Chosen (Renaissance: Taking on Challenge of Rebirth)* (Tokyo: Daiyamondo Sha).

González-Aréchiga, B. y Ramírez, J.C. (1989) 'La Inversión Asiática en Baja California: Un Caso Diferente de Especialización Regional', in *Seminario Reconversión Industrial, Inversión Extranjera y Territorio*, UAM y CIDE.

Graham, Laurie (1995) *On the Line at Subaru-Isuzu: The Japanese Model and the American Worker* (Ithaca, NY: ILR Press).

Grunwald J., Flann K. (1985) *The Global Factory*, Washington, The Brookings Institution Hall, E.T. (1976) *Beyond Culture*, Anchor Books.

Hao, Y. (1999) *Chugoku no Keizai Hatten to Nihon-teki Seisan Shisutemu*, Mineruva Shobo (*Chinese Economic Growth and the Japanese Production System*).

Hasegawa, Harukiyo (1998) 'Japanese Global Strategies in Europe and the Formation of Regional Markets', in Harukiyo Hasegawa and Genn D. Hook (eds), *Japanese Business Management: Restructuring for Low Growth and Globalization* (London: Routledge).

Heinz-Jurgen Stuting, Wolfgang, Dorow, Frank Claassen and Blazejewskim, Susanne (ed.) (2003) *Chang Management in Transition Economies: Integrating Corporate Strategy, Structure and Culture* (Basingstoke: Palgrave Macmillan).

Helper, S. and MacDuffie, J.P. (2000) 'E-volving the auto industry: E-commerce effects on consumer and supplier relationships', paper prepared for *E-Business and the changing terms of competition: a view from within the sectors*, Haas School of Business, UC Berkeley, April 24.

Helper, S. and Sako, M. (1995) 'Supplier Relations in Japan and the United States: Are They Converging?', *Sloan Management Review*, 36, no. 3, Spring.

Hualde, A. (2001) *Aprendizaje industrial en la frontera norte de México: La articulación entre el sistema educativo y el sistema productivo maquilador*, ed. Colegio de la Frontera Norte/Plaza y Valdes, Mexico.

Hudson, Ray and Eike W. Schamp (eds) (1995) *Towards a New Map of Automobile Manufacturing in Europe? New Production Concepts and Spatial Restructuring* (Berlin: Springer).

Humphrey, J. and Oeter, A. (2000) 'Motor Industry Policies in Emerging Markets: Globalisation and the Promotion of Domestic Industry', in J. Humphrey, Y. Lecler, M. Salerno (eds), *Global Strategies and local Realities* (London: Macmillan).

Hood, N. (2003) *The Multinational Subsidiary* (Basingstoke: Palgrave).

Iguchi, Yasushi (2000) 'Chutouou Shokoku niokeru Kigyou Senryaku Gijutsu Iten Niizu no Henka to Jinzai Ido' (*Changing Needs for Corporate Strategy and Technology Transfer in Central and Eastern Europe and Human Resources Movement: An Analysis Based on the Field Survey of the Japanese Subsidiaries*) Kansai Gakuin University, *Kansai Gakuin Economic Review*, vol. 54, no. 1.

Iori, Masayoshi (2002) 'Nikkei Seizo Kigyo no Han Oshu Senryaku', ('Pan-European Strategy of Japanese Manufactures'), Symposium to Commemorate the 10th Anniversaly of Waseda University's European Center at Bonn University Club, 22 March.

Ishida, Kazuo *et al.* (eds) (1998) *Kigyo Rodo no Nichiei Hikaku (Japan–UK Comparison of Industrial Labour*) (Tokyo: Otsuki Shoten Publishers).

Ishikawa, Kaoru (1981) *Nihonteki Hinshitu-Kanri: TQC toha Nanika, (Japanese Quality Control System: What Is TQC)* (Tokyo: Nikkagiren).

Ishikawa, Kenjiro (1990) *Japan and the Challenge of Europe 1992* (London: Pinter Publishers).

Ishikawa, Kenjiro (1991) *EC Togo to Nihon: Mo Hitotsu no Keizaimasatsu (The Single European Market and Japan: Another Economic Friction)* (Tokyo: Seibunsha).

Itagaki, Hiroshi (ed.) (1997a) *Nihonteki Keiei. Seisan Shisutemu to Higashi Ajia-Taiwan. Kankoku. Chugoku ni okeru Haiburiddo Kojo, (Japanese Management and Production Systems and East Asia: Hybrid Factories in Taiwan. Korea, and China*) (Kyoto: Minerva Shobo).

Itagaki, Hiroshi (ed.) (1997b) *The Japanese Production System: Hybrid Factories in East Asia* (London: Palgrave Macmillan).

Itagaki, Hiroshi (2000) *Keizai Kikika no Ajia niokeru Nikkei Kojo*, Musashi Daigaku Ronshu, vol. 40, nos. 3/4.

Itanii, H. (1987) *Jinpon-shugi (Peoplism)* (Chikuma-shibo).

ITI (2001) *Touou he no Chokusetsu Toushi to Keizai Kouzou ni Kansuru Chousa Kenkyu (Research Study Concerning Direct Investment in Eastern Europe and the Economic Structure).*

Jacoby, Sanford M. (1997) *Modern Manors: Welfare Capitalism Since the New Deal* (Princeton: Princeton University Press).

JETRO (1998) *Sekai to Nihon no Boeki: Ajia Tsuka Kiki no Eikyo to Sekai Boeki.*

Jurgens, Ulrich (1998a) 'Implanting Change: The Role of "Indigenous Transplants" in Tranforming the German Productive Model', in Robert Boyer *et al.* (eds) (1998) *Between Imitation and Innovation.*

Jurgens, Ulrich (1998b) 'Transformation and Mutual Interaction of the Japanese, American and German Production Regimes in the 1990s', paper presented at the conference 'Germany and Japan in the 2lst Century: Strengths Turning into Weaknesses' Max-Plank-Institut fur Gesellshafts-forschung und Japanisch-Deutsches Zentrum Berlin, Berlin, 22–24 January.

Jurgens, Ulrich, T. Malsch and K. Dohse (1993) *Breaking from Taylorism: Changing Forms of Work in the Automobile Industry* (Cambridge: Cambridge University Press).

Kagono, T. *et al.* (1983) *Nichibei kigyo no Keiei Hikaku (Comparison of Management Between Japanese and American Firms)* (Nihon Keizai Shinbun-sha).

Kamei, Hirokazu (ed.) (1992) *EC Togoshijyo eno Kigyo Shinshutu Senryaku (Strategy of Firms in the Single European Market)* (Tokyo: Nihon Keizai Shinbunsha).

Kamiyama, K. (1994) 'Japanese Maquiladoras in the United States and the Asian Countries a Comparative Study', paper presented at Seminar 'The Maquiladoras in México. Present and Future Prospects of Industrial Development', El Colegio de la Frontera Norte, Tijuana, April.

Kamiyama, K. (1998) 'Comparative study of Japanese Maquiladoras with Plants in the United States and Asian Countries', *Josai University Bulletin*, The Department of Economics, March.

Kamiyama, K. and JMNESG, (eds) (2005) *Kyodai-ka Suru Chugoku Keizai to Nikkei Haiburiddo Kojo (Toward Gaigantic Chinese Economy and Japanese Hybrid Factories)* Jitsu Gyo no Nihon Sha.

Kawabe, Nobuo (1979) 'Made in Japan: Changing Image', in James Soltow (ed.), *Essays in Economic and Business History* (Mich.: Michigan State University Press).

Kawabe, Nobuo (2002) 'Yuro Jidai ni okeru Nikkei Kigyo no Tai Oshu Senryaku-Genjyo to Tenbo', ('Japanese Corporations' Strategy in Europe in the Age of the Euro: Current Situation and Future Perspectives'), *Waseda Commercial Review*, vol. 394.

Kawamura, T. (ed) (2005) *Gurohbaru Keizai-ka no Amerika Nikkei Kigyo, Toyo Keizai Shinpo Sha (Hybrid Factories in the United States under the Global Economy)* (English edition is forthcoming from Oxford University Press).

Kazama, Nobutaka (1997) *Doitsuteki Seisan Moderu to Furekishibiriti (The German Production Model and Flexibility)* (Tokyo: Chuo Keizaisha).

Keeley, T.D. (2001) *International Human Resource Management in Japanese Firms* (Basingstoke: Palgrave).

Kenney, Martin and Florida, Richard (1993) *Beyond Mass Production: The Japanese System and Its Transfer to the U.S.* (New York: Oxford University Press).

Kenney, M. and Florida, R. (1994) 'Japanese Maquiladoras Production Organization and Global Commodity Chains', in *World Development*, vol. 22, no. 1, USA.

Kenney, M., Goe, W.R., Contreras, O., Romero, J. and Bustos, M. (1998) 'Learning Factories or Reproduction Factories?: Labor-Management Relations in the Japanese Consumer Electronics Maquiladoras in Mexico', *Work and Occupations* 25, (3).

Kenney, M. (2003) 'The Shifting Value Chain: The Television Industry in North America', in Martin Kenney with Richard Florida (eds) *Locating Global Advantage* (Stanford: Stanford University Press).

Kimura, Fukunari, Maruya, Toyojiro and Ishikawa, Koichi (2002) *Higashi Ajia Kokusai Bungyo to Chugoko (Intenrnational Division of Labor in East Asia and China)*, JETRO.

Kobayashi, Gen (1998) *Jinsei wo Tanoshimi Kenmei ni Hataraku Itariajin (Italians Enjoy Life but Work Hard)* (Tokyo: Nikkei Business Publications, Inc.).

Kochan, Thomas A., Katz, Hary C. and McKersie, Robert B. (1986) *The Transformation of American Industrial Relations* (Basic Books).

Kochan, Thomas A., Lansbury, Russell D. and MacDuffie, John Paul (eds) (1997) *After Lean Production: Evolving Employment Practices in the World Auto Industry* (Ithaca, NY: ILR Press).

Kogut, B. (2004) 'From Regions and Firms to Multinational Highways: Knowledge and Its Diffusion as a Factor in the Globalization of Industries', in M. Kenney with R. Florida (eds) *Locating Global Advantage: Industry Dynamics in a Globalizing Economy* (Stanford: Stanford University Press).

Koido, A. (1992) 'Between Two Forces of Restructuring: US–Japanese Competition and the Transformation of Mexico's Maquiladora Industry', Ph.D dissertation, The Johns Hopkins University, Baltimore.

Koike, Kazuo (1988) *Understanding Industrial Relations in Modern Japan* (London: Palgrave Macmillan).

Koike, Kazuo (1999) *Shigoto no Keizaigaku (Economics of Work)* (Tokyo: Toyo keizai shinposha).

Koyama, Yoji (ed.) (1999) *To ou Keizai (East European Economy*) (Kyoto: Sekai Shisosha).

Krafcik, John F. (1988) 'Triumph of Lean Production System', *Sloan Management Review*, autumn.

Kujawa, Duane (1986) *Japanese Multinationals in the United States: Case Studies* (New York: Praeger).

Kumazawa, Makoto (1993) *Nihonteki Keiei no Meian (Light and Darkness of Japanese Management)* (Tokyo: Chikuma Shobo).

Kumon, Hiroshi (1994) 'Eikoku no Nikkei Jidosha Kojo' ('Japanese Car Factories in the UK'), *Musashi Daigaku Ronshu (Journal of Musashi University)* 42(2/3).

Kumon, Hiroshi and Tetsuo Abo (eds) (2004) *The Hybrid Factory in Europe: The Japanese Management and Production System Transferred* (Basingstoke: Palgrave Macmillan).

Layan, J.B. (2000) 'The integration of Peripheral Markets: a Comparision of Spain and Mexico', in J. Humphrey, Y. Lecler and M. Salerno (eds), *Global Strategies and Local Realities* (London: Macmillan Press).

Lara, A. (2001) 'Convergencia tecnológica y nacimiento de las maquiladoras de tercera generación: el caso de Delphi-Juárez', in *Región y Sociedad*, El Colegio de Sonora, vol. XIII, no. 21, Jaunary–June.

Lara, A. and Carrillo, J. (2003) 'Technological Globalization and Intra-company Coordination in the Automotive Sector: The Case of Delphi–México', *Internatioanl Journal of Automotive Technology and Managment*, vol. 3, nos 1/2.

Lara, A., Trujano, G. and García, A. (2003) *Producción Modular y Escalamiento Teccnológico en la Industria Automotriz: Un estudio de caso* (Mexico: UAM – Xochimilco).

Lee, C. (1997) *Gendai Chugoku no Jidosha Sangyo (Contemporary Chinese Automobile Industry)*, Shin Zan Sha.

Liker, Jeffrey K., Fruin, W. Mark and Adler, Paul (eds) (1999) *Remade in America: Transplanting and Transforming Japanese Management Systems* (New York: Oxford University Press).

Louv, R. (1987) 'The Maquiladora Program in Tri-National Perspective', in *The Maquiladora Program in Trinational Perspective: Mexico, Japan, and the United States*, Border Issues series 2, SDSU Institute for Regional Studies of the Californias.

Lung, Y. (2000) 'Is the Rise of Emerging Countries as Automobile Producers an Irreversible Phenomenon?', in J. Humphrey, Y. Lecler and M. Salerno (eds), *Global Strategies and Local Realities* (London: Macmillan Press).

Lung, Y. (2004) 'The Changing Geography of the European Automobile System', *International Journal of Automotive Technology and Management.*

MacDuffie, John Paul (1996) 'International Trends in Work Organization in the Auto Industry: National-Level vs. Company-Level Perspectives', in Kiesten S. Wever and Lowell Turner (eds), *The Comparative Political Economy of Industrial Relations* (Wis: Industrial Relations Research Association).

MacDuffie, John Paul and Frits, Pil (1997) 'Changes in Auto Industry Employment Practices: An International Overview', in Thomas A. Kochan *et al.* (eds) (1987).

Mason, Mark (1997) *Europe and the Japanese Challenge: the Regulation of Multinationals in Comparative Perspective* (New York: Oxford University Press).

Mason, Mark and Encarnation, Dennis (eds) (1994) *Does Ownership Matter? Japanese Multinationals in Europe* (Oxford: Clarendon Press).

Matsumura, Fumito (2000) *Gendai Furansu no Roshi Kankei: Koyo. Chingin to Kigyo Kosho, (Contemporary Labor Relations in France: Employment. Wages and Negotiation Systems between Labor and Management)* (Kyoto: Minerva Shobo).

Matsuzaki, T. (ed.) (1996) *Chugoku no Denshi-Tekko Sangyo (Electronics and Steel Industries in China)* (Tokyo: Hosei Daigaku Shuppan Kyoku).

Maurice, Marc, Sorge, Arndt and Warner, Malcolm (1980) 'Societal Differences in Organizing Manufacturing Units: A Comparison of France, West Germany, and Great Britain', in *Organizing Studies*, 1/1.

Maurice, Marc, Sellier, François and Silvestre, Jean-Jaques (1986) *The Social Foundations of Industrial Power: A Comparison of France and Germany* (Cambridge, Mass: MIT Press).

Mertens, L. (1987) 'El surgimiento de un nuevo tipo de trabajador en la industria de alta tecnología. El caso de la electrónica', in Esthela Gutiérrez Garza, *Reestructuración Productiva y Clase Obrera*, Siglo XXI, México.

Milkman, Ruth (1991) *Japan's California Factories: Labor Relations and Economic Globalization* (LOS Angeles, Ca: Institute of Industrial Relations, UCLA).

The MIT Commission on Industrial Productivity (1989) *Made in America: Regaining the Productive Edge*, The MIT Press.

MITI (1999a) *Keizai Kozo Hikaku Chosa.*

MITI (1999b) *Ajia Tsuka Kiki Iko no Nikkei Kigyo ni Kansuru Chosa Kenkyu.*

Mori, Akio (1999) *Hangari ni okeru Min'eika no SeijiKeizaigaku (Political Economy of Privatization in Hungary)* (Tokyo: Sairyusha).

Morita, Tsuneo (1990) *Hangari Kaikakushi (History of Hungarian Reforms)* (Tokyo: Nihon Hyoronsha).

Munakata, Masayoshi (1998) 'The End of the "Mass Production System" and Change in Work Practices', in Harukiyo Hasegawa and Glenn D. Hook (eds), (1998).

Nakagawa, Yoichiro (1995) 'Furansu Kigyonai Soshiki ni okeru San Kaisokan no Danzetsu – Rodo shinshukusei no Ketsujo, sono Gen in to Kekka' (Gaps between Three Classes in French Corporate Organization: Lack of Labor Elasticity: Cause and Results), *Collected Theses of Economics* Chuo University, 36(1.2).

Nakamura, Keisuke (1996) *Nihon no Shokuba to Seisan Shisutemu (Japanese Shop-floor and Production System)* (Tokyo: University of Tokyo Press).

Nihon Rodo Kenkyu Kikou (1998) *Doitsu Kigyo no Chingin to Jinzai lkusei (Wage and Training Systems of German Companies)* (Tokyo: The Japan Institute of Labour).

Nishiguchi, Toshihiro (1994) *Strategic Industrial Sourcing: The Japanese Advantage* (New York: Oxford University Press).

Nishiguchi, Toshihiro (2000) *Senryaku-teki Auto Soshingu no Shinka (Strateglc Industrial Sourcing: The Japanese Advantage)* (Tokyo: University of Tokyo Press).

Norouha, C. (2002) *The Theory of Culture Specific Total Quality Management in Chinese Regions* (Basingstoke: Palgrave Macmillan).

Ogai, Takeyoshi (2000) *Kyoso to Senryaku no Gurobaruka: 21 – Seiki Takokuseki Kigyo no Tenbo (Globalization of Competition and Strategy: Prospect for 2lst Centuly Mutinationals)* (Tokyo: Chuo Keizaisha).

Ohno, Taiichi (1978) *Toyota Seisan Hoshiki (Toyota Production System)* (Tokyo: Daiyamondo sha).

Okamoto, Y. (ed.) (2000) *Hokubei Nikkeikigyou no Keiei (Management of Japanese Affiliated Firms in North America)*, Dobunkan.

Oliver, N. and Wilkinson, B. (1992) *The Japanization of British Industry*, 2nd edn (Oxford: Blackwell).

Onozuka, Tomiji (2001) *Kurafuto teki Kisei no Kigen (The Origin of Craft Regulations)* (Tokyo: Yuhikaku).

Ozawa, T. (1979) *Multinationalism, Japanese Style* (Princeton: Princeton University Press).

Park Sung-Jo and Rolf D. Schlunze (1991) 'Forschungs- und Entwicklungsmanagement japanischer Konzerne in der Bundesrepublik Deutchland', in Sung-Jo Park (ed.), *Japanisches Management in der Bundesrepublik* (Frankfurt: Campus Verlag).

Park, S-J. and Horn, S. (eds) (2003) *Asia and Europe in the New Global System* (Basingstoke: Palgrave Macmillan).

Parker, Mike (1993) 'Industrial Relations Myth and Shop-Floor Reality: The "Team Concept" in the Auto Industry', in Nelson Lichtenstein and Howell John Harris (eds), *Industrial Democracy in America: the Ambiguous Promise* (New York: Woodrow Wilson Center Press and Cambridge University Press).

Parker, Mike and Slaughter, Jane (1988) *Choosing Sides: Unions and the Team Concept* (Boston, Mass: South End Press).

Pil, Frits K. and MacDuffie, John Paul (1996) 'The Adoption of High-Involvement Work Practices', *Industrial Journal*, 35(3).

Piore, Michael J. and Charles F. Sable (1990) *The Second Industrial Divide: Possibilities for Prosperity* (New York: Basic Books).

Porter, M. (1990) *The Competitive Advantage of Nations* (New York: The Free Press).

Porter, Michael and Takeuchi, Hirotaka (2000) *Can Japan Compete?* (London: Palgrave Macmillan).

Pries, L. (2003) 'Volkswagen: Accelerating from a Multinational to a Transnational Automobile Company', in M. Freyssenet *et al.* (2003).

Raff, D. (1998) 'Models, trajectories and the evolution of production systems: lesson from the American automobile industry in the years between the wars', in Freyssenet *et al.* (1998).

Rinehart, James Christopher Huxley and Robertson, David (eds), *Just Another Car Factory?: Lean Production and Its Discontents* (Ithaca: ILR Press).

Robson, Graham (1997) *Cars in the UK, vol.1: 1945 to 1970 and vol.2: 1971 to 1995* (Croydon: Motor Racing Publishing Ltd).

Romijn, H., Van Assouw, R., Mortimore, M., Carrillo, J., Lall, S. and Poapongsakorn, N. (2000) 'TNCs, industrial restructuring and competitiveness in the automotive industry in NAFTA, MERCOSUR and ASEAN', in *Interregional Project on the Impact of Transnational Corporations of Industrial Restructuring in Developing Countries* (Geneve, UNCTAD).

Sadowski, B.M. (2001) 'Towards Market Repositioning in Central and Eastern Europe: International Coorperative Ventures in Hungary, Poland and the Czech Republic', *Research Policy*.

Saka, A. (2003) *Cross-National Appropriation of Work Systems* (Edward Elgar).

Sakaguchi, Yoshihiro (1992) *Hitachi Okoku: Eiko Karano Datsuraku (Hitachi Empire: Fall from Glory)* (Tokyo: Yell Shuppansha).

Sandberg, Ake (ed.) (1995) *Enriching Production: Perspectives on Volvo – Uddevalla Plant as an Alternative to Lean Production* (Aldershot: Avebury).

Seki, M. (2000) *Nihon Kigyo Chugoku Shin Shutsu no Shin Jidai: Dairen. (New Era of Japanese Companies Advancing in China/Dalian)* Shin Hyoron.

Schlunze, Rolf D. (1992) 'Spatial Diffusion of Japanese Firms in West Germany and West Berlin from 1955 to 1989', *Geographical Review of Japan*, (Ser. B), 65.

Schlunze, Rolf D. (1997) *Japanese Investment in Germany: A Spatial Perspective* (Munster: Lit-Verlag).

Schlunze, Rolf D. (2001) 'The Spatial Structure of Japanese Business Activities in Europe', TESG – Journal ofEconomic and Social Geography, 92, pp. 219–30.

Schlunze, Rolf D. (2002) 'Locational Adjustment of Japanese Management in Europe', Asian Business & Management, 1.

Schonberger, R.J. (1982) *Japanese Manufacturing Techniques: Nine Hidden Lessons in Simplicity* (New York: Free Press).

Shaiken, H. and Browne, H. (1991) 'Japanese work organization in Mexico', in Gabriel Székely (ed.) *Manufacturing Across Borders and Oceans: Japan, the United States and Mexico*, Center of the USA–Mexican Studies, University of California, San Diego.

Shibata, Hiromichi (1999) 'A Comparison of American and Japanese Work Practices: Skill Formation, Communication and Conflict Resolution', *Industrial Relations*, 38(2).

Shimokawa, Koichi, Ulrich Jurgens and Takahiro Fujimoto (eds) (1997) *Transforming Automohile Assembly: Experiences in Automation and Work Organization* (Berlin: Springer).

Shingo, Shigeo (1989) *A Study of the Toyota Production System, from an Industrial Engineering Viewpoint* (Portland: Productivity Press).

Shinohara, Kenichi (2003) *American Industrial Relations at a Cross Road* (Minerva Publishing Co).

Sorge, Arndt (1996) 'Societal Effects in Cross-National Organization Studies: Conceptualizing Diversity in Actors and Systems', in Richard Whitley and

Peer Hull Kristensen (eds), *The Changing European Firm: Limits to Convergence* (London: Routledge).

Strange, Roger (1993) *Japanese Manufacturing Investment in Europe: Its Impact on the UK Economy* (London: Routledge).

Streeck, Wolfgang (1996) 'Lean Production in the German Automobile Industry: A Test Case for Convergence Theory' in Berger and Dore (1996).

Strzelczak S. (ed.) (2003) *Economic and Managerial Development in Asia and Europe, Comparative Studies* (Karamist Ltd).

Sturgeon, T. and Florida, R. (1999) *The World that Changed the Machine: Globalization and Jobs in the Automotive Industry*, Final Report to the Alfred P. Sloan Foundation, Cambridge: Massachusetts Institute of Technology.

Székely, G. (1991) *Manufacturing Across Borders and Oceans: Japan, the United States and Mexico*, (comp.). Center of the USA Mexican Studies, University of California, San Diego.

Takahashi, Hiroo (2000) 'Yoroppa ni okeru Nihon Kigyo no Kenkyu Kaihatsu – Igirisu de no Kenkyu Kaihatsu' ('R&D in Europe by Japanese Corporations: R&D in the UK'), *Hakuo Business Review*, 9(1).

Takamiya, Makoto (1981) 'Yoroppa ni okeru Nihon no Takokuseki-Kigyo: Sono Katsudo to Kokyo-seisaku ni taisuru Gani' ('Japanese Multinationals in Europe: their Operations and the Implications for Public Policy') in Takamiya Shin (ed.), *Takokuseki-kigyo to Keiei no Kokusai-hikaku (International Comparison of the Multinational Enterprise and its Management)* (Tokyo: Dobunkan).

Tanaka, Hiroshi (1994) 'Hangari no Shisutemu Tenkan to Keizai Puroguramu' (System Change and Economic Program in Hungary) in Katashi Ono, Takeshi Okamoto, and Satoshi Mizobata (eds), *Roshia. To ou Keizai- Taisei Tenkanki no Kozo (Russian and East European Economy: Structure at the Time of System Change)* (Kyoto: Sekai Shisosha).

Tanaka, Takuo (1989) 'Nihonteki Keieigijutsu no Iten: Kanosei to Seika ni kansuru Tokeiteki Kensho', ('Transfer of Japanese Management: A Statistical Verification Concerning Possibility and Results') *Soshikikagaku*, 23.

Taylor, Billy, Elger, Tony and Fairbrother, Peter (1994) 'Transplants and Einulators' in Tony Elger and Chris Smith (eds), *Global Japanization?* (London: Routledge).

Totsuka, Hideo, Tsutomu Hyodo, Kikuchi, Mitsuzo and Ishida, Mitsuo (1987) *Gendai lgirisu no Roshi Kannkei, Jodosha. Tekko Sangyo no Jirei Kenkyu (Labor Relations in Modern Britain. Vol.1: Case Studies in Auto/Steel Industries)* (Tokyo: University of Tokyo Press).

Trevor, Malcolm (1983) *Japan's Reluctant Multinationals: Japanese Management at Home and Abroad* (New York: St Martin's Press).

Trevor, Malcolm (1988) *Toshiba's New British Company* (London: Policy Studies Institute).

Tsuru, T. (2001) *Seisan Shis-tem no Kakushim to Shinka (Innovation and Evolution of Production System)* (Nihon Hyoron-sha).

Tsurumi, Y. (1976) *The Japanese Are Coming: Multinational Interaction of Firms and Politics* (Cambridge, Mass: Ballinger).

Turnbull, Peter (1986) 'The "Japanization" of British Industrial Relations at Lucas', *Industrial Relations Joumal*, 1 7(3).

Udagawa, Masaru, Hiroki, Sato, Keisuke, Nakamura and lzumi, Nonaka (1995) *Nihonkigyo no Hinshitu-kannri: Keieishiteki Kenkyu (Quality Control of the Japanese Company: from the Historical Perspective)* (Tokyo: Yuhikaku).

United Auto Workers (1996) *What employers want in 1996 bargaining?.*

Wada, M. and Abo, T. (eds) (2005) *Chu-Tohoh no Nihon-gata Keiei-Seisan Shisutemu: Po-rando/Surobakia deno Juyo (The Japanese Style Management and Production System in Central and Eastern Europe: The Reception in Poland and Slovakia)* Bunshin do.

Uriostegui, A.R. (2002) 'Del Ensamble Simple de Componentes al Producto Final: El caso de Philips México', Tesis de maestría, Universidad Autónoma Metropolitana, Unidad Xochimilco; México.

Villavicencio, D. (2002) 'La configuración del Entorno Institucional de las Maquiladoras y las nuevas formas de interacción binacional', paper presenta at Seminario del Proyecto Aprendizaje Tecnológico y Escalamiento Industrial: Perspectivas para la Formación de Capacidades de Innovación en la Maquiladora de México, UAM, México, 5–7 November.

Villavicencio, D, and Lara, A. (2003) *Technological Learning and Industrial Upgrading in Maquiladoras: Towards a New Path of Industrialization?,* Document for Project Conacyt 35947, Mexico.

Welge, Martin K. and Holtbrugge, Dirk (1999) 'International Management under Postmodern Conditions', *Management International Review,* 39.

Westney, D. Eleanor (1999) 'Organization Theory Perspectives on the Cross-Border Transfer of Organizational Patterns', in Jeffrey K. Liker *et al.* (eds) (1999).

Wickens, Peter (1987) *The Road to Nissan: Flexibility: Quality. Team Work* (London: Palgrave Macmillan).

Whisler, Timothy R. (1999) *The British Motor Industry. 1945–94: A Case Study in Industrial Decline* (New York: Oxford University Press).

White, Michael and Trevor, Malcolm (1983) *Under Japanese Management: The Experience of British Workers* (London: Heinemann).

Williamson, O.E. (1975) *Market and Hierarchies* (New York: The Free Press).

Wilson, P. (1992) *Exporters and Local Development: Mexico's New Maquiladoras* (Austin: University of Texas Press).

Womack, James, Jones, Daniel and Roos, Daniel (1990) *The Machine that Changed the World* (New York: Rawson Associates and Palgrave Macmillan).

Womack, James P. and Jones, Daniel T. (1996) *Lean Thinking* (New York: Simon & Schuster).

Yergin, Daniel and Stanislaw, Joseph (1998) *The Commanding Heights: The Battle Between Government and the Marketplace that Is Remaking the Modem World* (New York: Simon & Schuster).

Yoshimori, Ken (1996) *Nihon no Keiei. Obei no Keiei, (Japanese Management versus Euro-American Management)* Course Materials of the College of the Air.

Yoshida. Nobuyoshi (1990) *EC Jidosha Daisenso (Great Auto War in the EC)* (Tokyo: Toyo Keizai Shinposha).

Yoshino, Michael Y. (1976) *Japan's Multinational Enterprise* (Cambridge, Mass: Harvard University Press).

Yuan, Z.J. (2001) *Chugoku ni Ikiru Nichi-Bei Seisan Shisutemu, Tokyo Daigaku Shuppan Kai (The Japanese Production System that Thrives in China)* (forth-coming).

Yuan, Z.J. and JMNESG (eds) (forthcoming) *Chu-Tohoh no Haiburiddo Kojo: Kakudai EU ni Mukau Iko-Keizai ni okeru Nikkei Kojo (Hybrid Factories in Central and Eastern Europe: The Japanese Plants in the Transitional Economies toward Enlargement to the East of EU),* Toyo Keizai Shinpo Sha.

White papers, directories, bulletins, newspapers, journals and others

Asahi Shimbun (newspaper).

Canon Inc. (ed.) (1987) *Canon-Shi – Gijutsu to Seihin no 50-nen (History of Canon: 50 Years of Technology and Products)* (Canon Inc.).

Economic Planning Agency (annual), *Sekai Keizai Hakusho (White Paper on the World Economy)* (Tokyo: Ministry of Finance Printing Bureau).

Economist Intelligence Unit (1999) *Motor Business Europe: The West European Automotive Industry worldwide*, 3rd quarter (London: The Economist Intelligence Unit).

FOURIN (ed.) (annual) *Oshu Jidosha Sangyo (European Automotive Industry)* (Nagoya: FOURIN).

Japan Automobile Manufacturers Association (annual) *Shuyo koku Jidosha Tokei (Automobile Statistics in Major Countries)*.

Japan External Trade Organization (JETRO) (annual) *JETRO Toshi Hakusho (JETRO White Paper an International Trade and Investment)* (Tokyo: JETRO).

Japan External Trade Organization (JETRO) (annual) *Kaigai Shijyo Hakusho (White Paper on Overseas Markets)* (Tokyo: JETRO).

Japan External Trade Organization (JETRO) (annual) *Kaigai Chokusetsu Toshi (White Paper on Foreign Direct Investment)* (Tokyo: JETRO).

Japan External Trade Organization (JETRO) *Economic Information Center (1995) Hangari ni okeru Chokusetsu Gaikoku Toshi to Goben Jigyo (Foreign Direct Investment and Joint Ventures in Hungaly, 1995)* (Tokyo: JETRO).

Japan External Trade Organization (JETRO) (annual) *Directory of Japanese-Affiliated Companies in the EU* (Tokyo: JETRO).

Japan External Trade Organization (JETRO) (annual) *Survey of European Operations of Japanese Companies in the Manufacturing Sector* (Tokyo: JETRO).

Japan External Trade Organization (JETRO) (1999) *Heisei 8 nendo Shijo Keizaika Jittai Chosa Jigyo Jisshi Hokoku sho: Jidosha Buhin (Hangari), (FY 1994 Report of the Implementation of the Research of the Transformation into Market Economies: Car Parts* (Hungary) (Tokyo: JETRO).

Japan External Trade Organization (JETRO) (annual) *Shinshutu Kigyo Jittai Chosa Oshuhen: Nikkei Seizogyo no Katsudo Jokyo (Survey of Japanese Companies Abroad. Europe: Activities of Japanese Manufacturers)* (Tokyo: JETRO).

Mainichi Shimbun (newspaper).

Ministry of International Trade and Industry (MITI) (annual) *Wagakuni Kigyo no Kaigai Jigyo Katsudo (Japanese Companies' Business Activities Abroad: Findings of Surveys on the Trend of Business Activities Overseas)*, Tokyo: MOF Printing Bureau.

NEC (ed.) (1996) *NEC no TPM (NEC – TPM)* (Tokyo: Japan Institute of Plant Maintenance).

Nihon Keizai Shimbun (newspaper).

Nikkei Sangyo Shimbun (2001) 17 January.

Nissan and AEEU (1995) *Agreement and Conditions of Employment between Nissan Motor Manufacturing (UK) Ltd./Nissan European Technology Centre Ltd. and the Amalgamated Engineering and Electrical Union*, January.

Sudwestmetall (1995) *Tarife Metall-und Elektroindustrie Sudwurttewberg-Hohenzollern*, Gultig AB, November.

Toyo Keizai Data Bank (annual) *Kaigai Shinshutsu-Kigyo Soran (Directory of Overseas Japanese Firms)* (Tokyo: Toyo Keizai Shinpo sha).

Toyota and AEU (1991) *Agreement on Procedures and Terms and Conditions of Employment between Toyota Motor Manufacturing (UK) Ltd. and the Amalgamated Engineering Union*, 31 October.

Toyota Motor Corp. (1988) *Toyota: A Histoly of the First 50 Years*, Toyota Motor Corp.

UNCTAD [annual], *World Investment Report.*

Index